High Praise for the Author
and Prospect & Flourish (alphabetically by source)

"Prospecting is the number one concern for any sales professional—or for that matter anyone who is looking for new career opportunities. That's why I started Big Fish Networking in the first place. And I have to say, when it comes to tackling this challenging issue, Prospect & Flourish nails it better than any resource out there. Luscher takes a complex topic and keeps it simple, both in his book and in our workshops."

—*Steve Baldzicki, Founder & President, Big Fish Networking*

"Keith Luscher's 'wedge' strategy works! Although this isn't the norm, one of the recipients of a recent letter, the president of the organization, organized a meeting with his leadership and me after I made the initial contact. He informed his assistant to contact me, to arrange a time for five of us to meet at once!"

—*Merri Bame, Executive Communication Coach, Breaking Down Barriers*

"I've been in sales and business for more than thirty years. Luscher's step-by-step, proactive approach to generating referrals alone makes Prospect & Flourish highly worthy of its modest investment."

—*Wayne Booker, Vice President at Gottesman Company*

"After retiring from a successful forty-year career in the life insurance business, I wasn't ready to just play golf. I wanted to pass along to others in the industry the knowledge of how to effectively prospect for new clients. Achieving this goal required more than just having this knowledge—I needed some direct guidance and assistance in packaging it, and combining it with the input of other colleagues in the industry. This is where Keith's service was invaluable. With Keith Luscher's help, my resulting program and textbook, Prospect or Perish, is taking the financial services industry by storm. He is truly gifted, on many levels."

—*I. David Cohen, CLU, ChFC, LUTCF; Adjunct Faculty Member, The American College*

"Keith Luscher is among the best in the business, having worked with him for more than ten years. His exceptional skills in listening and framing, not to mention his supreme expertise in marketing and communication technologies have made him an integral part of many successful campaigns. He gets my heartfelt recommendation and upmost respect."

—*Joseph S. Czarnecky, Senior Consultant, Geottler Associates, Inc.*

"Prospect and Flourish! This is also a book title from Keith Luscher that I recommend for new and old. His approach is straight forward and ties together a lot of things we get comfortable with over time and stop doing."

—*Fred Dempster, Capgemini, Sr. Manager, Finance Transformation*

"New Horizon Press seeks authors who strive to improve the human condition, and Keith Luscher's book, Don't Wait until You Graduate, now in its second edition on our backlist and translated into Chinese, continues to be an important book for young people who want to enrich their own lives by enriching the lives of others. We are proud to have Keith Luscher as an author at New Horizon Press."

—*Dr. Joan Dunphy, Editor-in-Chief and Publisher, New Horizon Press*

"*Prospect & Flourish* is simply the most focused, and best resource on learning how to prospect I have ever seen. I highly recommend it!"

—*Jo Ann Florey, Branch Manager, Allied Home Mortgage*

"I know Keith both personally and professionally. He is one of the most thoughtful, and thought provoking businessmen I've ever met. He has an uncanny ability to uncover the needs of his clients and the sincerity in which it is done is a breath of fresh air. His talents can be enjoyed by reading any of his published books; which in itself is an illustration of his professional ability. In economic times like these, I can recommend Keith and his services without reservation to anyone."

—*Chris Gardner, Principal/Executive Recruiter, Artemis Consultants*

"Prospect & Flourish is an awesome book and a tremendous program! The part on 'wedging your foot in the door' is, by far, the best assembled and explained prospecting strategy I have ever seen. This specific strategy addresses the #1 concern of sales professionals."

— *Kim Gerhart, National Account Executive, SCG Services, LLC*

"When Keith Luscher first came to work for our firm back in the early nineties, one of the challenges we faced was marketing—both in doing the right things, and in doing them right. Keith played a leadership role in creating a consistent marketing structure that allowed us to take full advantage of the resources at our disposal, and has produced results. We continue to use this structure to this very day. Further, his expertise in marketing and media has proved invaluable through many highly successful client engagements spanning more than ten years."

—*John Goettler, CFRE, President, Goettler Associates, Inc.*

"When we were looking for assistance in growing our organization, we interviewed several firms, most of whom reflected only a superficial understanding, recommending their standard approach to solving our problem. We hired Keith Luscher for one reason: he listened. He invested the time necessary to understand our organization, our mission, and where we were coming from. Keith asked questions we hadn't even asked ourselves—demonstrating not only an understanding, but an investment in a shared approach."

—*Julie Harmon, Ph.D., Executive Director, IMPACT Safety*

"Keith is an expert in the field of planning for a career after college. His books and workbooks are superb. He is a good speaker and relates well to the students."

—*Lin Hess, The Columbus College of Art & Design*

"Anyone wishing to take their business to the next level in these challenging times can truly benefit from Prospect & Flourish. One of the habits Keith stresses in his book and the program is that of social mobility, which is being visibly active and engaged in one's community. It's a value that I have lived and worked by throughout my career, and one to which I owe much of my success."

—*Jon Kirk, Realtor®, RE/MAX Premier Choice*

"We have used Keith for a number of marketing related projects. Keith designed our web site and has helped with periodic updates. He has been helpful in strategic discussions on how best to market our services to our target audience. Keith has good business instincts. We have always felt that with Keith we have received more for our money than we expected to get."

—*Mark Palmer, Principal, The Joseph Group Capital Management*

"A big obstacle we often face to growing our business is actually running it. We always knew we had to continuously seek out new client relationships, but until we brought Keith Luscher in as our consultant, we didn't give this activity the focus it deserved. With Keith's ongoing counsel and interventions, we are focused! We are growing our bottom line and have raised our sights in where we want our business to be in the years to come."

—*Matthew Palmer, CFP, President, The Joseph Group Capital Management*

"Keith has a God given talent for converting the complex into their simplest form so everyone can understand and learn. He is a great speaker and someone that makes you believe in yourself."

—*Thomas W. Parry, Community Strategist*

"Keith is a trust worthy person who cares about helping people! I know Keith on both a professional and personal level. I would recommend him to anyone who needs his services and know that that they would be well taken care of in every possible way."

—*Chris Pedon, Associate Real Living HER Pedon & Page Office, Real Living HER*

"When our company made a significant investment in a new tradeshow display, we knew we wanted some kind of video element to achieve maximum impact on prospects, customers and the manufacturers whose products we distribute. However, we couldn't quite put our finger on the right solution. After one short meeting with our staff, Keith Luscher was able to recommend, design and create just the solution we needed. Tradeshows are a big part of our ongoing marketing. Thanks to his assistance, we continue to create maximum results from our investment. In fact, it's already been copied by some of our competitors."

—*Craig Peterson, Vice President, Webster Veterinary*

"Keith is not only a genuinely caring and 'give first' oriented guy, he is an exceptionally gifted author and strategic thinker about growing your business via prospecting...which every business must do. He example of being a consummate networking professional is one to follow as well. He is a 'go to' guy on many fronts. Get to know him!"

—*Jon Price, Director of Business Development, Phylogeny, Inc.*

"I've had the pleasure of working with Keith a number of times over the past decade and have enjoyed the experience each and every time. He is the consummate professional. He always looks to add value to any project or relationship he is a part of and has done so every time that we've worked together."

—*Steven Rothberg, President and Founder, CollegeRecruiter.com*

"Two producers in my former office increased their production by fifty percent in six months, after Keith helped them define their value proposition to their niche market and focus their sales efforts accordingly. I highly recommend him!"

—*John Stewart, Financial Advisor*

"Whether you are just starting out or growing your practice—the key activity is prospecting. Otherwise you plateau and then go downhill. Luscher gets right to the point, and keeps you focused on what should be your number one activity."

—*Erick Zanner, Registered Investment Advisor, JDM Investment Counsel for Dad*

Cataloging in Publication Data

Luscher, Keith F.

Prospect & flourish: how to conquer the "weakest link" in the sales process - 4th ed.

1. Sales/Prospecting   2. Marketing
3. How-to   I. Title.

International Standard Book Number:
978-0-9625977-3-2 (print)
978-0-9625977-5-6 (digital)

© 2014 by Keith F. Luscher.
All rights reserved.

Published by K&L Publications (SAN 297-2484)

Prospect & Flourish

How to Conquer the "Weakest Link" in the Sales Process

Fourth Edition
version 4.0

KEITH F. LUSCHER

Columbus, Ohio
prospectandflourish.com

Contents

Introduction 11

Chapter 1: The Prospecting Enigma 15
    I. What is Prospecting? 15
    II. The Five Hurdles
        to Successful Prospecting 18
    III. Your Psychological Keys
        to Success 41
    Conclusion 44
    Chapter Review 44

Chapter 2: Not Everyone is a Prospect 47
    I. Your Market 47
    II. Narrowing Your Focus with Niche Markets 54
    Chapter Review 61

Chapter 3: Building Prosperous Relationships through Networking 63
    I. Networking through Centers of Influence and Social Mobility 63
    II. Networking Organizations 83
    III. Referral Groups 89
    IV. Your Personal Board of Advisors 93
    Chapter Review 98

Chapter 4: Sharpen Your Point of Contact 101
    I. Identify Your Value Proposition 102
    II. Know What to Say Before You Say it! 107
    III. The Power of Subtext 115
    Chapter Review 126

Chapter 5: What Do You Want? 129
    I. No Shortcuts, No Quick Fixes 129
    II. Your Goal is Not to Solve Your Problems 142
    III. How Much Do You Want to Earn? 146
    Conclusion 155
    Chapter Review 155

Chapter 6: Your Moment of Truth 159
   I. Service and Prospecting 159
   II. How to Provide Outstanding Service 169
   III. The Eight Rules of Outstanding Service 173
   Conclusion 179
   Chapter Review 179

Chapter 7 Prospect and Flourish Everyday 183
   I. What Next? 183
   II. A Quick Recap 185
   III. Green, Red, and Yellow 192
   Conclusion 195

Bonus Section I: Serve Your Prospects BEFORE They're Customers! 197
   Part 1. Define Your Message 197
   Part 2: Leverage Your Media 206
   The Bottom Line 224

Bonus Section II: To Get Your Foot in the Door, Use a Wedge™. 227
   The Typical Obstacles 228
   Using the Wedge:
      An Eight-Step Strategy 229
   Why the Wedge Does and WILL Work... 241
   Where Do You Go from Here? 242

Bonus Section III: From Screen-2-Screen to Face-2-Face: 245
   Leveraging Social Media to Identify, Qualify and (Yes!)
      MEET New People 245
   How Can Social Media Help Us Prospect? 247
   Linking Up with LinkedIn 249
   Facebook 257
   Twitter: Can You Say it in 140 Characters or Less? .. 260
   The 12 Laws of Social Media Prospecting 266

Afterward: Thinking About Giving Up? 279

Index 283

About the Author 292

Introduction

Today's sales professionals are facing an educational crisis. As business continues to change, and in many cases converge (we have seen it in financial services and communications, just to name a few) the focus of most companies has been diverted from sales support and education for their representatives, to primarily *product development*. With some exceptions, sales forces have transitioned from internally driven, company-specific sales teams to a largely outside, independent base.

For example, most of today's insurance companies see themselves as product manufacturers. Those insurance products are then distributed through whoever will ring doorbells on their behalf. This has led to a common pattern of heavy recruitment (with high emphasis on quotas and limited advanced screening), nominal training, and then thrusting novice representatives out into the proverbial waters with little instruction or over-the-shoulder guidance on how to keep one's head afloat, let alone how to swim.

A similar dynamic can be seen among some investment firms, with their investment products being various funds from which to choose, or platforms that independent agents then use with their clients. Real estate is another industry that has been impacted by a reduced emphasis on personal development.

As a result of these trends, many industries have devolved into a numbers game, which has had negative consequences on business and the general public. For example, according to the Life Insurance Marketing Research Association (www.limra.org), **out of every one-hundred sales agents recruited, only nine will still be in the industry in four years.** This attrition adversely affects the companies, their customers, as well as the lives and families of the representatives themselves.

Introduction

What is the number one reason so many sales professionals fail in business? Why is turnover so great? The answer is simpler than you think: *it is lack of prospects.* Many would concur that selling is easy, but it's the prospecting activity that causes most people to trip. It's the weakest link in the selling process.

I. David Cohen, a highly respected 50-year veteran of the life insurance industry recognized this problem, and also realized that something had to be done about it. David and I had known each other for many years, and had worked on some previous projects together. He was also aware of my work as a consultant, and an author of other books that address the various dynamics of interpersonal communication as they pertain to both our personal and professional lives. Knowing that I had already significant experience in tackling this difficult subject, he approached me about creating a program *to attack the prospecting enigma head on.*

> ...selling is easy, but it's prospecting that is difficult. It's the weakest link in the selling process.

The result of that effort was ***Prospect or Perish: A Success Guide for Financial Services Professionals.*** This program (along with the textbook under the same name, and published under I. David Cohen's byline) made its debut in September, 2005 as a curriculum course offered for professionals through Capital University in Columbus, Ohio.

In the time since, *Prospect or Perish* was acquired by The American College in Bryn Mawr, Pennsylvania. **There, it has become a permanent course for all agents who wish to attain both the Life Underwriter Training Council Fellow (LUTCF) and the Financial Services Specialist (FSS) designations.**

While originally conceived for the insurance industry, the fundamental challenges and principals in *Prospect or Perish* can be applied equally to anyone involved in sales of some kind. These include real estate, other professional services, personal services, law, medicine—you name it. Further than that, as our economy has continued to endure a slow, painful recovery, countless people (many for the first time) have found themselves out of a job and having to search for work...*to prospect* for new employment.

For this reason, I am pleased to introduce *Prospect or Perish's* "younger sister" program: ***Prospect & Flourish.***

Further, the principals of prospecting apply equally to the process of job hunting and advancing your career. Indeed, many of the concepts presented in this book originated in a career book I wrote for college students and had published ten years earlier.

That book is called *Don't Wait Until You Graduate!*...and since its initial publication has been released in its second edition (with a third on the horizon) and has also been translated into Chinese.

As we did before, we will continue to attack the prospecting enigma directly. The principals are the same. Indeed, I created this material not as a financial services professional (which I am not), but as a management consultant helping organizations grow their bottom lines, through growth through prospecting every day.

So, I thank you for your attention. I also hope you will share your thoughts, experiences and comments on this material as you apply the principals to your professional life.

Keith F. Luscher
mobile (614) 205-0830
Keith@ServeYourProspects.com

Don't miss out on free updates!

Be sure to register your copy of this book at
www.prospectandflourish.com

Chapter 1:

The Prospecting Enigma

I. What is Prospecting?

What do you think when you hear the term "prospecting"? Does it bring negative images or feelings to mind? Most people have their own personal definition of what is prospecting, just as they do for so many other terms that tend to be thrown about too loosely in business.

That's why it's important for us to quickly review some other terms and concepts that affect your work in prospecting for new customers and clients. Before we go into the ins and outs of prospecting, we must make sure that all of us have a shared understanding of where prospecting stands in the "sales and marketing" process.

Marketing, Selling, and Prospecting

You have no doubt heard expressions similar to "I'm going to market this product," or others that equate marketing with selling. Marketing and sales are tied together, but still have very specific definitions in relation to one another.

Marketing is the planning and implementation of a process that involves:

Chapter 1

- Identifying specific customer wants.

- Defining groups of people who have those wants.

- Customizing (or creating) a solution that grants those wants.

- Articulating and delivering messages that focus on what the customer wants.

- Creating awareness in the prospective customer's mind of the messenger/seller as the source for providing for those wants.

- Laying the groundwork for making the sale.

Marketing takes a *macro*-view of the whole process. Its efforts are directed toward a *group*. Marketing is about the forest. It involves processes and activities such as advertising campaigns, publicity campaigns, outreach efforts (which may involve a little more personal touch), all directed toward *delivering a compelling message to a specific audience.*

Selling, on the other hand, takes the *micro-view.* It focuses more on the individual. If marketing is about the forest, then selling is about the tree. *Selling is the process of asking the prospect to buy—to become a customer.* It involves greater interaction between the seller and the prospect/customer.[1]

> Prospecting is the continuous activity of exploring for and qualifying new people to meet and talk with concerning your business.

Effective marketing fuels the sales process. Marketing helps build product and/or brand awareness, and it aids the representative in attaining an audience with the prospective customer. However, it is the skill of the representative that closes the sale.

To get a better sense of how marketing and selling relate, imagine what it might be like to try to sell with absolutely no marketing efforts to fortify you. *It would be like trying to move a sailboat without any wind.*

If marketing takes a macro view, and selling takes a micro view, then prospecting bridges the gap. **Prospecting is the continuous activity of exploring for and qualifying new people to meet and talk with concerning your business.**

Prospecting starts with the market. Individuals in this group are not even *considered prospects* unless they:

- Need and want the value your products and services deliver

- Can afford to pay for it

- Can be approached by you on a favorable basis[2]

Let's review these criteria in a little more detail:

Needs, wants, and value. Need is important, but value is critical. Value determines want, and the reality is *people will most often buy what they want before what they need.* Wanting is the key, and people want that which adds value to their lives.

Affordability. A suspect cannot be promoted to the status of a prospect unless you are confident that he can afford what you offer. While issues of affordability can be resolved on many occasions, there are two factors that can impact this challenge:

1. Budgeting can only be accomplished when there is enough "wiggle room" to pay the price.

2. Whether the prospect *wants* what you offer badly enough to pay the price.

You can save yourself and others much time and effort, by being tactfully realistic with people in determining whether or not they can afford what you offer.

Approachability. In lines of business where relationships drive most activity, this is critical. A prospect may meet all the other requirements, but if you cannot approach him in a favorable manner, *then he is not your prospect—at the moment.* Don't throw the name away—because something may change in the future that may qualify him.

> Rapport is crucial, especially when you're in a business that gets personal.

Rapport is crucial, especially when you're in a business that gets personal. Legal, insurance and financial services people get about as personal with their clients as one can. In fact, the only people getting any closer usually are their health care professionals.

Now that we all have a shared understanding of what prospecting is, and how it relates to your other sales and marketing efforts, we can move forward in addressing the many challenges—and opportunities—that exist when you unlock the key to prospecting.

II. The Five Hurdles to Successful Prospecting

Selling is easy. But prospecting? That's difficult. It's the very reason you are reading this material today. Prospecting is the enigma that every sales professional must confront. It is also the number one reason why sales people fail, or leave their respective businesses. They simply cannot master the art of prospecting.

This is well documented in the insurance business and other financial services. **The number one reason people leave the insurance business is lack of prospects.** According to the Life Insurance Marketing Research Association (www.limra.org), only nine out of every one hundred sales agents recruited will still be in the industry in four years. This adversely affects not only the companies, but also their customers, as well as the lives and families of the representatives themselves.

The reason so many sales professionals run out of prospects is that they never learned how to make prospecting an ongoing habit. However, learning how involves much more than memorizing the "techniques." If it was all technique, everyone would be doing it, and succeeding.

So, why is it that you don't prospect? Each of you has your own personal reasons or hang-ups. Your reasons probably fall under **five primary hurdles to successful prospecting:**

1. You don't understand the value of what you are selling

2. Fear of rejection

3. Not knowing exactly what to do or how to do it

4. Laziness

5. Overcoming the difficulty (whatever the nature of that difficulty may be)

Do some soul searching into why you don't prospect effectively and make a list of your reasons. By identifying some of the root causes, you can then begin to address them.

Assume that your list is similar to those issues we just identified. Look at each one a little more closely, and then we will consider some "action steps" you can take to overcome them and jump-start your prospecting engine!

> The reason so many sales professionals run out of prospects is that they never learned how to make prospecting an ongoing habit.

Hurdle #1: You Don't Understand the Value of What You Are Selling

It's a fact of human nature that you wouldn't start asking people to meet with you if you knew *nothing* about what you have to offer. But think about it for a moment: *Do you really understand what it is you are selling?*

Are you focused solely on your products or services? Or, do you truly understand and grasp *the value* your products or services deliver to your clients?

> If you do not understand the value—the related buyer benefit—you cannot truly appreciate the impact you can have on their lives.

If you do not understand the value—that is, the related buyer benefit—that your products bring to your clients, you cannot truly appreciate the impact you can have on their lives. By learning your portfolio you will gain confidence and begin to believe in what you and your company have to offer. You will also believe that you can really make a difference in the lives of your customers. Your excitement will become infectious, and people will automatically be drawn to you! Learn facts! Sell benefits!

Product versus Value

Have you ever encountered a new acquaintance at a social or business gathering and when you ask them about what they do, they trivialize it? These include responses such as...

- ☑ "I'm just an accountant."
- ☑ "All I do is sell building materials."
- ☑ "I'm only a broker."

Have you ever responded in this manner? Do you trivialize what you do or the services that you offer? If this is true, then your first job is to MODIFY YOUR BEHAVIOR! You must take a serious look at what you offer and learn the difference between *what you sell* (your product or service) and the *value it delivers* (why people would want it).

As you review the examples table to follow, keep in mind that we will delve much further into helping you discern your value—and more importantly your *value proposition*—in Chapter Four.

For you to consider for now:

As you can see, the issue of "understanding the value of what you offer" applies to many callings. Think about *that* the next time you encounter someone who, when asked what he does, pre-qual-

Chapter 1

ifies his response with the expression "just." It will be *your* opportunity to enlighten them!

If You Are:	What You Offer (Product/Service)	Why People Want It (Value)
An accountant	Advice and services on taxes and cash management	You help individuals and/or businesses make the best use of their earned capital and achieve the maximum savings and benefits under current tax law.
A financial planner	Advice on managing assets, investments, and other financial-related issues.	People want security and piece of mind in knowing that their hard-earned dollars will provide security and comfort for themselves and their children.
A cabinet maker	Custom-designed and built cabinets for the home or office; high-end quality	People want efficient storage, long-lasting quality, and added beauty to their homes— not only for their enjoyment, but also for friends and guests
An exterminator	Services that wipe out threatening insects, rodents and other unwanted pests	A person's home is likely their biggest investment. Many insects and other pests threaten the safety, stability and even the beauty of this possession— you offer protection from this threat and enhance its value.

Take a look at the portfolio of products or services you offer the public. What excites you about these products or services? Perhaps you do overall financial planning and your particular software program is truly outstanding. You feel it can help people identify, set, and achieve their financial goals. If this is important to you, share that sense of importance with others. Create an excitement for the company you represent and your particular services. It will go a long way toward overcoming any reluctance you may have, and help you develop a clear sense of *how your products and services improve people's lives.*

You can increase your value understanding in several additional ways:

> Talk to others who have succeeded in your business. Capture their passion!

Talk to your current clients and customers.

Want to gain a better understanding of how your services help people? Ask the people you are helping now! You can learn quite a bit by just having a conversation with your clients—ask them about how your services are meeting their needs, or enriching their lives. Find out how you can do better, or if there are any concerns or issues they might like to discuss. You may be surprised at how much praise you will hear, by simply asking if there is anything you can do better. Take their suggestions seriously and make certain you implement them (and be sure to get a testimonial from them in the process—more on those later in the book).

Talk to others in your business.

Seek out possible mentors and others whose success you would like to emulate, and ask them what they like about their work. Beyond the financial rewards, what do they receive? Why did they pick this business? Why not something else? Ask them to share stories of their favorite clients (minus the names, of course), about their relationships, and the essence will probably go much deeper than the nature of the product or service they provide. Capture their passion!

Look at the product and how you deliver.

Can your customer get what he needs from anyone? Do you provide outstanding service? Do you work to ensure that your customer receives not just the product, but the benefit your product in intended to delivery? There is no question that how you view your role, your relationship and your contributions to the lives of your clients will impact the quality of the service you deliver.

Understanding the value of what you are selling is vitally important. If you cannot get excited about what you offer people and, how you help people, you will have a very difficult time making it in our (or any other) business. Further, you will find that as your enthusiasm builds, it will have a tremendous impact on your capacity to overcome other obstacles that hinder your prospecting efforts.

Hurdle #2: Fear of Rejection

No one likes to be rejected in any of life's situations. Rejection is an emotional experience, and we go to great lengths to protect our fragile egos. However, in our business, where we must continuously ask people to meet with us, rejection comes with the territory. In retailing, the customers have already determined that they have an interest in your product or service when they come into your location. With services, there are not too many people who stop by and ask you to sell them. We seek out customers, and that fact is not going to change over our careers.

> Rejection is an emotional experience, and we go to great lengths to protect our fragile egos.

Fear of rejection is a manifestation of our insecurity. Most of us are insecure about *something*. We all have issues, whether it is about our appearance, how much money we may earn, or just an overall lack of faith in ourselves to accomplish and get what we want.

There is a measure of detachment that we must adopt if we are to overcome any inherent insecurity within ourselves. There is a simple truth which we must accept, and it is:

"It's not about you, so get over yourself."

When it comes to rejection, remember, it's not you. It's your product or service that is being rejected. Don't take it personally. One of the biggest excuses heard for nonperformance is that our business is so negative! If you think the business is negative, it's not the business—it's you!

A point that too many people in our business fail to understand is that the world is a surprisingly *impersonal* place. The laws of nature play no favorites. There is no such thing as a "born loser" (which we all feel like from time to time) and a "born winner" (a label we tend to lay on the other guy).

By making this point, we are not indicating that your personality, your "like-ability," and your capacity to build rapport with others aren't important. You can offer the most beneficial product in the world, but if you are not particularly pleasant to be around, you won't have success. Our goal is to help you see your own insecurity and simply put it in perspective with the thought, "It's not about me."

That said, let's address fear in general. Let's get it out in the open. What frightens you?

So many people are afraid of so many different things. The fear of prospecting evokes thoughts such as:

"I am imposing on people."

"No one wants to buy from me."

"What if I say something wrong?"

"What if they say no? Will they not like me? I can't risk the rejection!"

"I am sure they already have all they need."

Fear is normal. It is said that the two greatest fears are death and giving a speech—and more people are afraid of giving a speech than they are of dying! Death is inevitable—a speech is optional.

A key question to explore: What system or structure can we put into place that can help us get over the fear? Until we tackle this issue, all the techniques you learn won't mean a thing because you will be too afraid to apply them. Look at it this way:

"What's the worst that could happen?" Let's consider some answers.

If I telephone a person and request an appointment, *what's the worst that could happen?*

If I approach an individual at a social gathering, and gently start up a conversation, *what's the worst that could happen?*

If I send a letter, perhaps enclose a copy of a helpful article on a topic that relates to what I do, and then follow up with a phone call, *what's the worst that could happen?*

These are NOT near-death experiences! Why are we so afraid?

We are all afraid of rejection, of embarrassment, of suffering or pain. We are only human.

Think about other things you have accomplished in life—things when first approached made you afraid. Have you ever...

- ☑ Spoken before an audience?
- ☑ Bought a house?

> Death is inevitable—
> a speech is optional.

Chapter 1

- ☑ Taken on an exciting new job?
- ☑ Gone sky-diving?
- ☑ Ridden a bike?
- ☑ Learned a new language?

Not everyone reading this will be able to say "yes" to all of the above—but they are all activities that many people do every day.

When we learned how to ride a bike, that itself was our goal. Once we mastered the skill of bike riding, it became a means to a greater goal—as a child, bike riding was our first step towards independence!

You have ridden a bike. There is also a good chance that as an adult, those of you with children have also taken your own kids through the process of learning to ride a bicycle. To this end, you had to teach your own children (just as you learned as a child) how to overcome their fear.

Let's explore this example a bit further. Imagine you're a kid again. You want to get up on that big bike without the training wheels, but you're afraid. You are afraid it will topple over and fall, and take you with it. No matter how many other kids and grown-ups you see riding their bikes on just two wheels, you know, you insist, it just will NOT work for you.

It's a belief that many children have, despite the fact that evidence to the contrary is all around them.

These fears stemmed from a faulty belief system. Do you have these same fears today? Of course not. Today, you operate with different beliefs. Think about that the next time you get on a bicycle.

> You don't fail until you quit. You quit your business. Your business doesn't quit you.

Once mastered, bike riding was like walking, jumping and climbing. It became second nature. **So too will the case be with prospecting.** You will always be prospecting. It will become second nature. Prospecting, like bike riding, eventually comes down to one thing: *practice.*

Fear is a factor you can overcome with a sustained effort. If you do not overcome your fears, there will be consequences.

Forty years ago, a well-known general insurance agent from Cincinnati offered advice for agents who *could not* overcome their fears and were destined to quit:

Let's make it simple. We all know fear is a factor. If you are not going to address your fear, then how will you explain it to your family that you have left the business? Let me help you with some explanations...

- ☑ Lousy company, lousy products
- ☑ Manager was a moron
- ☑ Economy is slow
- ☑ This time of year is a bad time to sell
- ☑ People have other priorities

or...

If you don't want failure to happen to you, then get to work! You don't have to fail. It's your choice!

You don't fail until you quit. You quit your business. Your business doesn't quit you. There are many people who succeed—you must emulate what they are doing. As you will soon learn, examples are all around you.

Hurdle #3: Not Knowing Exactly What to Do or How to Do It

In conversations with sales professionals, I am constantly asked, "How will I know what to do?" and then the follow up question: "How do I do it?" While there are dozens of ways to prospect, you MUST make a choice—you must have the goal to *keep it simple*. **Until you determine a few approaches that work well for and produce positive results, you will always be in a fog.**

This gets into the "techniques" side of the issue. Let's quickly review just a few of the steps you can take now to begin prospecting.

Cold Canvassing

Also known as "cold calling" or "door knocking," it is perhaps the least popular of all prospecting techniques. It is challenging, tedious, and regarded as the least productive method to generating leads. This does not mean that it should not be considered seriously in certain circumstances.

Once mastered, bike riding was like walking, jumping and climbing. It became second nature.

So too will the case be with prospecting.

For example, if you are new to a market or neighborhood, a sensible way to start meeting new people may be to begin making calls in that area. Stop in local businesses, not as a solicitor, but as a visitor. You may visit the lobbies of area office buildings and see who is listed on the directory board.

Make a note of the "suspects" that merit further exploration. Visit the office, briefly introduce yourself, and ask for an appointment. Be prepared for a conversation should that first chat turn into an impromptu interview. When visiting in person, be sure to have sales and informational materials handy. Always leave your business card, and follow up with a phone call or letter after making the initial contact. Doing so will confirm you are interested and serious about learning more about the prospect's needs, and how you can address them.

Pre-Approach Letters with Follow-Up Calls

A pre-approach letter is a short note that the suspect receives, containing a brief introduction, perhaps a tidbit or two of value, and information indicating that the signer will be contacting the recipient by telephone. The idea is to "warm up" the suspect before you make that first phone call.

Many factors determine the effectiveness of this approach, including:

- ☑ The source and nature of the mailing list (Are they properly qualified? Is the list accurate?)
- ☑ The crafting of the letter (This includes the message and voice.)
- ☑ The offer (Does the letter deliver or offer anything of *value* to the recipient?)

The method is straightforward: send the letter, and then follow up a few days later by phone with the aim to schedule a meeting. This begs the question: **Have you ever sent out pre-approach letters, yet failed to make all the necessary follow up calls on those letters?**

You invested the time in the process, and the money in the letterhead, materials and postage. Doing all these steps probably made you feel good, like you were doing something important to growing your business. Given this investment, why have you not called? You know that your prospects will not call you.

> Cold canvassing is challenging, tedious, and regarded as the least productive method to generating leads. This does not mean that it should not be considered seriously in certain circumstances.

Perhaps you have not tried this approach because you have felt hindered by the cost of postage and a list, or maybe you are just not very good at writing (more on this later). However, these factors amount to little more than excuses, as resources abound that you can use to get the job done. The next step is up to you: send out the letters, then pick up the phone and make the calls. You can learn more about becoming more effective in your follow up calls in Bonus Section II.

Public Speaking

> Making yourself available to speak is an excellent way to spread your message

In addition to being another method of prospecting, public speaking is a double-whammy because it is also one of life's greatest "fear factors." Doing so places you in front of a captive audience, either in an informal group discussion, or as a highly structured seminar on the topic of your service.

Making yourself available to speak with groups at churches, civic organizations and other community-based and business groups is an excellent way to spread your message—especially if you are not yet well known in the community. What are the potential results of giving a public talk? Consider these...

- ☑ As the result of a seminar or speech, members of the audience *request* more information—you send them materials that provide value and initiate a relationship.

- ☑ Upon reading your materials, they have more questions about their situation. They call you, and you set up an appointment.

- ☑ You meet with them at a mutually convenient time. You listen to their needs and concerns. You provide feedback. They get to know you and trust you.

- ☑ They become your clients!

What Should You Talk About?

Obviously, this depends on two factors: the focus of your business and the interests of the group to which you will be speaking.

The age range of the audience will likely determine much of what they will want to hear. For example, younger people (let's say singles) will want to know about the first steps of starting a savings plan. Married couples (especially those with children) will be interested in creating a solid financial plan. This will lead to other concerns, such as life insurance and planning for college tuition

Chapter 1

and retirement. Senior citizens will be interested in health-care issues and succession planning.

Business groups also provide a tremendous opportunity. These include management conferences, industry trade associations, professional specialty groups, and even university management extensions. In many circumstances, personal finance topics such as those above may be very appropriate; however, you have additional opportunities to address more business-related topics if that is part of your focus.

How to Get Started on the Program Circuit

Getting in front of these audiences can be surprisingly easy. Program chair-people and group leaders everywhere are always on the lookout for new ideas, new speakers and information that offer value and is of interest to their members. Ask your clients, neighbors and friends if they belong to any groups—social, professional or otherwise—that would find the type of information you offer to be helpful. Think about conversations you have with people—issues or problems that are of popular discussion among people may often present a special opportunity to create a powerful presentation. For a comprehensive list of organizations, both local and national, refer to the *Encyclopedia of Associations*—found online and in your local library. Online social networks such as LinkedIn and Facebook make finding these organizations, and their leaders, easier than ever!

Presentations must be informational, offering value and benefits to your audience. Promotional material should be kept at a very minimum and saved for your closing. **Do not jump into a sales pitch of any kind!** Focus on delivering valuable content—information that your audience may benefit from right here, right now. Serve your prospects.

When you present to a group, always hand out business cards, have plenty of literature available, and be sure to collect the names and contact information of your audience members. Before you know it, you will be off and running with a cost-effective means to prospect through mass-marketing in person!

Referrals

You have heard it said a hundred times, and in a hundred different ways: referrals rule. If you don't have a systematic referral program, you are missing one of the simplest, lowest cost ways to generate your highest quality clients.

Program chair-people and group leaders everywhere are always on the lookout for new ideas, new speakers and information that offer value and is of interest to their members.

Obviously, referrals are by far the most popular and among the most efficient means of generating prospective client contacts. For our purpose, a referral is a person to whom you are directed by someone who knows you and values what you offer.

Trust plays a critical role in this process, and when a stranger accepts you on the word of a common friend or acquaintance, you are actually "borrowing" the trust of the referrer. As a result, it is up to you to ensure that the trust is not broken.

Referrals are powerful for one simple reason: they typically come from a credible third-party that has experienced first hand the benefits of doing business with you.

For the prospect, a referral is even more powerful when it comes from a friend, because the prospect knows that his friend has only his best interest at heart. Referrals are also valuable because they are completely free. How would you like to receive the benefits of the most compelling sales advertisement on earth for absolutely nothing? You can through referrals.

Furthermore, clients and friends who give referrals become more loyal to you and your business. Once someone stands up and makes a public statement about you, psychologically they will become more loyal to you and your business. *It strengthens the emotional bonds.*

Referrals from clients are endorsements of the value you offer, and the quality of your work. Compare that to a cold call, and you can plainly see that in building trust with your prospects, referrals are powerful.

The biggest mistake sales professionals make when it comes to referrals is not asking for them. Too many believe that referrals will happen on their own. Nothing can be further from the truth. Clients as well as friends will not necessarily think to recommend you to other people they know (whom you may contact on a favorable basis, using the name of your common friend) unless you ask!

To get referrals, start with your most important group: *your clients.* When they refer you, your clients are not just doing *you* a favor—they are also doing every person to whom they refer you a favor as well: their friends, family, and colleagues.

While clients may not necessarily offer unsolicited referrals, they will often expect you to ask for them. By always reinforcing the idea that your business is based on your capacity to meet and

Chapter 1

build relationships with new people, you can prepare clients to always be on the lookout for someone you can help.

We will talk much more about referrals in the next chapter, as well as their most powerful form, personal *introductions*.

Introductions

An introduction is the best kind of referral you can imagine. We highlight this concept on its own, because we feel that the power and dynamics of a personal introduction go way beyond that of traditional referrals.

> An introduction is the best kind of referral you can imagine.

Put yourself in a prospect's position for a moment. You are at your desk. The phone rings. It is an agent making a cold inquiry, indicating at the outset that she received your name and number from a common friend.

You are receptive and willing to talk. But even in these situations, there is still some measure of skepticism (or at least a little hesitation, depending on your current list of priorities).

Now back up, and imagine you are again sitting at your desk, and the phone rings. Instead of the agent, it is your friend calling!

The momentary resistance or any hesitation about taking the call disappears. You and your friend chat for a moment, and then he says that he has a person whom he thinks you should meet.

The story continues, and so too will we get further into these dynamics later. However, we hope from this brief illustration that you see the tremendous and powerful difference between a traditional referral and a personal introduction.

It is like driving a sports car. Referrals keep you in fourth gear—which is not bad. You can move just fine in fourth gear. But introductions get you out of fourth and into fifth gear. The RPM drops, the power increases, and all the lights are green!

Personal Observation

One point we hope that you will glean from this curriculum is that prospecting has more to do with detective work than with sales.

If you want to increase your luck, personal observation is the key. Earl Nightingale often defined luck this way: *When preparedness meets opportunity—and opportunity is there all the time.*

The mistake too many people make is not being able to recognize the opportunity when it is staring them in the face. Their eyes cannot see; their ears cannot listen. Opportunity passes them by.

How does one not miss the opportunity? The answer is simple. *You observe.* You look for it. This is accomplished through:

- ☑ Talking with your friends and neighbors, and being aware of what is happening in their lives.

- ☑ Becoming involved in area clubs and groups, and becoming engaged in the life of the community.

- ☑ Mastering the art of listening (see Chapter 3).

- ☑ Reading local media about people and events in your community.

Social Mobility

In the same vein, as you work to become a better observer, becoming *socially mobile* allows others to increase their observation of you. You must let people know who you are and where to find you. You must get involved in your community; allow others to see you working at their sides, for common interests.

> Personal observation is the key to getting lucky.

This includes activities and volunteer opportunities in local clubs, the chamber of commerce, professional organizations, or even your place of worship. Your children's school is also a great place to meet other parents to learn about what is happening in their lives, and to seek out opportunities where you may be of service. If you serve seniors, volunteering in age-related organizations is a good way to enhance your visibility. This greatly warms the approach, because in such cases, your prospects know you *first* as a friend and neighbor, rather than for what you do professionally.

Social mobility is part of the overall process of *networking,* a topic we will address much more deeply in the next chapter.

Hurdle #4: Laziness

According to Merriam-Webster, to be lazy is to be "not easily aroused to action or activity." We have all had times when we have felt lazy—just not motivated to do anything. *Chronic laziness,* on the other hand, is definitely a problem, and if you find yourself feeling "lazy" more often than you should, perhaps it's time to make a change.

Chapter 1

The cure to laziness is to *do it*. You need to become a *doer*.

What Makes Up a Doer?

You may have heard the following expression:

There are three types of people in the world:

1. Those who make things happen
2. Those who watch what happened
3. Those who wonder what happened

There are many ways to observe and define the traits. For our purposes, we can define ten traits of "doers."

1. Doers Are Passionate.

If you really want to succeed in this business, to become a top producer and to make tremendous changes in many peoples' lives, then you must look inside yourself and become very passionate about your goals. Business is challenging, with lots of competition and its fair share of bad days.

You must want it and care about it so deeply that you will rise above the bad days. You must look past them, learn from your mistakes and bad experiences and focus on your goals. Passion energizes our spirit, gets us up early in the morning, and frees us from being a prisoner of the moment. When we are focused on the big picture, it doesn't matter if we're tired, if the house is messy, or if our car breaks down. Passionate people are not excuse makers—they are constantly moving forward. They are proactive; they take responsibility for the results they produce, both good and bad.

> Passion energizes our spirit, gets us up early in the morning, and frees us from being a prisoner of the moment.

How many of you think that successful entrepreneurs are passionate about earning money? According to Steve Mariotti (founder and president of the National Foundation for Teaching Entrepreneurship), most successful entrepreneurs are *not* focused on the money. They are indeed passionate about their work, what they do, and how they are serving people. If they reach some level of financial security or independence, they are passionate about what they are able to do with their lives as a result of their success.

There is a story of a person who sought out Picasso to draw him a portrait. When the artist completed the drawing, which took thirty minutes, the man received his picture. Picasso then said, "That will be $2,500."

"What?!" the man gasped. "But it only took you thirty minutes to do this drawing! You expect $2,500 for thirty minutes' worth of work?"

"Not thirty minutes," Picasso replied. "Thirty years."

Picasso began preparing for his assignment long before the visitor ever stepped foot onto his world. Was Picasso an overnight success? Of course not, but he had a passion for his work. *He had paid the price, and it was his time to be rewarded for all of his hard work and to reap the benefits.*

> The most successful entrepreneurs are passionate about their work, what they do, and how they are serving people.

2. Doers Believe.

There is a powerful quote: "What the mind can conceive and believe, it can achieve." Perhaps you've heard another one (attributed to Henry Ford): "Whether you believe you can do something or you can't do something, you're probably right." Every religious tradition gives testimony to the power of our own beliefs.

We will get further into how beliefs affect our careers later. Rest assured, they play a big role in our daily lives. The choices we make and the results we produce play a much bigger role than you might realize.

Ask yourself, what are my beliefs? Have you ever felt that you really weren't good enough to get what you want? If you embark upon a challenge with the inward belief that you will not succeed, it becomes a self-fulfilling prophecy! One belief that doers share is this fact: *The world plays no favorites. It doesn't care whether you get what you want or not.*

"Wishful thinkers" talk about what they are going to do tomorrow (while waiting for the phone to ring); doers talk about what they are doing today.

3. Doers Plan.

One of my favorite quotes is from Gloria Steinem: "Rich people plan for three generations; poor people plan for Saturday night." What are you planning for? Do you have any plans in your life? Just as doers see a worthy goal realistically, with all the challenges and opportunities it presents, they also plan a course of action that will direct them to their goal. They look at it from the perspective of where they are now in relation to where they want to be. They navigate a path and a plan that will get them there. *They build structure.*

But it takes more than a plan. Remember, doers do, wishers wish. "Wouldn't it be nice…" "If only…" "One of these days…" This occurs not only in individuals, but also in organizations. Many companies and organizations, with the same idea of creating the future and planning for the long-term, engage in what's called "strategic planning." It's a long, drawn out process, which typically costs lots of money in consultant's fees and then results in a printed STRATEGIC PLAN in a big heavy binder. When this plan is completed, what do you think happens?

> "Rich people plan for three generations; poor people plan for Saturday night."

In many cases it becomes a very expensive bookend on the CEO's bookshelf! It sits there, and doesn't get used. People don't follow it. Instead, they are mired in meeting the demands of the day. They are "stuck in the mud" so to speak—and that mud is their problems. It takes more than having a plan—*you must execute it.*

Let's make one more observation about planning. Most of the time, things do not turn out exactly as we plan. It's important to have a "road map" approach. If you are driving somewhere, even across town, you might decide the best way to get there is on the major freeway. However, as you head for the entrance ramp, you discover that the ramp is closed—it's blocked off.

What do you do now? Do you give up on reaching your destination and retreat back home? Of course not! You look at a map, and determine your detour. All this time, what is on your mind? *Your ultimate destination.* If we all had a simple game plan for getting what we want, wouldn't life be easy! There are no cookbooks. No simple recipes. But it will come to you if you are focused on what you want.

4. Doers Are People of Strong Character.

A primary factor in the value that anyone can offer to someone ultimately comes down to one thing: strong character. People of strong character have integrity, which means that they are true to themselves and everyone else with whom they come in contact.

Integrity means the value of a promise or commitment kept. You might find that people of integrity make promises sparingly. But when they do make them, they keep them. You can have the most valuable skills on earth, but if you cannot be trusted, what good are you to anyone?

Character is what gives all people, young and old, the power to make the right choices. Again, this gets into the realm of personal responsibility. The course of our lives is determined by our choices, and our choices are determined by the depth of our character. Author Thomas Stanley, who has spent thirty years observing and writing about the habits of our nation's millionaires, observes in his book, *The Millionaire Mind,* that a majority of millionaires (who also live frugally, drive American-made cars, and enjoy long-term marriages) regard honesty and integrity as a major part of their success.

5. Doers Have Energy.

How many of you are tired? It's been a long day, you were at work or dealing with your kids. You're pooped! How many of us feel that we are always tired? We are just living day by day, ever focused from the time we get out of the bed, to the time we can get back in. We are exhausted. We are drained.

Your body is like a battery. You know the Energizer bunny? He just keeps going and going and going. Did you know that right now, every cell in your body is generating power? The food you eat is the fuel. In fact, the issue most people face is how to tap into each cell and generate even more energy. Ask yourself this question: what did I eat for breakfast? Did I eat breakfast at all? What about lunch and dinner? What do I eat every day? How about exercising?

> You can have the most valuable skills on earth, but if you cannot be trusted, what good are you to anyone?

Your body is the only tool you have. From your brain to your feet it needs constant care. If you don't look out for your body and treat it with respect, it will not perform the way it should. Imagine, there are people who take better care of their cars than their bodies! Eating right, exercising regularly (several times a week), reading good books and exercising your mind are all practices not of "losing weight," but of being healthy. There is plenty of information on how to live a healthier life. When you are healthy and taking care of yourself, you have the energy you need to realize your goals.

6. Doers Communicate.

What would you say is the most important communication skill? God gave us two ears and one mouth. Therefore, it is vitally important to listen twice as often as we speak. Of all the communication skills that we have, the most important is our capacity to listen. We don't mean just hearing the other person, we mean actually listening to what is being said.

When people speak with us, tell us their point of view, share their concerns, frustrations and joys, the most important thing we can do for our fellow human beings is to understand them. Even in conflict situations, it's not nearly as important for two people to come to an agreement, as it is for them to understand the other person's feelings and point of view.

How many of you can recall having a conversation where, as you heard the other person speak, you were thinking about what you were going to say? We have all done it! That's a bad habit for a lot of people. When another person is speaking with you, it is time to give him the stage. Just for a moment, put your own agenda aside, and try to imagine yourself in his shoes. When you respond, your response should first be what the other person just told you. When you have made that person know that he is being understood, then you open the door for him to listen to what you have to say.

> When you are healthy and taking care of yourself, you have the energy you need to realize your goals.

If more people made the habit of listening more often to their children, it could greatly reduce drug abuse and teen pregnancy and all the other ills that plague our youth. Sales professionals would greatly increase their commissions; countless marriages would find healing and begin to thrive! In situations of conflict, we are not talking about winning an argument (when was the last time you actually won an argument?). We are simply talking about understanding one another, with empathy, with love, and with compassion.

7. Doers Take Responsibility.

Taking responsibility for your life is very liberating. Doers assume full responsibility for the results they produce. It is often said that the moment John F. Kennedy became a true leader was during the Bay of Pigs crisis. As president, he ordered a military operation that shamelessly failed. When it came time for him to answer, he didn't beat around the bush, he didn't look to blame anyone else. His answer was simple: "I am your president. I am responsible."

In your life, you will make mistakes and you will have successes. Assume responsibility for each.

8. Doers Have Courage.

Let's face it: to succeed in this business requires stepping out of your comfort zone. When we set foot into a realm where the results of our actions are not predictable, it is scary. We have fear, and we must summon our courage.

Courage is defined as "mental or moral strength to venture, persevere, and withstand danger, fear, or difficulty." When you have courage, you will persevere; and you will overcome whatever obstacles you face.

Are you afraid? Sure. That's normal. But when you are blessed with passion, vision and integrity, you will look past the obstacles; you will become courageous.

9. Doers Do It.

This sounds obvious. People who decide that they really want to do something, don't wait until certain events occur—they do it. The proof is in their actions, not in what they say. The world allows you to get anything you want—nobody cares; and no one is holding you back.

Doers don't make excuses. How many of us, when faced with a seemingly daunting project or task, have procrastinated, only to rationalize or make excuses to ourselves or to others? However, when we have passion, we don't care about excuses. We don't wait for something to happen. We only know that the best time to act is NOW. There is no "some day"—there is only today.

> Of all the communication skills that we have, the most important is our capacity to listen.

Think about these attributes, and ask yourself objectively how you stack up. *Are you a doer?* Maybe some days are better than others. Don't get us wrong: doers who have all the attributes we discussed still challenge themselves on a daily basis. They are not perfect people. Some days, they may feel like victims when their plans don't go well; other days they may feel less motivated.

Is there dreaming going on when you are a doer? Of course. Dreaming is linked to creativity. To become a success, to get what you want, to be a creator, you need to *know* what you want— where you are in relation to what you want and have a plan to achieve it. When you are sailing, you typically have your eye on a destination, or a point up ahead. But you never move in a straight direction— you are probably off course most of the time. When you are steering the boat, you are constantly anticipating and responding to your environment, the waves, the water currents, and the wind. You are always compensating to make up the difference. As you move, even though you may be off-course, you never lose sight of your destination. You never lose sight of where you are going, which leads us to our final attribute...

10. Doers Know What they Want!

That's the bottom line. As you read the text, do you know where your career is headed? The question ultimately comes down to: "What do I want?"

You are reading this textbook because you have decided that you want to greatly improve the effectiveness of your prospecting and sales efforts. Do you have goals that are more specific? Consider them. Decide what your goal will be for the next thirty days, six months and even three years from now. Begin mapping out a plan to get there. As we continue, you will learn the formula.

> The world allows you to get anything you want—nobody cares; and no one is holding you back.

Hurdle #5: Overcoming Difficulty

If prospecting were easy, everyone would be good at it, and this textbook would not be necessary. However, it is difficult and only those who are dedicated will overcome the difficulty. Think about all the things you first tried that were difficult:

- ☑ Playing golf or tennis
- ☑ Learning a language
- ☑ Playing bridge or chess
- ☑ Flying an airplane
- ☑ Playing a musical instrument

In each case, with practice, dedication, and hard work, you overcame the difficulty to the point that today it seems effortless.

What's difficult for one person is easy for another. By breaking down how many prospects you may need in order to acquire a client or customer will be helpful. When you focus on one or two prospecting techniques and practice them, the difficulty will slowly disappear. Soon, you will become a pro.

For example, years ago, George, a fairly new insurance agent in Columbus, Ohio was struggling to improve his business numbers. Prospecting, as with most agents new to the business, was George's weakest link. He lacked focus. "Everyone needs insur-

The Prospecting Enigma

ance," so he thought, "so everyone is a prospect." As we have already established, if everyone is a prospect, then *no one* is a prospect. With such a mindset, where do you begin?

This represented his *first* area of difficulty. But that wasn't the whole story.

When asked, "Do you believe in what you offer? Do you truly believe in your heart that your products and services make a difference in peoples' lives?"

"Yes, I do!" George replied.

Next question: "Are you afraid of rejection? Does calling or visiting people frighten you?"

"No," was his honest response. He felt that fear wasn't a big factor.

Then the next question: "Are you active? Are you working every day, and not goofing off or sleeping in?"

"I'm busy; I'm not slacking off," George responded.

This led naturally into the final question: "What are you doing?"

"I'm lost. I really don't know what specifically to do, or how to do it."

George faced two areas of difficulty:

1. A lack of focus in who his best prospects would be.

2. Knowing the *specific* steps in how to approach them.

> If prospecting were easy, everyone would be good at it, and this textbook would not be necessary.

The advice we gave George: "Would you—could you—call your very best friend and client, and request a meeting?"

"Sure," George answered. "I could call Rick."

Our response: "Great. Now, if you want to ask for a referral--or better--an introduction, this is the conversation you want to have with him:

George: "Rick, we've known each other for a long time, and you have been happy with my service, right?"

Rick: "Sure, George. As far as I'm concerned, you're the best in the business. I wouldn't work with anyone else."

Chapter 1

George: "It really pleases me to hear that—which is why I am coming to you. My business is going great, and I am working hard to grow it further. But to do so, I really need your advice, counsel and help."

Rick: "Okay, George. What can I do?"

George: "First, while I'm happy you have been pleased with my service, is there anything else I could do to improve my service? Is there anything that I could, or should, be doing differently?"

Rick may or may not have some constructive advice to offer—and if there are any issues—your best friend and client is the best person to call them to your attention. After an honest and open discussion, you take the conversation a step further.

> What part of the overall process of prospecting do you find the most difficult?

George: "Rick, I deeply appreciate your advice. As I move forward, I was also hoping that you might be able to help me not only to improve my business, but also to expand it."

Rick: "Okay, I'd be happy to help."

George: "Who do you know that may be able to benefit from what I have to offer, in the same way that I have benefited you? I was really hoping that you may be able to introduce me to some of your other friends and colleagues."

Rick: "You know, George, I can think of three people right now whom you really ought to meet!"

George: "Excellent! Can we call them and set up a meeting?"

The rest is history. By starting with his best friend, by taking a single first step, George was able to get out of his "rut" and today, he is doing very well.

As we said before, what is difficult for one person is easy for another. Your "difficulty" hurdle probably has something to do with one of the previous four. Perhaps your difficulty lies in interpersonal communication skills or in overcoming fear. Perhaps it is discipline—having the focus to do what it takes, when it's required, regardless of how you may feel at the time.

As we move forward, ask yourself this question: What part of the overall process of prospecting do you find the most difficult? Identify your weakness, and focus to the point that it becomes your greatest strength. What was once difficult will become easy. I guarantee it!

III. Your Psychological Keys to Success

In business, there is a popular tendency to separate emotion from business—to deny the role that our emotions play in our business relationships.

This is a paradox, because without emotions, you cannot have relationships. *You can have transactions,* but these are short term, and do not have any significant, positive long-term impact on your life or the lives of your clients.

People want to deny the role emotions play because they are fixated on the negative: fear, anxiety, and rejection.

Look at the most successful people in business and in your industry. Are they cold, heartless corporate salespeople? No! They are passionate about what they do! Does this mean that they are passionate about life insurance, annuities, real estate, or whatever they sell? Yes—because they understand the value! Highly successful sales professionals are passionate about helping people!

If you are passionate about helping people, you can be successful at anything, as long as you look at your role in this light. It is a set of beliefs. This set of beliefs is what empowers us to overcome our fear, anxiety and insecurity.

If you care and want to help people, yet find yourself in a job in which you *cannot* see yourself making this contribution, then you should examine your options.

> Highly successful sales professionals are passionate about helping people!

Why Do People Buy?

Earlier in the chapter we talked about why people buy. Look back. Was it logic (what they need) or emotion (what they want)?

People will typically buy what they want rather than what they need. Examples surround us. Look at the exploding market for sport utility vehicles—these are products that go way beyond what people need (how many people do you know are planning to drive to the top of Pikes Peak?).

Unfortunately, in our country, too many people allow their "wants" to be dictated by their next-door neighbor. This is human nature. We live in a country in which most of us have all that we need. When our basic needs, for food, shelter and cloth-

Chapter 1

ing are met we get spoiled. *We start to focus on what we want.*

That is also the nature of capitalism and what has created the highest standard of living on earth.

Why Do People Buy from *You*?

When we like another person, we enjoy being around them.

Ask your clients: "There are many people who can provide you with what I offer—why do you do business with me?"

> People will typically buy what they want rather than what they need.

It's likely the answers will not lie within the realm of logic, such as "You had the right product to meet my needs," or worse, "Your price was the lowest." While the "logical" buyers are there, most will not respond this way.

Most clients will respond with answers such as:

"I like you."

"You're a professional."

"I feel comfortable with you."

"I feel as though you understand my needs and care about me."

"I trust you."

Ask yourself this question: have you ever done business with another person or place of business because you *liked them* better than the other, even cheaper alternatives?

Your answer is "Yes!" Most of us have. The reason is simple. When we like another person, we enjoy being around her. If that person were to become overtly negative, we will *not* be drawn to her. This isn't exactly rocket science, is it?

The Power of Likability

To encourage others to do business with you, and to be successful in your ongoing prospecting efforts, you must be likable. To this end, we offer up four recommendations:

1. Be Punctual.

Show up on time. Don't make people wait. Doing otherwise is a sure sign of disrespect. When you make a habit of not showing up on time, you send messages such as:

- ☹ I am lazy.
- ☹ I am disorganized.
- ☹ I have no regard for your time.
- ☹ I have no respect for myself or you.

Wow! That's heavy, isn't it? It's also the truth. Punctuality is tied to so many of our character traits.

When we are punctual, we express other important traits of strong character and likability, which include:

- ☑ *Humility*—we are not seen as arrogant, selfish or conceited. We do not see ourselves as the center of the universe, and we keep our egos in check.

- ☑ *Empathy*—because we respect other people and their time, we place ourselves in their shoes. We are constantly working to see things from other people's point of view.

- ☑ *Caring*—we care about others.

2. Be Honest.

> Honesty is about saying what you mean, and meaning what you say.

Honesty is about saying what you mean, and meaning what you say. It's about truthfulness, character and integrity—just as we indicated earlier when we talked about being a *doer*.

If you are not true to yourself and everyone with whom you come in contact, everything else you offer is worthless. What good are you if you cannot be trusted and cannot be relied upon?

3. Be Polite.

Treat others as you would like to be treated. Always say please and thank you. Be positive, laugh often and be upbeat. *Act likable!* Be the kind of person that others enjoy being around!

4. Be Responsive.

Reply immediately to all telephone, voice, pager, fax and emails. In the minds of your clients, friends and prospects, a prompt reply is a welcome gesture. Follow through on your promises. Responsiveness is a strong character trait that you should always emulate.

Chapter 1

Conclusion

We have delved into some very deep issues and have encouraged you to look at yourself, your own strengths, weaknesses and fears, and begin to identify them with genuine objectivity. Perhaps it's been difficult, but it is important to address these issues up front. Do so, and the rest is smooth sailing!

As we move forward, you will, as we indicated earlier, come to see prospecting in much the same way that you view riding a bike. Our objective is to get you past looking at prospecting as an end-goal, but as a life-long habit—as a part of your daily routine. *Prospecting is not an end—it is a means!*

(Chapter 1 Endnotes)

1 While this is true in general, there is a dimension of marketing that involves some measure of interaction—it's called *relationship marketing*. However, this is the subject for another discussion. For the sake of argument, relationship marketing serves the same function as our defined term of marketing in this overall process.

2 Okumura, Kirk S. and Glenn, Stevick E. Jr., *Techniques for Exploring Personal Markets, Chapter 2*, ©2001 The American College Press. All Rights Reserved. Used with permission.

Chapter Review

1. Define the following:

    a. Marketing _____

    b. Sales _____

    c. Prospecting _____

2. What are the five hurdles to successful prospecting?

    a. _____

    b. _____

    c. _____

    d. _____

    e. _____

The Prospecting Enigma

3. What is the difference between product and value?

> Responsiveness is a strong character trait that you should always emulate.

4. Share some fears, and explain how you can overcome them.

5. Why are introductions preferable to referrals?

6. List the four ways to become likable.

   a.

   b.

   c.

   d.

7. What did you gain most from Chapter One?

Chapter 2:

Not Everyone is a Prospect

I. Your Market

In the first chapter, we discussed the various psychological issues surrounding the process of prospecting, addressing your fears, learning about the various issues of why you don't do what you know you should, and also having a better understanding of where prospecting stands in the overall sales and marketing process.

What was covered in chapter one, while it contained quite a bit of theory and psychology, is highly relevant to the upcoming information. From this point forward, we will be moving away from the theoretical side of prospecting, and putting more and more emphasis on *action*.

Whether you are an industry veteran or a rookie, one issue that must remain at the forefront of your mind is *your market*.

Do You Know Your Market?

Earlier, we discussed how important it is to understand the value that your product or service brings to your clients. You cannot gain such knowledge without having a clear understanding of your ideal client's profile, his or her wants and needs, and most importantly, how to find them.

Chapter 2

These issues concern not only prospecting but also marketing. Effective marketing must deliver a compelling message to a defined audience. The actual definition of that audience may be wide, or it may be very narrow. Your company's marketing efforts may very well be targeting a wide range of people—however as an agent, you must make two choices:

1. Who among a wide range of people will make your best prospects

2. How you will find them

> It is a fundamental first step in any sales and marketing effort: Identify your prospective client.

Who Will Make Your Best Prospects?

It is amazing how many sales professionals—and job seekers—fail to understand this crucial dynamic. It is a fundamental first step in any sales and marketing effort: Identify your prospective client.

To gain some perspective, consider the four basic models for products and markets:

1. Wide Product → Narrow Market

The first model illustrates when a business or individual decides to target a specific group of people, such as physicians, homeowners, or any other group, and wants to meet *all* of their needs within some reasonable parameter. One example is a representative who handles *all* financial services for high-income-earning professionals.

2. Narrow Product ➜ Narrow Market

The second model exemplifies one person or business deciding to provide a specific need or product to a narrowly defined group. This group can be defined by almost anything, such as a profession or a location. An common example of this model is a sales professional who serves customers within a specific region, or specializes in the needs of a particular group or industry (known as vertical market).

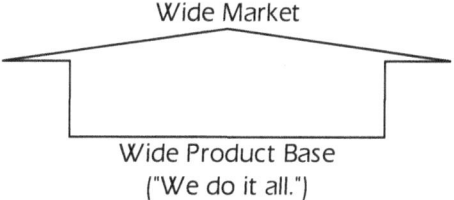

3. Wide Product Base ➜ Wide Market

The third scenario describes a "trap" into which too many sales professionals can fall into if they lack focus—especially if they offer a product or service with a fairly wide appeal. This is the least preferable model because—as we have already discussed—if everyone is your prospect, then *nobody* will be your prospect.

> If everyone is your prospect, then nobody will be your prospect.

4. Narrow Product Base ➜ Wide Market

In this model, your business provides a fairly specific product or service to a wide, yet still well defined market base. This base may consist of retirees, working professionals, or any other group that can be defined by one or more parameters.

Taking these models into account, how wide or how narrow do you wish to define your market? Then, how will you approach that market?

Chapter 2

Discovering Your Natural Market

In exploring for your customers and clients, you will also need to consider the fact that while a large number of people may need or want what you offer, they may not all be suitable prospects. A prospect is someone who wants what you offer, and can be approached *on a favorable basis*. The last factor is vitally important in helping you determine what we call a *natural market*.

A natural market is a group of people with whom you have a natural *affinity*, or *access* because of similar values, lifestyles, experiences and attitudes.

Affinity. When you have an affinity with a certain group, you have something in common. Perhaps it's as simple as living in the same neighborhood, or attending the same place of worship. Other bases for affinity include lifestyles and interests, such as:

- ☑ Sharing marital status
- ☑ Being parents of young children
- ☑ Being parents of grown children
- ☑ Being grandparents
- ☑ Sharing enthusiasm for certain sports or hobbies
- ☑ Having graduated from the same high school or college

A big part of having affinity with others depends largely on your stage of life. You like and feel more comfortable with others who share similar values, concerns and interests.

They, in turn, feel more comfortable with you. Such is the foundation for creating new relationships.

Access. The second factor that can define a natural market is ease of access—those people to whom you can reach with greater ease, other than direct personal knowledge and acquaintance. Access means that you can approach a group and gain entry with greater ease because you have something in common. It could also mean that you can approach a group from its point of view, with a greater understanding of its needs, wants, and concerns.

Example: if you worked as a teacher before joining the real estate industry, you may have greater access to other teachers, not only because others you may know, but also from your own understanding of what it is like to be one of them.

> When you have an affinity with a certain group, you have something in common.

Why Consider Natural Markets?

In our business, most accomplished professionals will be the first to tell you: Start with whom and what you know. These people make up your natural market. You can begin prospecting and approaching them with the *least resistance*.

Further, natural markets offer the following benefits:

- ☑ You have a higher capacity to understand that market's needs, wants, attitudes, and concerns because you are "one of them."
- ☑ You feel more comfortable around them, which gives you more confidence.
- ☑ You will experience less rejection and frustration.
- ☑ You step into your prospect's world with increased credibility and trust.
- ☑ You will experience greater success in serving your prospect's needs, because you have a greater understanding of those needs from personal experience.
- ☑ You will need to do less cold calling and receive more referrals and introductions.
- ☑ Your connection with your prospects and clients will be more personal, more sincere, and you will make new friends and have more fun!

How to Identify Your Natural Markets

Natural markets can develop in many ways. Sometimes you pick your natural market; others will say that the natural market picks you. It really depends upon how you look at it. However, if you take a proactive approach to defining your market, it will save tremendous time and lead to greater long-term success and career satisfaction.

Ironically, the first step to identifying your natural market is not to look outward, but to look inward, and to do so using two criteria:

1. Personal attributes
2. Previous successes and failures

Sidebar: Sometimes you pick your natural market; others will say that the natural market picks you.

Personal Attributes

To put it plainly, if you have never mingled with corporate CEOs before, you may find that going after this group may not be your best starting point. Why? Your lack of experience dealing with them may show through, and this will prevent you from building rapport. It is very important to examine your own background, service history, and accomplishments, as well as your personal strengths and weaknesses.

Your values, when it comes to business, family, money and other life issues, may also come into play. If you do not have anything in common with your prospects, it will also hinder you from building a successful rapport.

Questions to further explore your personal attributes in your natural markets are:

1. What occupations have I worked well with in the past?

2. In what social organizations/associations have I been successful?

3. With what types of people do I enjoy associating?

4. What businesses or industries do I know and understand fairly well?

5. In what organizations, businesses, associations and other circles am I fairly well known and/or recognized?

> Who are the top 20 clients you enjoy working with the most? We are not necessarily talking about your biggest buyers.

Previous Successes and Failures

Your past service, accomplishments and successes will also play a telling part in where your natural markets may lie. This information provides a clearer indicator of where you are confident you can do well, based on past experience. Take a look at your previous sales records (if you are newer to the business, use your most promising prospect list), and ask yourself the following question: *Who are the top 20 clients you enjoy working with the most?*

We are not necessarily talking about your *biggest buyers*. We want you to consider those clients with whom you have the greatest rapport, and enjoy their company. From such a list, gather the following demographic information:

1. Age

2. Income level

3. Occupation or Profession (be as specific as possible)

4. Personal attributes, including:

   a. Employer

   b. Community

   c. Family status

   d. Life values

   e. Lifestyle

5. Interests, including:

   a. Community interests

   b. Social organizations, religious groups, clubs

   c. Alumni and/or professional organizations

   d. Ethnic or cultural background

6. Wants and needs (the *emotional* reason they purchased the product or service)

7. Referrals—did they refer or introduce you to any other prospects or clients?

With the information gathered, look for any trends (while excluding exceptions or extreme circumstances). Seek out commonalities in:

1. Age

2. Income

3. Occupations and professions

4. Interests and associations

5. Wants and needs

Just as you have done with your previous successes, consider your previous failures. Not understanding where you "underperformed" in the past can only lead to a repeat of such performance. You must be aware of people with whom you have had difficulty connecting. Have you changed since then, or will including them in your market cause history to repeat itself? Failure is not a dirty word if you take the opportunity to learn something. No inventor ever produced a success with his first attempt. Rather, he succeeded by refining and adapting his methods based upon their past failures.

Comparing the Results—Discovering the "Path of Least Resistance"

Carefully examine the results of the questions in both "Personal Attributes" and "Previous Successes and Failures." This will help you to gain a better insight into some possible markets where you will have greater success, given your affinity and access. Ask yourself the following questions:

- ☑ What markets appear in both exercises?
- ☑ What markets are there, that have not been fully explored?
- ☑ Why have I not explored them?
- ☑ What would it require to penetrate those unexplored markets?

These valuable questions may uncover aspects of your life and your career of which you were not previously aware. In the process, by exploring your existing relationships, your current life structure and the community of people with whom you live, work and operate, you will have greater success in opening new opportunities, and developing new natural markets. As a result, you will have discovered the starting point on the prospecting "path of least resistance."

> Niche markets are groups of people defined by certain criteria.

II. Narrowing Your Focus with Niche Markets

While exploring your natural markets is a strong first step, you may find even more potential by identifying additional markets. Niche markets are groups of people defined by certain criteria. These groups are large enough so that you never run out of names and small enough so that the members are interrelated to the degree that your reputation can precede you. The group is identifiable, is accessible, and has members with common traits and needs. They also may communicate with each other on a regular basis.

For instance, if you sell office supplies, you may wish to focus on companies of a certain size. An attorney may develop a "specialty" by addressing the specific needs of people within a certain profession or industry, such as engineers or home contractors.

Exploring niche markets and your capacity to serve them may create opportunities that you never realized existed. Furthermore, you can begin exploring potential niches within the realm of your current natural markets.

Benefits of Niche Markets

Some may think it counter-intuitive to actually *decrease* the number of people you target for prospecting (niche markets are also commonly referred to as *target markets*). However, when you effectively target your prospecting efforts to predefined niches, several things can occur:

You Become a "Specialist" for Your Niche

To effectively target a niche market, you must first tailor your *service* to meet the specific needs of that market. When you become educated about the goals, challenges and wants of a certain group, you become a specialist. This gives you a tremendous competitive advantage.

Your Name Becomes Well Known

People in groups talk! Doctors talk with other doctors; lawyers talk with other lawyers; clergy talk with other clergy. If you are exceptional in what you do and serve your niche clients well, word gets around.

You Will Stand Out Among the Competition

By narrowing your focus, there will be less competition for the same audience. Indeed, if you become a dominant player in serving the needs of your niche market, it will greatly deter others from intruding. Less competition means more business with less effort.

Prospecting Will Become Much Easier

As these other factors fall into place, identifying and contacting your prospects on a favorable basis will occur with greater ease. The more clearly defined your group, the more targeted your efforts and your marketing message—the less time and money will be wasted on "mass marketing" efforts.

When you become educated about the goals, challenges and wants of a certain group, you become a specialist.

Chapter 2

Types of Niches

Niche markets can be defined using four basic criteria:

1. Occupations

These are people who all share the same, or similar, job or profession. They can be widely or narrowly defined (such as all architects or broken up further into specialties). Because these people share the same job or profession, we can assume that they all share similar problems, concerns, needs and wants. Products and services can be tailored (or positioned) to address the needs of these people.

> The more clearly defined your group, the more targeted your efforts and your marketing message.

2. Demographics

A demographic niche consists of people who share one or more of the same characteristic, such as age, gender, income level, ethnicity, or any number of other criteria. This group may also be defined by stage of life, such as singles, married parents of young children, single parents, widows and widowers, and retirees.

3. Geographics

As you may expect, geographics are determined by people living in the same neighborhoods, subdivisions, school districts, voting districts, suburbs, apartment complexes, zip codes, counties, cities, states, or countries.

4. Psychographics

Psychographics is the study of how people think, what they like and dislike. People who share the same psychographic profile often have similar interests, values, passions, and hobbies. Another term for this definition is "subculture," which can be broad (all democrats) or narrow (all model plane enthusiasts between the ages of 30 and 45).

With Greater Focus Comes Greater Clarity

Now that we have surveyed the various ways you can better define your best potential prospects, it is time to take things a step further. You may recall in the beginning of this chapter, we placed the burden of two choices on your shoulders:

1. Who among a wide range of people will make your best prospects
2. How you will find them

How *will* you ever find your prospects? It's like searching for a needle in a haystack!

Suppose someone hands you the telephone directory and says, "Here are your prospects." In reality, they are just names of people, businesses, charitable organizations and professionals. Your mission is to change those names into prospects and the million dollar question sales professionals have always asked: **"How do I do that?"**

It's just like fishing. There are many fish in the ocean, but to catch those particular fish you want, you need the following:

1. The right fishing spot
2. The correct bait
3. The proper equipment
4. The proper discipline

1. The Right Fishing Spot (or Know Where to Find Them!)

When you have decided upon "your fish of choice" (discussed in your natural markets and your niche markets), you must also determine where you will find them. If you are looking for marlin, you won't catch them by fishing in Lake Erie. In the same way, if your niche market includes working professionals, you won't find them mingling at the mall during the day.

> If you are looking for marlin, you won't catch them by fishing in Lake Erie.

Understanding "where" to find your prospects means more than just a physical location. If you are targeting a niche based on *geographics,* the question of where to find them has already been answered. However, if your criterion is *demographic* in nature, such as a niche market of retirees, you can find retirees in various communities and social clubs. You can also reach them through publications that are tailored to their particular interests.

2. The Correct Bait (Offer Value in Your Approach, Presentation and Closing)

You have worked diligently to enhance your knowledge level pertaining to the products and services that you offer, and now you

Chapter 2

are ready to make that first approach. How will you "hook" the interest of your prospects?

Should you stand on the corner and say to each passerby, "Psst! Hey! Want to buy some life insurance?"

Probably not. Let's examine our fishing metaphor a little more closely. You have a fish hook and a nice juicy worm. The worm goes on the hook; the hook goes in the water. Why will the fish come after the hook?

The fish wants the worm. The fish *values* the worm. The worm is food. Have you ever tried fishing without bait? It doesn't work.

What does your prospect value? What does he or she want? At the risk of sounding too manipulative, what "bait" can you offer to hook your prospect into a productive, meaningful conversation—your primary objective. (Remember, you are not seeking to close a sale...yet!)

The *means* of piquing the interest of your prospects are endless—however they all follow the same rule: offer value, especially if you want to *reduce or avoid resistance.*

When most of us encounter another person, or a marketing message that we perceive as being manipulative, we raise our guard. Our attitude is, "All right, what are they trying to sell me this time?"

However, let's suppose *you* are approached by someone who was referred to you by another person whom you know and trust. That representative is completely non-confrontational and only interested in learning about what *you* want. Perhaps he makes his inquiry based upon something he knows concerns you; or maybe he is offering you a complimentary book, CD or DVD, well packaged and professionally produced, with a title that empathetically conveys value, with no strings attached. What happens?

You lower your guard. You show interest.

We are discussing offering value—fishing with the right bait. When you begin to offer and *deliver* value, even if it is simply in the form of greater knowledge, you build relationships. Where relationships are in place, there is credibility and trust, and before you know it, the fish is on the hook. Now it's time to reel it in, which leads us to the next point...

> Have you ever tried fishing without bait?
> It doesn't work.

3. The Proper Equipment (Your Own Knowledge and Expertise)

If you are hunting for whales, you wouldn't use a fly rod. You would use a harpoon. Your equipment is the basic knowledge of your products and services, and the value they provide to people. It's not difficult to determine that if you are seeking prospects that are older and wealthier, you need a different set of skills than if you are seeking newly married couples. It's just common sense.

Earlier, when helping you to decide your natural markets, we asked you to take an objective look at your skills level to make certain your skills match the profile of the people you are seeking. It makes no sense to prospect in an area where you have little or no knowledge about what motivates the buyer, or the knowledge base needed for you to communicate effectively.

4. The Proper Discipline

Prospecting, like fishing, is no different than many other activities. It requires that you do certain things consistently. Ask yourself the following questions and see if you have the "stuff" of which sales professionals are made:

1. Do you make a favorable impression?
2. Do your presentations evoke an emotional response from your prospects?
3. Do you enjoy helping people reach their goals?
4. Are you constantly rehearsing your material?
5. Are you seeking mentors and advisors?
6. Do you believe that what you are doing makes a difference?
7. Do you support your industry and profession by involvement with associations?
8. Do you look at your work as a career, not a job?

In summary, do you have the passion necessary for your industry, and *are you constantly working* to improve each and every aspect of your business life so that *no name ever gets wasted?!*

If you are not passionate, and not doing what you know must be done on a daily basis, your problem may be a lack of discipline.

When you offer and deliver value, even if it is simply in the form of greater knowledge, you build relationships.

Chapter 2

A famous coach once said "If I have to choose between the player who's high on skill, low on discipline, and the one who is low on skill and high on discipline, I'll take the latter—because I can make him a star."

In essence, people who get what they want are not always the smartest, the best, or the brightest. *They have discipline.* It's not enough to know *who* you want to target, or *what* you need to do to reach them. To achieve your business objectives, you must also have the discipline and self-sacrifice to do what you know it takes. *You have to be willing to pay the price.*

> People who get what they want are not always the smartest, the best, or the brightest...
>
> They have discipline.

Even the most successful people will admit that discipline alone can be a daily challenge. Often, the results are not immediately visible. It builds over time in small, hard-to-see increments.

When we hear others around us complaining, feeling defeated, and talking like a victim, it isn't hard to understand the critical role of discipline. Have you ever thought this yourself or heard others lament:

- ☹ I couldn't force myself to get out of bed in the morning. *I was late for work.*
- ☹ I couldn't control my anger at work. *I got fired.*
- ☹ I neglected to follow up with my prospect. *I lost the sale.*
- ☹ I couldn't walk away from work to be with my family. *I am divorced.*
- ☹ I ignored problems hoping they would go away. *They only got worse.*
- ☹ I just didn't eat right, I let myself go. *I'm overweight.*
- ☹ I couldn't keep my credit card spending under control. *I am deeply in debt.*

Many of these sound familiar, don't they? Most of us struggle with discipline in one way or another. We must remember that building discipline is a process. It is the result of daily decisions and habits rehearsed over a lifetime. Each time we see discipline pay off we strengthen it as a character trait and get closer to achieving our goals.

Chapter Review

1. Do you have a natural market? Explain your answer.

   _____
   _____
   _____

2. Name the four basic models for products and markets:

   1. _____
   2. _____
   3. _____
   4. _____

3. Name the four basic criteria of a niche market.

   a. _____
   b. _____
   c. _____
   d. _____

4. If you want to catch a particular fish, you need the following:

   1. _____
   2. _____
   3. _____
   4. _____

5. What did you gain most from Chapter Two?

   _____
   _____
   _____

Chapter 3:

Building Prosperous Relationships through Networking

I. Networking through Centers of Influence and Social Mobility

Networking is one of the most nebulous subjects when it comes to career development. Why? Because it deals with intangibles. In this text, you will:

- ☑ Gain a clearer idea of what networking is and what it isn't.

- ☑ Learn to make networking a daily habit rather than a short-term effort (and one that is often the result of desperation).

You have probably already heard quite a bit about networking. Indeed, there are many good books written on the subject. However, the essence of it is very simple and does not require hundreds of pages of explanation.

Chapter 3

Networking is:

- ☑ Sharing knowledge, resources, and contacts
- ☑ Receiving advice and assistance from people you know
- ☑ Giving advice and assistance to people who know you
- ☑ Leveraging your time for increased productivity
- ☑ Seeking out and building long-term, prosperous relationships

On the other hand, networking is not:

- ☒ Selling something
- ☒ Receiving a job
- ☒ Seeking monetary compensation, donations, or funding
- ☒ A business transaction
- ☒ Manipulating others

> As you have heard a million times, it's all about who you know...
>
> ...or is it something that runs much deeper?

Traditional networking regards people as contacts, describing a process in which you call people you know to find out who they know. The classic rationale is as follows

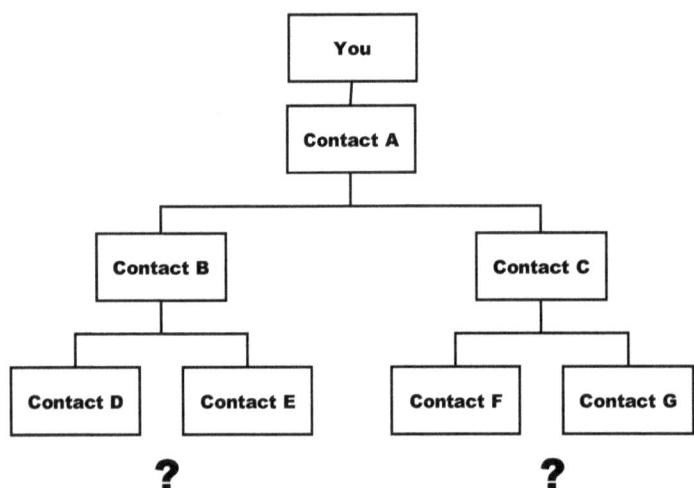

- ⮕ You know Contact A.
- ⮕ Contact A knows other contacts, and gives you the names and numbers of Contacts B and C. You get permission to call them, using Contact A's name as a reference.
- ⮕ You call Contacts B and C, talk with them, indicating that Contact A gave you their names and that since you were in the process of seeking advice and counsel, A thought that B

and C would be good people to speak with for advice or possibly any additional leads.

- You meet with Contacts B and C, and by the end of those meetings you learn what might be happening in each of their respective worlds, and the names of four more individuals. You call them (as well as the other leads from Contact A) and the process continues. It becomes an endless chain.

- From one individual, you received six potential prospects!

There you have it. That's networking. Pretty simple? As you have heard a million times, it's all about who you know.

But it goes much deeper. These objectives (collecting names and phone numbers) are important but too often are over stressed and overrated because the techniques and steps required to achieve them are easy to explain and presumably simple to follow. Books and articles vary in how they recommend to specifically go about networking, but the bottom line is the same: to become acquainted and share information with as many people as possible. It works beautifully.

As simple as it sounds, networking can still be a painfully frustrating effort—especially when your goal is to find immediate prospects. Be patient—it takes some time and effort to fully implement.

> If you were growing your own food, would you wait until you were hungry to plant your seeds?

The "Two Faces" Networking

Look at it this way: if you had to grow your own food, would you wait until you were hungry to plant your seeds?

Certainly, you would not! Why? Because of simple laws of nature. When you plant seeds, you have to nurture them and wait for them to grow. There is nothing humanly possible that you can do to accelerate the process. You water them, make sure the soil is rich, and allow time and nature to do the rest.

That's where networking suddenly becomes frustrating and difficult for so many people. It's also why you need to start doing it sooner rather than later. Networking really has two faces. The more common face is building a list of "contacts."

What doesn't get as much attention and is more effective yet more challenging, however, is turning those contacts into relationships (the other face).

Chapter 3

Building relationships is a long-term goal. Building contacts is often regarded as, although mistakenly, a short-term goal.

The common mistake, and the point of frequent frustration, is most people don't make an effort to make contacts until they have an immediate, short-term objective:

- They need a job.
- They need clients.
- They need something!

Building contacts, or collecting names and phone numbers, theoretically takes a few simple steps. Building relationships requires more than passing and collecting business cards. It isn't the occasional phone call, the holiday greeting card, or remembering names of individuals you met at last week's soccer game.

Building relationships takes more time and work. You cannot possibly build as many deep relationships in your life as you may be able to cram names into your address book. Yet one friend who will help you is often worth more than dozens of names you barely know and have little in common.

In essence, we are speaking of quality over quantity. It is an old theme. But it is also valid. Before we discuss more about building relationships, let's think about the dynamics involved in building contacts: the most visible and elementary part of networking.

> One good friend who will help you is often worth more than dozens of names of people whom you barely know.

Building Contacts

In his book *Sharkproof*, author Harvey Mackay suggests that to build contacts, you start with whom you know. If you belong to a club or fraternity, every member, nationwide, is a contact worth calling.

He suggests that you should collect five contacts a day.

It's possible, but it is also difficult. If you are calling a complete stranger who is busy, you had better have a strong means of linking yourself to him. You might belong to a common professional organization. But your involvement in that organization may be much stronger than his. Other members may not be as involved, nor do they feel the ownership. They may only belong because their employer makes it a requirement. You don't know. Therefore, don't be surprised if you call a fellow member, and his response is, "Yes, we are both members. So what?"

His lack of commitment to the organization makes it easy to dismiss your call.

Your best connection with a stranger is another human being whom you both know on a favorable basis. Contact her using the name of one of her good friends, and she is more likely to receive your call and arrange to meet, based on the fondness and respect she has with her friend.

One of the most common processes used in networking is what we call the informational interview. It is a simple meeting between two or more individuals to share information, insights, opinions, advice, and names. Some people call this a "tip club."

It is here that you discover the "awful truth" about networking: *not everyone you meet will feel comfortable putting you in touch with everyone they know.*

Let's face it. Suppose you were to give a complete stranger another friend's name, telling him to use you as a reference. What are you really doing?

You are putting your reputation—and your relationship—on the line!

What happens if your friend does business with this stranger, who then turns out to be unreliable and untrustworthy? How does that make you look?

That can be a difficult situation for you. Have you ever met people whom you would not DARE pass along to trusting colleagues? We all have.

Some people are more trusting than others. But we all have to use discretion when meeting new people and introducing them to our friends. After all, the two of you just met. The contact may know a little about you, and he hopefully knows the person who gave you his name (that relationship can have a strong bearing on your meeting, as we will see).

Still, there is something missing...a deeper familiarity...an element of trust...*a relationship.*

Building Relationships: Simple, But Not Easy

Building relationships is the much deeper side to networking, and it is a little more challenging. It is also better and more powerful. Here's why:

Relationships are ongoing and more sincere.

You usually have some kind of continuing contact or involvement with a person with whom you have a relationship. It doesn't mean you see her or talk with her every day or necessarily every week. Your association, however, does reach beyond a first-time meeting in her office.

You may have heard the expression: "When you meet someone, find a way to stay in touch with him!"

It is very important to stay in touch with people, but don't wait until you want something.

> Stay in touch with people, but don't wait until you want something.

People know you as a person, not a name.

Through ongoing interaction and involvement, people begin to know and understand you. They are aware of your strengths and weaknesses. They understand what's important to you, not from what you communicate through your words, but through your actions. They have an understanding of the depth of your character. You need to create trust.

When you are seeking opportunities, people with whom you have built strong relationships can give you as good a reference as your mother would, without the obvious bias. This takes time to develop.

In the following pages we will address specific starting points where you can begin building your network today. However, building relationships, stresses quality over quantity. You can't possibly chum up to every person you encounter. It is neither practical nor sincere.

The Fundamental Differences

Let's quickly review the main differences between building contacts and building relationships.

Building contacts is a short-term process. It usually focuses on trying to meet as many people in the shortest amount of time. If a person you meet does not have an immediate need for your services, nor can they lead you to anyone else, there is little foundation for a long-term relationship.

Building contacts emphasizes quantity. Again, you are trying to collect as many names of people as possible. The more you collect, the deeper your network of contacts becomes.

Building contacts is based upon the age-old premise of "It's not what you know but who you know (and who they know!)." You must make as many acquaintances as you can to ensure that the right opportunity will come through at the right time. It is strictly a numbers game.

On the other hand, building relationships is long term in nature. When starting your career, you are taking active steps to prepare for the future. The people you meet and develop bonds with will hopefully be with you for the rest of your life.

Building relationships emphasizes quality. You can't form deep relationships with every person with whom you come in contact. That should be, however, an underlying goal. Keeping this in mind will help you notice opportunities to nurture those relationships that are influential to your success.

Building relationships puts the "who you know" attitude into perspective. In reality, it is not just "who you know." It often comes from three elements:

- ☑ It is who you are (your integrity).
- ☑ It is what you know and can do (your qualifications).
- ☑ It is how well another individual **knows you** (your relationships).

These elements get you through the door and keep you there.

Don't be discouraged by this "awful truth." Yes, relationships do take time to develop. **The good news is there is a shortcut.** If you do not have many deep relationships in place, you can start building them by leveraging the relationships that other people have. These people are what we call *Centers of Influence.*

> Building contacts is about who you know.
>
> Building relationships is about who knows you.

Networking, Newtonian Style

According to the natural laws of physics, in space, every object (planets, moons, stars, asteroids, etc.) has *mass,* which is another word for "substance." Simplistically speaking, the greater the mass of an object, the greater the gravitational pull it manifests on other objects nearby.

Our moon has one-sixth the mass of the earth. It has one-sixth the gravity, and as a result, an object that weighs 100 pounds on earth only weighs about seventeen pounds on the moon. **This gravitational pull is an *influence* that is far reaching. It is the** earth's gravity that keeps the moon in orbit around the earth; it's the sun's gravity that keeps the earth and all the other planets in orbit around the sun. In our solar system, the sun is our "center of influence."

When it comes to interpersonal relationships, people are like heavenly bodies. Some people are more influential than others. When these people speak, others listen. These influential and often dynamic individuals are called "Centers of Influence (COI)." They also represent the key to effective networking—and successful
prospecting.

> The Center of Influence must know you favorably and be willing to introduce and refer you to others.

To help you in your prospecting, the COI must know you favorably and be willing to introduce and refer you to others. However, like we mentioned, not just anyone who likes you can be *your* COI. To receive this informal title, an individual must:

- ☑ Be active in a community or other sphere of influence (such as an organization or industry)
- ☑ Be highly regarded and sought after for advice by others
- ☑ Be active in communicating with other people and visible in myriad ways
- ☑ Be givers, not takers

COIs know you well enough and have enough confidence in your abilities that they are willing to refer—or introduce—you to their friends, business associates and colleagues. **Furthermore, your relationship with the COI should be one of a mentor.** Your COI develops an ownership in your career and thus has an interest in seeing you succeed.

Where do you find such a person? You probably know at least a few. Consider all the people you know, and ask yourself, "Who among these people meet the criteria of being a 'center of influence?'"

The first group from which to choose would be your active client base. Are any of your clients influential, involved and visible in the community? A COI doesn't necessarily need to be a client. Perhaps it is a friend of the family or someone with whom you have worked well in the past.

Once you identify a potential COI, you need to cultivate the relationship. Consider that person's interests, and what you possibly can do for them. If that person is a client, you already have established the relationship. If he is not a client you need to cultivate a relationship through referrals and introductions.

Mentoring: A Powerful Role for the Center of Influence

A mentor is usually a center of influence whom you have "adopted" as an informal teacher and advisor. Most of today's successful sales professionals will attribute some of their success to at least one mentor who guided and, more importantly, introduced them to other prospects.

By seeking out a COI's advice, you are already fulfilling one of your mentor's very important needs—*the need to be needed.*

Consider the following: regardless of what stage we are in during our careers, we all like to be appreciated, to feel needed, and to make a positive contribution to others. We get a natural sense of euphoria when we know we have made a difference. Think about a time when you "saved the day" for someone else. It was a very satisfying feeling!

When your COI refers or introduces you to other prospects, you are carrying the "weight" of your center with you. For example, let's suppose you know an influential corporate executive. Because you are both well acquainted, you ask the executive for advice as you build your client base. You ask to be introduced to people who may also benefit from your products and services.

The executive gives you the names of five other people. When you call each person, it is the executive's influence (and relationship) that wins you an audience with the prospect—and it will remain so until the prospect is impressed and accepts you for who you are, and what you offer (this is the case, regardless of whether the prospect becomes a client or not).

When seeking centers of influence as mentors, you will want to look for individuals who:

Inspire genuine respect and for whom you feel a level of trust.

Because someone is successful doesn't automatically qualify the person to be your mentor. All people deserve our respect as human beings. However, we respect some people more than others. People may be professionally and financially successful, but are they honest? What was their key to success? How a person conducts himself in all roles makes a difference. In the words of

Gandhi: "Life is one indivisible whole."

When you are evaluating a person who may have a significant role in your life, you must respect that individual or you will not respect his or her counsel. Seriously consider this quality when searching for a mentor.

Display character traits and values similar to your own.

You needn't agree on everything or do everything alike. But whether or not the person possesses qualities you admire helps to determine whether your prospective mentor makes a good role model for you. We will discuss later about how community service and other forms of local involvement can help you meet people who share similar values to your own and have reached admirable heights. You may also seek mentors in your university, professional clubs and organizations, and previous employment.

> The key to cultivating centers of influence is to think of the interests of the other person.

Can connect you with other significant people and meaningful opportunities.

This is vital, and one positive lead can make a profound difference in your future. Your mentor will be able to provide you with guidance and leads through his or her own network of clients, colleagues and friends. As your relationship with your mentor strengthens, you will most likely be introduced to or come across these people naturally.

How to Get Started with Your Centers of Influence: Two Approaches

The key to cultivating centers of influence is to think of the interests of the other person. If you consider their needs and interests, then you have the foundation for a symbiotic relationship. Consider these steps:

1. Define, to the best of your ability, the type of client you want to serve.

You should have already gone through this process in the earlier part of the chapter. That information is very important so that you have a better understanding of *whom you seek*. When you meet with your COI, you can be assured that he or she will ask you, "What type of person are you looking for?" Make sure you know!

2. Review your client lists.

Go through your lists and mark the ones who may meet the criteria for being a center of influence, and possibly a mentor. Will these individuals also be able to direct you to prospects that fit in your market? Using index cards or your contact manager, record your information: age, profession, social circles, associations, hobbies, interests, education, or any other important factors.

3. Highlight three to five potential Centers of Influence.

For each of these potential centers, list as many people as you can whom you believe that individual knows, or may know. These may be attorneys, doctors, accountants, and other people in his or her respective industry (or company).

4. Contact each of these potential centers, and ask him or her for a meeting.

When you call him (again, this is someone you know), you indicate to them that you are looking to expand your business, and that you would like their assistance and counsel.

Another Approach...

Here is a second approach, if you have a more defined target market. Let's assume that your target market consists of people within a certain industry. In this case, potential centers of influence will be others in that industry you know. You ask each of them for their help.

1. You prepare a list of ten other people whom you would like to contact, but do not currently know.

2. You sit down with your center of influence, present the list and inquire if he has any rapport with any of them.

3. Your COI indicates to you that he personally knows three, and is willing to connect you.

4. You show the same list to your next COI and ask the same question. He indicates that he knows four of the people very well. You are on a roll!

5. You continue this process with each COI you have chosen—let's assume that you have five meetings and from the same list, three names are mentioned by all five of your centers. You have hit a home run.

As your relationship with your mentor strengthens, you will most likely be introduced to or come across new people naturally.

Chapter 3

Note: Another approach similar to this can be utilized using LinkedIn. If your Center is also on LinkedIn, and you are both connected (you should be), you can review his/her connections before your meeting and identify those with whom you might wish to connect yourself. Take that list to the meeting and proceed accordingly.

During each of these meetings, it is important to learn as much about these new names as possible, from the people who know them personally! What are these individuals like? They may be married, own their homes and have children—all easy information to obtain. Use this opportunity to dig a little deeper. For example:

- ☑ What are their hobbies?

- ☑ What charitable organizations do they support?

- ☑ What causes are they passionate about?

- ☑ Where did they receive their education?

Armed with the information you obtained from your centers, you are now ready to use whatever approach you choose to contact them. When you make the call:

- ☑ You have the use of five centers of influence who know you well and trust that you will treat these prospects with respect and dignity (they were on everybody's list)

- ☑ You have the confidence that your product or services really can help those prospects (centers of influence won't help you with foolish ideas)

- ☑ It shows the prospect how important he must be because of all the effort you took before you ever made the contacts.

Once you receive a name or recommendation start networking with everyone you know to find out everything you can about the prospect. The process could take from one day to one month.

Never underestimate the value of a new prospect—it could be worth literally millions!

> Never underestimate the value of a new prospect—it could be worth literally millions!

Social Mobility—Staying Visible, Mobile, and Active

As we briefly indicated in the previous chapter, another powerful means of networking is through *social mobility*. These activities allow others to see you in the community, be it in the business community, in the schools or on other fronts. People know who you are and where to find you.

If you want to build a strong, integrated network of contacts and friends, the time to start is now. These are all steps that you can take today to guarantee a great payoff tomorrow.

Volunteering.

Volunteering is one of the most effective ways to build relationships with people. Your involvement with an organization bonds you to other members or volunteers with that same organization. By working together to reach a common goal, you automatically build relationships.

That doesn't mean you have to associate with these people every weekend, or even see them on a weekly basis. If you have the opportunity to connect with them regularly, which volunteering allows, you automatically get to know them better. People discover your talents, your values and your character, which cannot normally be accomplished through a single thirty-minute meeting.

Before you start getting involved with an organization, remember to focus on something that interests you. Make sure that it involves work and activities that you enjoy.

If your heart isn't really into something, it will show in the quality of your work and in how you relate to people. That will reflect badly upon you and do much more harm than good.

The opportunities are endless. They include activities and volunteer opportunities in local clubs, the chamber of commerce, professional organizations, or even your place of worship. Your children's school is also a great place to meet other parents, and learn what is happening in their lives, and to seek out opportunities where you may be of service.

Consider your market, and look for opportunities that afford you greater exposure in those markets. Remember, wherever there are opportunities to serve, there are friends to be made. Not superficial acquaintances. Not names to just jot down. Not temporary contacts...but friends. They are all around you.

Wherever there are opportunities to serve, there are friends to be made.

Chapter 3

Writing

Would you like to see your name and picture in the newspaper or online without having to purchase ad space? Write an article! Print publications of all sizes are seeking quality content for their space—content that serves the interests of their readers. Their need is your opportunity to get your name and company in front of a large number of prospects in a highly cost-effective manner.

When you write an article or a book, and it is published, you are regarded as an authority. This gives you the credibility you need to build relationships with unknown prospects. It does not cost anything in advertising dollars; it only requires an investment of your time to write and research publishing opportunities. Be warned: this investment can be significant—but so can the payoff.

> When you write an article or a book, and it is published, you are regarded as an authority.

When you publish an article in a community newspaper, a trade magazine or an industry newsletter, you can leverage its marketing value beyond the time that the publication is in circulation. Collecting extra copies, distributing them to new friends and acquaintances, and mailing them to people you know is a great way to use them as "personal brochures," instead of a purely self-promotional piece, prospects are receiving information that delivers value. When the time comes for the prospect to call someone, you have increased the odds in your favor!

If you want to get published, consider these points:

1. Research publications, websites and blogs that your prospects and clients read. You want them to see your name in a new role.

2. Explore these publications; contact the editors and inquire about *their* needs. Remember, they are not interested in promoting you, (even if you may be an advertiser!). They are only interested in serving their readers—help them achieve that objective, and they will help you achieve yours.

3. When writing, don't attempt to sell anything or pitch your product or service. Editors understand this and will not run your piece. Your article should offer useful information (if you can tie your advice to current events or market trends, it is even better). Place yourself in the prospect's position—what does he care about? What does he want? Address these issues.

4. If you're feeling stuck, tell a story. Has one of your clients or associates experienced a life event that would relate to others?

5. Another approach to writing is to present solutions or a message in numbered points, such as *The Ten Secrets of Estate Taxation,* or *Ten Steps to Selling Your House.* Such a method makes writing easier for you, and the learning easier for the reader!

6. Reprint your articles yourself, in your own newsletter and/or on your company's website. You wrote it—you own it. Leverage it for all the value it's worth!

7. Make sure credit is given where it is due. This not only includes other experts or publications you may reference, but also yourself. At the conclusion of every published article should be two or three sentences about you, who you are and what you do, and at least, an email address, and preferably a phone number. It should be noted that you are available for any questions, or to speak publicly. This leads us to our next point...

> *Place yourself in the prospect's position—what does he care about? What does he want?*

Speaking

In the first chapter we introduced the concept of public speaking, and the role that it plays in prospecting for new clients. Let's recap a few of these points, and take it a bit further.

If you are not yet well known in your community, being available to speak at churches, civic organizations and other community-based and business groups is an excellent way to spread your message. What happens next?

- ☑ As the result of a seminar or speech, members of the audience *request* more information—you send them materials that provide value and initiate a relationship.

- ☑ Upon reading your materials, they have more questions about their situation. They call you, and you arrange an appointment.

- ☑ You meet with them at a convenient time. You listen to their needs and concerns. You provide feedback. They get to know you and trust you.

- ☑ They become your clients!

This sounds great, doesn't it? The best part of speaking is that it is interactive. You have a live exchange, a dialog, with your audience. This gives you the opportunity to build rapport and have spontaneous exchanges with people who could become your clients! However, because some aspects of speaking may not always be rehearsed, it is important for you to *know your material,* and know it well. The depth of your knowledge and understanding will reveal itself in how well you field questions, and reach a shared understanding with your audience.

Your presentation is vitally important. People will not only be seeing you, but also the company you represent. You will be representing your entire industry—always be a professional!

To this end, here are some additional guidelines:

Know your audience. Discover who will be attending, and do it weeks in advance—not the night before. If you actually have a list of people who will be attending, review it to see if anyone stands out—if you know more about specific people, you may have the opportunity to meet top prospects, and centers of influence!

Be prepared. It's the Scout motto. Have you ever listened to a speaker or presenter who was NOT prepared? Most of us have, and it's typically a waste of our time. Know what you are going to say, before you say it! Ad-libs are for amateurs!

Look sharp. This should be common sense. Packaging is half of the presentation—it's about first impressions. Dress appropriately, and if you are unsure of what your audience expects (for which there is no excuse), you are far better overdressing than doing the opposite.

Survey the setting in advance. Know the room where you will be speaking. Make certain that all the equipment is available and functioning properly. This isn't the time for surprises—whether or not a mishap is your fault, you will be the one looking like a fool and wasting everyone's time. Also, don't be interrupted. Loudspeakers should be turned off, as should your mobile phone or pager.

Serve your prospects, not yourself. Presentations must be informational, offering value and benefits to your audience. Promotional information should be kept at a minimum. It's acceptable to have "a word from our sponsor," just keep it short and at the end. If people want more information, they can contact you.

Tell stories. People love stories; it puts a human face on your subject matter. Stories are like pictures—if you are making a point, illustrate that point or lesson with a story as an example (the same stories can be used in, or taken from, articles you write!)

Don't speak over their heads. Remember, your purpose is to

> Know your material, and know it well. The depth of your knowledge and understanding will reveal itself in how well you field questions, and reach a shared understanding with your audience.

communicate and serve the audience, *not show off your expertise.* Avoid jargon, and illustrate complex issues with metaphors when possible. No one likes to be made to feel stupid.

Have contact and follow-up materials available. *Every* member of the audience should leave with, at minimum, your business card. Preferably, they should take something else of value with them, such as a Q&A brochure or something tangible that is less likely to be discarded. Obviously, your contact information should be present on everything you distribute.

"What if I'm afraid of public speaking?"

We discussed fear at some length in the first session, but here is a quick recap. Of course, public speaking is one of the biggest fears many people have, which is most likely rooted in the fear of embarrassment. While some people choose to practice speaking by joining a group or even hiring a coach, you may find the process much easier by doing the following: *speak from your heart.*

There is a saying among public speakers: *the audience will not care what you know until they know how much you care.* Speak about what you know. Speak from your experience. Carry yourself as though you were conversing with another individual, not a group.

Serve your prospects; not yourself.

How to Get Started

As we indicated in the first session, addressing audiences can be surprisingly easy. Program chair people and group leaders everywhere are always on the lookout for new ideas, new speakers, and information that offers value and is of interest to their members. Ask your clients, neighbors and friends, and your centers of influence if they belong to any groups—social, professional or otherwise—that would find the type of information you offer to be helpful.

Board Service

This obviously has much in common with volunteering, with one key difference. You can serve on the board of a corporation as well as a nonprofit. Serving in such a capacity is an excellent way to benefit other people with your expertise, as well as connect with other key leaders (centers of influence) in your community.

There are typically two kinds of boards—a board of advisors and a board of directors. Advisors are responsible for advice and counsel, while directors are accountable for major financial decisions, as well as advice. With the exception of special circumstances, your best method to beginning such a role would be on a board of advisors.

In an advisory position, you will be mingling with other important and influential individuals. You will need to be careful to not over-commit yourself, because these responsibilities can be time consuming. As you can imagine, individuals are typically invited to sit on local boards based upon their influence, affluence and relationships.

Joining Professional Associations

Professional associations, either in your own industry or in the industries of those for whom you prospect, are another positive and often overlooked opportunity. Your involvement and membership can help you expand your business, your expertise, and your contribution *back* to an industry in which you work.

- Associations have regular meetings, which offer opportunities for you to speak.

- Associations have their own publications, which offer opportunities for you to get published.

- Associations have development programs, which allow you to increase your expertise.

- Associations have leaders, which allow you to meet potential centers of influence.

> There is a saying among public speakers: the audience will not care what you know until they know how much you care.

In short, virtually everything we have spoken about can be achieved through professional associations. Look into them! Join at least two, and get involved!

Who Else Do You Know? (We had to Ask!)

You may be tired of asking this question. However, it must be continually asked: *Who else do you know?* Through your friends and family you probably already have a strong network in place. Some of the more typical entries on your list:

- ☑ Your immediate family members (parents, siblings, grandparents)
- ☑ Your extended family members (uncles, aunts, cousins)
- ☑ Your previous teachers (both high school and college)
- ☑ Your bosses from past jobs
- ☑ Your landlord
- ☑ Your lawyer and accountant
- ☑ Salespeople, beauticians and barbers
- ☑ A member of the clergy
- ☑ Members of your religious congregation
- ☑ Your banker
- ☑ Others with whom you volunteer or serve your community
- ☑ Former classmates from high school and college
- ☑ Fellow members in your professional association

Individuals are typically invited to sit on local boards based upon their influence, affluence and relationships.

So what do you think? Possible network? Not a bad start? The only challenge is that it is "asleep." Most of the people in your network may not necessarily see you in terms of what you offer. Instead, you are to them whatever is the nature of your relationship: the niece or nephew, the client, the patient, the fellow club member, the person next door. If you have a network that is "asleep," what you must do is to "wake it up!"

In other words, you want those around you to be aware of all you can do—of what kind of services you can provide for them and other people as you build your career.

There are many ways to accomplish this. Your value depends on several factors, which include the nature of your relationship with each person, what his or her specific needs are and the services you can provide.

No matter how well someone knows you *personally*, it is always better to *demonstrate to them* what you do and turn them into a client. Most people, whether they are neighbors, uncles and aunts or fellow church members, will have a much stronger opinion of your professional abilities if they have benefited from your services, rather than *simply being told* about the benefits you could provide.

Imagine that your uncle owns a dry-cleaning business, and you are a financial advisor. In the interest of building your network, you want to contact him to explain to him your business goals and services. There are two possible approaches.

One can be to set up a meeting, where you might sit and talk and perhaps ask for some advice. You might even pass on some literature for him to display for his customers. Of course, you also want to know if he has any contacts that you may call upon.

The second approach would be different. Instead of calling on your uncle and asking for advice and names, you ask your uncle about his business. Many scenarios can be imagined. For instance, you probably wouldn't have known without asking him that he was seeing a portion of his business slip away because of new competition. Perhaps he has been trying to upgrade his equipment but has struggled to find the capital required.

> No matter how well someone knows you personally, it is always better to demonstrate to them what you do and turn them into a client.

By asking about his business, you are actually inquiring about his needs. In response, you can lend your talents to examining his financial situation, and help bring him closer to his financial and business goals.

Now what do you think will be his impression of you?

He will definitely be impressed. **He will be sold on, not to mention indebted to, your abilities.** But what kind of connections does a person who operates a dry-cleaning business have that can help you? The answer is hanging on those racks in the back of the store. What do you see?

Men's suits. Women's suits. Your uncle has some influential people walking through his doors every day. If he is a good businessman, he knows most of them by name. After you have helped him resolve various financial goals, how enthusiastic do you think he will feel about suggesting your name to others? A lot more than if all you did was hand him your information and walk out while he remained preoccupied with his own challenges.

You may read this and think, "That is so hypothetical. How can it relate to me?" Sure, it's a fabricated story. But the principles apply everywhere. As you network, you search for needs. You provide for needs. You benefit people. You build relationships. Then, when opportunities arise, you get rewarded.

Because personal relationships are at the heart of successful prospecting, in recent years we have witnessed a growth in networking organizations and referral groups in metropolitan areas around the country. Another driver behind this growth, in my opinion, is the recent recession, with a mixture of professionals having to work harder at feeding the relationships that in turn feed their businesses, as well as the onslaught of networking newbies who have been forced into the job market and must now go out and sell themselves (many for the first time).

Moving forward, we will now cover three basic structural models designed to help you network, and are likely being used in your community. They are networking organizations, referral groups and your personal board of advisors.

II. Networking Organizations

Based on what I have seen, most networking organizations (typically localized to a specific geographic market) can trace their roots to a single individual in that region who wanted to explore and qualify new people with whom they could meet and talk with concerning their business (sound familiar?).

That person may have been a financial advisor, a real estate agent, or in one example I know, a professional carpet cleaner. They wanted to meet new people, but at that time, could find no satisfactory forum through which he or she could do that. So they went out and created one on their own.

By asking a person about his business, you are actually inquiring about his needs.

In central Ohio, we have several examples...and one I will give is Big Fish Networking (bigfishnetworking.com). This organization was started by Steve Baldzicki (I have remarks from Steve later in the book about social media)—a partner in a title agency here in central Ohio. His interest was to go out and meet people in the real estate industry, and so he began to organize ongoing events and fund raisers aimed at the local business community.

Despite its labeling as an "organization," there is no fee to become a member. Want to participate? Sign up for the email newsletter, and attend and participate in the networking functions. You can sponsor specific events or the organization itself and gain visibility and recognition for doing so.

The events are typically open gatherings (most free to attend), with door prizes from sponsors and, as I indicated, often include a fund raiser component as well. Networking for charity is a good excuse to get out and shake hands with people. Since Big Fish events tend to attract a lot of people, Steve usually does not have trouble partnering with other organizations to provide venues, light catering and door prizes. Those partners see the benefits of building relationships by delivering value—by demonstrating what they can do for people, they serve their prospects. It's win-win all around.

Networking organizations are pretty diverse. They can be for-profit or not-. Some focus primarily on key demographics, such as women, age groups, or even faith. Many events they organize will be free, some will require a fee or even advance registration (although in most cases, anyone who shows up at the door is unlikely turned away unless there is a compelling reason to do so).

> Networking organizations are pretty diverse.

In Denver, Colorado, there is the Certus Professional Network. Founded in 2004 by Sabrina Risley, Certus not only organizes a wide range of events that are open to all (most require a nominal fee to attend), but there are paid memberships available as well. Memberships have privileges that include (besides access to events at a greatly reduced cost) discounts on services and products from other members, access to member-only events and resources as well as being listed in their member directory.

Like many others have in the past, Sabrina began the Certus Professional Network out of an observed, genuine need in the community. "As a business professional, I as well as many other colleagues were seeking opportunities for sincere, genuine networking," Sabrina recalls. "All we found were gatherings where the attendees were there with one intent: to sell. Personally, I found it repulsive," she states bluntly.

"Genuine networking is not about trying to sell, but about building long-term relationships that lead to business and making money--both in the short and long term," Sabrina continues. "So I began to organize events with that spirit in mind. Today, I am pleased to say that helping business professionals connect with each other is how I earn my living. It's become an exciting and rewarding business."

As I indicated, Certus Professional Network events typically are not free. "It is amazing how a nominal charge to get into an event will impact the quality not just of the attendees, but of their intentions at the events as well," Sabrina adds. "Certus networkers are givers. We focus on listening to each other, and on learning how we can help one another."

"People often compare Certus to that of local chamber or commerce or business association. It truly is a community of givers," she says. And for one who visits an event and suddenly becomes panicked about what to say? "Then you are only thinking about yourself," Sabrina advises. "I distinctly remember during my novice networking years, I met another business professional who did nothing but listen to me for quite some time. She asked questions; she showed she cared, and that made a huge impact. It helped me learn how to be a giver."

Additional advice for new networkers: "Don't go to an event without a game plan. You don't want to just collect cards. Instead, consider what industries or professions that compliment what you offer and attempt to seek those people out—or someone who can connect you with them. Be strategic."

Can Networking Events Really Pay off? Here are Five Tips.

Open networking events are *always* happening. Which means only one thing: They *do* pay off!

Recently a friend of mine (who at the time was looking for a new job) decided to attend her first networking event to start prospecting for new opportunities. It was an after-hours social mixer that was bound to have a pretty robust attendance. "Any advice for a networking newbie?" she said. Here's what I had to share, which are really in the form of mistakes to avoid:

> "Genuine networking is not about trying to sell, but about building long-term relationships that lead to business."
> —Sabrina Risley

Tip 1: Check negative emotions at the door; rather, bring a smile.

I will be the first to admit it: I have had plenty of times when I have had an event to attend (or worse, an audience to speak before) and, for any number of reasons, I just wasn't up to it. We all have days when we feel that way–but there is no place for it when we are making first impressions. Further, that first impression is how we make others feel. Bad emotions and negativity are toxic. If you find yourself in this spot, before stepping in, stop. Take a deep breath, and offer a prayer of gratitude for the opportunity to meet new people (whose lives you just might be able to touch in a positive manner). Then smile, and carry your body language as you would if you were feeling positive and upbeat. You may be surprised on how this makes you feel.

Tip 2: Do not talk too much about yourself; instead, listen.

This is one of the most common mistakes we make–especially when we are nervous. When engaging others, don't jump right in to your own elevator pitch. Rather, ask others about them and what THEY do. Remember what we said in the last chapter about listening: put your personal agenda aside first, focus your attention on what the other is saying and then repeat back what they told you in your own words. Have them confirm your understanding of what they shared. This will make a strong emotional connection, because nothing beats the feeling of being understood.

Further, when that other person knows and feels that you both care and understand, they will be much more inclined to learn more about you and what you have to say.

> Open networking events are always happening. Which means only one thing: They do pay off!

Tip 3: Don't focus on who can help you; rather, seek opportunities to help others.

Once you get accustomed to attending meetings you will quickly spot those who are just in it for themselves. These are the people who, when engaging in conversation, will quickly screen you and others out if they don't see you as an immediate sale. If such a person screens you out, consider yourself fortunate.

Ultimately, we are all in it for ourselves in one way or another, but we also know that what goes around comes around. The purpose of getting people together to network is to make new friends and plant the seeds for long-term relationships. This happens when we listen, and in doing so we discover opportunities to build relationships by delivering value. An example of this might be hearing about another person's issue or business goal, and passing on a helpful resource, or introducing them to another person who might help them reach their goal (if you cannot help them directly of course).

Tip 4: Focus on quality over quantity.

So often, networking newbies work a room and collect business cards. While growing a contact base is not in itself bad, this should not be your primary goal. Try to have a handful of decent discussions (without dominating one person's time–after all they want to mix with others also). If you have a half a dozen good conversations and subsequent opportunities for follow up, then that's a good night. My personal opinion is that business cards should get exchanged at the *conclusion* of a conversation, not at the beginning (although some people will use it as an ice breaker—and if that's what makes *them* more comfortable, then just roll with it).

Tip 5: Follow Up.

It's amazing how many people never follow up–which makes the whole effort rather pointless, does it not? Let's say you attend an open networking event (or just meet a new business contact in some other context). Generally speaking, here is what you should do:

1. Within 24 hours, mail a hand-written follow up note (keep a stash handy that you can write up and send out quickly). You can also use an online service like SendOutCards.com—which I like and use myself—however I still prefer something truly hand-written for new contacts.

2. Assuming you have their business card, enter their contact data into your address book (I am partial to Plaxo.com—a live, online address book that will sync with Outlook and your mobile device). If you carry an iPhone, use CardMunch to scan their business card into your address book. The app is owned and distributed by LinkedIn. It's not a card reader...it's a free service offered by LinkedIn that sends the card image to a *human being* who in turn types the contact data in for you and sends it back to your device—often within minutes! You'll love it—especially when you find yourself with a dozen or more business cards to process.

   Additional note: When entering a new contact's information, be sure to include the date and place of the first meeting in the notes section of your address book. As you meet more people, trust me—you will be glad you took this extra step.

3. Speaking of LinkedIn...look the contact up on that network and extend a *personalized* invitation. (CardMunch will look them up on LinkedIn for you and even automatically extend a connection invitation to those with whom you are not already Tier 1 connected, but I strongly recommend not using this feature until it permits you to add a custom note with the invitation. If this all sounds Greek to you, the flag this page for revisiting after you read more about LinkedIn later in the book in the section called "From Screen2Screen to Face2Face."

> The key to successful networking is building relationships; and the key to building relationships is helping others.

4. Call or email the contact to schedule a follow-up meeting right away if you both concurred that it would be mutually beneficial during your first meeting (this may not always be the case). If a follow up visit isn't possible right away, add that person to your mailing list, be it for electronic or postal.

5. If you can deliver some value to that new contact to build the relationship, what might it be? What did they share with you about their needs, wants and concerns?

These are some of the fundamentals, especially for one who is new to networking. Consider these five simple points, and you may just turn what might have been an evening of anxiety and frustration into one of enjoyment and success!

A Note About Meeting for Coffee... Be Sure to Have a Cup.

As I indicated, it's important to have follow up meetings with new contacts, when possible and appropriate. Many of us whose jobs involve being out and about, prospecting and meeting people will often do so coffee houses. Here in Columbus, Ohio, I am partial to Panera in particular.

Recently I was in a Panera Bread store that I frequent on the east side of Columbus. When I ordered a cup of coffee, Dan, the general manager told me it was on the house because he sees me in there so often.

As much as I appreciated the gesture, I couldn't accept it. "Why not?" Dan asked.

"For as much time as I spend in here," I answered, "I feel like I should be ordering more than just coffee." Sometimes I would order something else, but the truth was, for the free wifi, the crackling fire and the relaxing atmosphere, all I was paying for that "office space" was about two dollars—which included all the refills I wanted. And I wasn't just ordering it for show: the truth is, I'm a coffee lover; it was a win-win arrangement.

Dan chuckled at my response, acknowledging that the place was very popular for one-on-one business meetings. "Last week," he told me, "our district manager was here. Late one morning we looked out at the dining room and saw perhaps ten to fifteen people sitting, meeting and working, and not a single coffee cup on the table! The DM went out and politely asked them all to leave if they were not going to order anything."

When entering a new contact's information, be sure to include the date and place of the first meeting in the notes section of your address book.

I replied that I could understand the DM's point of view. "Me too," Dan countered, "However I don't think I would have gone that far. I'm happy to fill the seats. If you can do that, you'll make money. That point in time may have just been a fluke."

Dan probably has it right—bring people in, provide value, and you'll build customer relationships. However, it begs the question: If you use someone else's business, such as a coffee shop or restaurant, to build your own, yet you don't patronize that business, what does that say about you—especially in circumstances when you are meeting prospects for the first time?

This gets into subtext here. It's the difference between being a giver and a taker. It's also a measure of showing respect for the people and resources at your disposal to help you do business. If you appreciate those establishments being available for you to meet others and conduct business of your own, don't they deserve the respect of your patronage?

Not a coffee drinker? Fine! Order tea, juice or a soft drink. Order something—and while doing so, encourage your guest to order as well and pick up the tab (By the way, that's a cardinal rule if you extended the invitation.).

III. Referral Groups

Another popular model for organized networking are what I will refer to as Referral Groups. These are typically tightly managed groups of non-competing professionals who meet on a regular basis to share ideas, contacts and referrals for potential business opportunities. Essentially, when you join the group, the group becomes your extended set of eyes and ears in the community, as you become for every other member.

Always send a personalized invitation when connecting with someone new on LinkedIn.

There are several national models for these groups, such as AmSpirit, BNI, LeTip, Business Leads of America and Gold Star Referral Clubs. I will say up front that there are a lot of people out there who will swear *by* these groups; and still some others who will swear *at* them. As most group leaders and organizers will acknowledge up front: it's not necessarily for everyone. Here is why:

- First of all, it does require a financial investment. To join a club, you pay a fee that is either monthly or annually, or both. It is typically between two and four hundred dollars per year.

Chapter 3

- Second, just because you are willing and wanting to join, doesn't mean you will be accepted. The most reputable referral group organizations have a screening process that they adhere to not just to protect their members, but also to protect their brand. They won't take just anyone—nor should they.

- Third, most referral groups hold weekly meetings at a set time and place. Membership in the group requires mandatory attendance in most cases. You need to be committed.

- Fourth, the basic structure of the referral group are individuals in different professional categories. So each group will have just one financial advisor, one insurance representative (with possibly one who does life, another doing property and casualty, another doing health, etc.), one mortgage broker, one real estate professional, one banker, one plumber, one butcher, one baker, one...well, you get the picture. The categories I suggested first are typically the ones that fill up the fastest, and don't be surprised if the leader/organizer is in one of them. The idea is that the members *compliment* each other, rather than compete. Which leads to the next point...

- Fifth, the basic premise of most referral groups is built upon members helping each other build their respective businesses. So, in order to receive referrals from members of your group, you need to be willing and able to *give* them as well. Some—but not all—have requirements that as a club member, you need to provide a set minimum number of referrals to fellow members. These quotas may be on a weekly, monthly or annual basis. As you provide referrals to others, referrals in turn will come your way as well. Obviously, the larger the group, the more professions and industries represented, and the easier it should become for you to spot opportunities for fellow members as you go about your weekly routine.

> Referral Groups meet on a regular basis to share ideas, contacts and referrals for potential business opportunities.

These are the basic tenets that most referral group organizations have in common. Each model and organization is going to differ in some fashion, ideally to make themselves stand out among the competition. However, if you read the points above, one might wonder: why should I *pay* to join an established club rather than just starting my own?

This is a key question that a lot of people ponder. Greg Leffel is a Director with Gold Star Referral Clubs and hears these kinds of questions all the time. "Essentially, it comes down first to you deciding what you want," Leffel points out. "Our purpose is to grow business—pure and simple."

"With Gold Star, we emphasize this sense of community—of truly wanting to help each other grow, not just ourselves. And you will find that to be the case with the most enduring models that are out there," Leffel continues.

"Secondly, to achieve this purpose, a club must follow a structure," Leffel says. "It's like any other organization—when you become a member there are certain criteria that may need to be met, and expectations for what is very much a reciprocal relationship." All of the successful models like the ones listed earlier have such guidelines, which include fee structures, expectations and requirements for continued membership and participation. Sure there are similarities, but there are differences as well.

"Some groups are stricter in their requirements than others," Leffel points out. "When making a choice, it's really up to you to evaluate those criteria and decide for yourself what suits you best. But the choices are out there."

Leffel adds that among all the differences, there is one trait that most—if not all—have in common: the meeting agenda. "Everything revolves around the meeting," Leffel states with conviction. "If your meetings are not successful—that is, resulting in productive referrals for your individual members—then your group will not succeed, nor will it grow."

> Among all the differences between referral groups, there is one trait that most have in common: the meeting agenda.

Requirements to run successful meetings include (but are not necessarily limited to):

- ☑ **A good location.** Location is very important—it must not only be practical and accessible, but it should reflect the spirit and culture that the group hopes to emulate to the public and to potential members.

- ☑ **An agenda.** For productivity and timeliness, an agenda is crucial. It keeps the pace of the meeting on track, and it also ensures that the purpose is served for every member attending. It helps the facilitator make sure that discussion topics stay on track as well.

- ☑ **A positive spirit that makes ALL feel welcome.** The small group model of mutual support for a common purpose is ancient. This dynamic is very important to furthering a spirit and attitude of brotherly love, personal growth, and

Chapter 3

☑ **Attendance and participation.** Why is this last? Well, if you haven't gotten these other factors lined up correctly, it becomes a mute point. If your group members are focused on meeting each others' needs then attendance and participation will not be a problem. Everyone has choices as to how they will invest their time—and if members receive a "payback" for their investment in the group, they will not only return—but they will spread the word!

abundance for all. When members and visitors feel this spirit and experience the measurable, positive results it creates, they will be back and your group WILL thrive. This leads us back to the final requirement…

So this all appears simple enough, one may observe. This brings us back to the question: Why might one use a model like Gold Star or AmSpirit? Why not just create a group on your own?

"That's one of the most commonly asked questions," Leffel says. "Sure, you can do it yourself—and I'm sure many have in situations where the conditions are right. But it is a process of being part of—if not running—an organization. Adopting a model that is time-tested keeps you from reinventing the wheel. You have the guidelines, the step-by-step plans, and the information tools not only to run the organization with minimal work and time, but to bring in new members and help them share responsibilities."

Most of my colleagues who have been actively engaged in referral clubs have said how valuable they can be. But as I said before, that is not to say that it is for everyone—but there is no doubt that for many of us who face the ongoing challenge of prospecting for new clients and seeking referrals to help us grow our business, considering such a group can be a great way to leverage the resources, the time, and the relationships that we have for our benefit and for the benefit of others.

As Leffel tells all his members and fellow directors: "You will grow your business, because that's what we are all about. But this will happen only as much as you focus your heart on helping others."

IV. Your Personal Board of Advisors

To be prepared also means to be accountable. This will require a team effort on your part and on the part of an *elite group* of your most important centers of influence.

Companies, universities and nonprofit organizations have boards of advisors, directors, or trustees. It's required by law. Why? The answer is simple: **accountability**. After all, leaders in positions of power cannot have *absolute* power. They must answer to *someone*—especially in situations where the leaders are responsible for managing assets that belong to others (such as publicly held companies and nonprofit organizations). There is a process of checks and balances that occurs in effective boards—which creates the sense of accountability that holds senior management's feet to the fire.

This is the value in creating a **personal board of advisors**: a group of three to five (or more) centers of influence who share your vision and want to see you succeed. To this end, your board should be available to give you:

1. Advice

2. Counseling

3. Encouragement

4. Pressure to follow through on your commitments

To begin, ask three to five of your *best*, most influential **clients** to serve on your board. Why clients? The answer is simple: only a client can truly grasp and understand the value of what you offer.

You share your mission statement and business plan with your board. Their commitment is to meet with you as a group two to three times a year.

This is not a new concept. In his book *Love the Work You're With*, author Richard Whiteley describes six key "jobs" that together, can make up an effective board of advisors:[3]

1. Mentor. We have already discussed the valuable impact that mentoring can have on your career. In many ways, your board is a group of mentors; however some members may take this role more seriously than others. Your mentor should care about your success and have ownership in your future development.

2. Strategist. What makes a good strategist? It's a person who can anticipate future challenges and opportunities, and can then alert you to them. It's a person who can teach you to do the same—to look beyond *the next step* to *the next five or six steps,* and evaluate all the possible outcomes. Talk about being prepared!

3. Solution Provider. This individual would be more focused on the present, helping you confront more immediate challenges so that you can move forward with achieving your goals.

4. Coach. We all need a coach from time to time—it's someone who helps us stay focused on what we want to achieve and how we are going to achieve it. Coaches are immensely valuable in situations when we begin to feel as though the world is bringing us down.

> Companies, universities and nonprofit organizations have boards of advisors, directors, or trustees. It's required by law. Why? The answer is simple: accountability.

5. Butt Kicker. This is the person you do not want to tick off—because you know that if you let him down, you will either get an earful, or worse, they will sever his ties with you. He or she can also motivate you to challenge yourself in ways you never imagined.

6. Cheerleader. Your cheerleader should always reinforce a positive attitude—not only in a "Pollyanna" sense but also to always help you to see problems as opportunities and to look for the positive side of every "issue" you may face in your career.

Enlisting Board Members

We indicated earlier that your board of advisors consisted of elite members of your centers of influence. They can be suppliers, clients, or work associates. One thing to remember is that movers and shakers are typically asked by many organizations to join their boards, so being asked will be nothing new to them.

The Secret to Effective Board Meetings: Big Deal It!

Serving on your board should be a pleasant experience—not something that your members should do with hesitation or regret. To maintain the maximum benefit from your board meetings, you must be prepared to provide maximum input—you must be prepared to **Big Deal It!**

What do we mean when we say to Big Deal It? It's simple: you make your meeting, the activity and the advice your members are sharing something special. This isn't some ho-hum boring routine board meeting that occurs within so many organizations. **Your board meeting is the *willing* assembly of some of the greatest minds you know—and such a gathering should be given appropriate seriousness and respect.**

The more seriousness you give the process in front of your board, the more seriously your attendees will take their roles as members. They need to see that you mean business.

How do you take the Big Deal Approach to planning your board meeting? We recommend that you consider the following steps. What we are suggesting is no different than what you would see from a first-class corporation. There are no gimmicks; however if you think some of them seem like going overboard, think again about the impact (or subtext message) they will have on your members:

1. You respect them, their time and their counsel

2. You respect your mission and your business, and

3. You respect yourself.

Following are the specific steps to scheduling, preparing, and administering a successful meeting of your Personal Advisory Board:

Scheduling (two to three months in advance)

1. Schedule your meeting at least two to three months in advance. We all know how challenging it can be to assemble a group of movers and shakers together in a single place and at a single time. Pick at least three options, and find out which choices are the best for *all* your members (ask them to indicate to you which ones work—and emphasize that it is important that they choose more than one, if possible). The more options you offer, the better your chances of having full attendance.

2. Choose a business setting for your meeting. If your idea of a good meeting location was in your dining room with screaming kids running loose, think again. Meeting rooms are not difficult to obtain, whether rented in a hotel or simply at your corporate offices. Remember, this is business. Choose an environment that is first class and matches the impression you want to create.

3. Once the time and place is set, send out letters to confirm. When we say letters, we mean LETTERS! In the age of email, letters have increased perception of formality and respect. Tak-

---

Only a client can truly grasp and understand the value of what you offer.

ing the time to send out a personalized letter on your company stationery sends the *subtext* message that you appreciate their time and respect.

Preparation (from scheduling until days before meeting)

4. Prepare Information Packets. A complete information packet should include the following:

a. A **personal brochure** describing your services, qualifications and how you meet the needs of your targeted market. This may be a single page, a double sided page, or an 11x17 half-fold newsletter format. It should have a clean design and some color as well.

b. A **statement of objectives.** Remember, your statements should follow the **SMART** formula: **Sensible, Measurable, Attainable, Realistic, and Time-specific.**

c. A **meeting agenda.** This document may open with specific indicators as to what results you wish to achieve through the meeting. Is it feedback on a sales and marketing plan? Is it "business intelligence" on what's happening in the community? The more tangible ideas you offer for feedback, the more effectively you will elicit responses from your board members.

d. A **one-sheet indicating time and place.** This clearly states the time and place of the meeting, with a map indicating the location and directions.

e. A **pocket folder.** It's all about presentation. All of the above items, and anything else you may choose to include, should be neatly arranged in a crisp, attractive 9x12 pocket folder.

5. Hand-deliver (if possible) the information packets to your board members. This should be done one-to-two weeks prior to your meeting. They should know what to expect at the meeting, and how long it will last. This will not guarantee that they will review your information—although a crisp presentation will improve your chances.

6. Call each member personally to confirm receipt of the package and of their plans to attend. It never hurts to make an extra call, and many of your members will appreciate the reminder. It also is the best way to ensure the highest attendance possible. An office assistant can do this if you wish.

Administering the Meeting

7. Arrive early to properly set up. You do not want to arrive at the same time as everyone else. When your guests arrive, they should find you there to receive and greet them.

8. Have the following items available for your meeting:

a. **Extra information packets** for the board members who inevitably leave their packets at home or the office.

b. **Pens and notepads,** just as a precaution.

c. **Refreshments** that you are confident your members will enjoy, that will not interfere with the progress of the meeting; nothing alcoholic.

d. **Thank-you gifts.** These needn't be anything elaborate or expensive. It may be a personalized pen or gift certificate to a restaurant. Whatever it is, it should be sincere and send a message that says, "thank you!"

9. Lead the meeting from your agenda. Outline where you are, where you have been, and where you want to go. Use your materials to back up your information. Tape record your meeting if it's okay with your members. Get productive feedback, and stay focused on creating the results you intended.

10. Keep the momentum going. In other words, while everyone is in the same room, arrange the next meeting on everyone's calendar. Afterwards, begin the same preparations for your next meeting! Keep the process alive and make it part of your routine, and theirs! Your results will be staggering!

At each meeting, you share "all your numbers." The more concise you are, the better the advice you will receive. Many successful sales professionals have followed this procedure, and in almost every case, each member of the board has acted as a true COI and has given many, many introductions.

Sound like too much? If you make it important, so will your board members also feel its importance. They will take your work, your intentions, and your inquiries seriously, will not hesitate to give you the best guidance, and will connect you to the best prospects available.

Chapter 3

Chapter Review

1. What is networking, and why is it important to your career?

2. What are the "Two Faces" of Networking?

3. Do you have centers of influence? How many?

4. Why have a mentor?

5. Define social mobility.

6. According to Sabrina Risley, what is Networking NOT about? Why should one network?

Building Prosperous Relationships Through Networking

7. List the Five Tips to make networking events pay off.

   1. _____
   2. _____
   3. _____
   4. _____
   5. _____

8. Name three ways in which referral groups are typically different from open networking organizations.

   1. _____
   2. _____
   3. _____

4. What do virtually all referral groups have in common?

   _____
   _____

5. A personal board of advisors will give you:

   1. _____
   2. _____
   3. _____
   4. _____

6. What did you learn most from Chapter Three?

   _____
   _____
   _____
   _____
   _____
   _____
   _____

Chapter 4:

Sharpen Your Point of Contact

Up until now, we have focused primarily on issues of making contacts, generating referrals and meeting people. However, that is only part of the challenge. You may be great at meeting people—but how do you handle yourself at the moment of contact? Last chapter, we were outwardly focused. Now we must direct your attention inward.

After all, if you screw it up at the point of contact, it is all for nothing. First impressions matter. For example, do your eyes verge upward when asked, "What business are you in?" Consistency is vitally important when meeting and speaking with others. There is nothing insincere about rehearsing what you say, so long as you actually know what you are talking about.

In the previous chapter we covered the essential points of networking and finding the right centers of influence; and we learned the importance of building relationships.

One might complete the previous chapter and think that's all there is. **Nothing could be further from the truth.**

You may know how to *seek* people whom you can approach on a favorable basis—which begs the question: *how do you approach them?*

Chapter 4

You have only one chance to make a good first impression. If your first impression is negative, it could be your last! This is your chance to shine—or make a total fool of yourself.

In this chapter you will be focusing *inward*—if you don't, everything you have learned so far will be for naught. It's time to look at yourself, your presentation, and that all important first impression.

Before we get into style, we need to address substance. We need to address one question: *Why should a prospect even **want** to have just a twenty-minute conversation with you?*

I. Identify Your Value Proposition

> You don't determine your value; your clients do.

For many of you, the value proposition will be the most challenging step, because it is amazing how many people in business have never honestly and inwardly evaluated the **value** they provide for others. If you have worked in competitive, often price-driven industries, such as commodity supplies and services, you know what a challenge this can be.

This is not just a challenge—it's an *opportunity* to talk and listen to your most recent clients. Here's the truth: you don't determine your value; *they do.* Every customer values something different—although they will have much in common as well. Make a list of those individuals, and invite them for a cup of coffee. Then, your job is to find out what they value, why, and use that as a foundation for:

1. improving or optimizing your own service (more of that in a later chapter), and

2. building a true value proposition that gives prospects and potential centers of influence a reason to *want* to have a conversation with you

Let's review item number two again. This is what it all comes down to. This is what a value proposition is, in its simplest form: **Your prospects must have a reason to want to have a 20-minute conversation with you.** They have to *feel* as though they have more to potentially gain than they do to lose by giving up 20 minutes of their precious time.

In most cases, your value proposition must be tied to your prospect's bottom line. Your product or service must, in some way, either increase revenue, reduce costs (or both), or improve their life in some compelling way. It also makes your prospect's life easier and makes them more successful.

So, how are you going to achieve this? How are you achieving this right now for your present clients? It may be direct or indirect. You may not be the cheapest in selling and delivering office supplies, but your customers value your service and time saved in fulfillment. Or, perhaps you provide access to a particular niche of products that help your customers do business profitably.

And if your prices or fees are competitive, that opens the door to forging a business relationship that can lead to delivering higher-margin products and/or services. It is about leveraging prosperous relationships for every piece of potential value you can deliver to your clients!

When talking with clients, you will find that different people value different things. In professional services, such as insurance, investing, accounting, information technology, real estate, health and wellness, and multiple others, value is most often found in trusting relationships. In business-to-business relationships, do not underestimate this dynamic in how it impacts your client's profit margin. **In fact, just three or four testimonials on how your service makes a business-owner or executive's work life easier and more successful can be a powerful value proposition.** Saving time, reducing stress and anxiety, or helping your business clients provide better service to *their* customers is worth its weight in gold!

So remember, your value proposition is your prospect's REASON to WANT to have a conversation with you. It is your job to give them that reason.

Further, you may need to go through this process more than once because:

1. it is likely that you have more than one market, and

2. prospects in each market will likely have a different reason to want to meet with you

For example, if you deliver telecom services (offering cable television, voice and data), the owners and managers of restaurants and bars will have a different reason to want to talk with you than will professional service firms, such as those in law and accounting. Each market has an interest in different products and/or services.

Just three or four testimonials on how your service makes a business-owner or executive's work life easier and more successful can be a powerful value proposition.

Chapter 4

Two Approaches to Presenting Your Value Proposition

Approach #1: Tell a Story

In developing your value proposition, what positive, measurable result can you create for someone else?

This question presents a challenge for many people. Such was the case for Chad, a job seeker who approached me after leading a discussion. He had a diverse background, largely in information technology. "I've been instrumental in deploying updated systems for one employer; at another I developed new protocols for support teams…"

As he recited his background interwoven with jargon that went over my head, part of me wanted to just hold up my hand and say, "Dude, you're losin' me."

Mind you, this impulse (which I withheld), was not out of indifference. Rather, it was in Chad's focus on tasks, rather than *results*. Instead, I engaged Chad by pausing him and replying: "Really? You did that? WHY is that important? Can you tell me a story?"

What stories can you tell? People love stories because they can relate to them. A concise, results-focused story will enable you to emotionally connect with your prospect, and define your value proposition at the same time.

If you are prospecting for a job or client, here is a template that might help you develop a story from a previous engagement:

> **"Not long ago, one of our clients was facing the problem of [identify the issue here], and it was causing [articulate, in measurable terms (time, money, lost sales, etc.), what the issue was costing them]. The client invited us to sit down and focus in on what the real issue was, and together we [describe the solution that was implemented], which led to [state your measurable, positive results, and the impact it had on all stakeholders]."**

How many stories or scenarios from your service history can you develop and share? Develop three and then compare and determine what all of these stories have in common. List them out.

Important Note: This need not always be told from the negative (which is reactive in nature). It can also be told from the positive (proactive). Instead of a "problem" that is addressed, you may do yourself better by telling the story of an opportunity (which is what problems are)–indeed that should be the ultimate lesson learned: how was this problem translated into an opportunity to create a positive result?

To engage with a story is the first step. Tell your story, and then follow up with the statement: **"What this means to you is…"**

Approach #2: Before & After

Once I recalled the comments of a colleague in the tax, accounting and payroll service as he pondered, "How can I *show* people what I do, as opposed to just telling them?"

You might think that this question is answered more easily than others. For example, a graphic designer can show a portfolio of work; a writer can show what she has written and where it's been published (Although, in both cases, prospects should be more interested in what tangible results the writing and designs helped to produce.). You are charged with engaging your prospects by showing them what you offer. If you are an accounting and tax professional, an insurance professional, or an IT consultant, this question is: How do you *show?*

If you are having trouble identifying your value proposition, then stop trying. Instead, think in two simple terms: *before* and *after*.

Start with a blank piece of paper. Lay it in front of you horizontally. Across the top, write down the name of just ONE previous (or current) business relationship.

Divide the page into two columns, by drawing a line down the middle. The left column will be labeled "Before;" the right "After." By now you are starting to figure this out...?

Under "Before," list between three and six conditions that were in place before your involvement. These could be profound problems or simple inefficiencies. It may be a simple status quo—conditions that were in place and never questioned or challenged simply because no one ever thought to do otherwise. For example, before my work as a creative director at a fund-raising consulting firm, marketing programs (the campaign message and the corresponding print and video tools) often required six months to assemble and get distributed to their users. It was costly and time consuming, but that was how it was always done at that point.

In the right column, indicate the condition "After." Here it is very simple: how much did you reduce expenses? How much time did you save? How did you increase revenues and/or profits? How many people benefited from your work? If you don't know the measurable answers to these questions, ask the person who would. In my example, after my involvement as a creative director, I was able to leverage my diverse media background and expertise in then-emerging technologies to reduce production schedules from *six months* to as little as *six weeks*—and slash budgets accordingly. This saved the company money, the clients money, and helped them raise more money much faster. Did it happen overnight? No—but by the time of my departure, procedures were far different and more efficient than when I began.

Keep it simple and brief. Use bullet points. Are you a job seeker? Create a "before & after" version of your résumé in this fashion—that will make it stand out. Simply indicate: "Here is what conditions were like before my involvement...and here is what they were after."

"Really?!" your prospect will respond. "How did you do that?"

Your response: "Great question! Let's set up a meeting and I'll tell you!"

Further, if you are already in a meeting, by all means share the *solution*. I emphasize this last, however, because too often, it is where job seekers will get bogged down FIRST (hence my story earlier about Chad).

Articulating the solution is more than just telling another person about what you did. Indeed, it is an opportunity to reveal *who you are*. For example, as you devised and implemented a solution:

What challenges did you encounter? No plan ever turns out just as we expect, so what were the bumps in the road? Were they budget constraints? Technical issues? Bad weather? How did you work around these hurdles? *This illustrates your capacity to improvise on the fly, making use of the resources at hand and keep your eye on the ball when something or someone is attempting to throw you off course.*

Who all was involved? No man is an island, so the saying goes. Chances are that you didn't achieve these results single-handedly. Give credit where credit is due. Praise your colleagues for their contributions. *In doing this, you demonstrate your role as a team player (or leader) and that you see the bigger picture of serving the needs of the group as opposed to striving for singular glory.*

> Why should a prospect even WANT to have just a twenty-minute conversation with you?

How long did it take? Some of your Before & After stories may only have taken a week; others, years! Common time frames are typically in the months-to-years time scale. *Knowing and communicating the duration will demonstrate you to be someone who can take the initiative and then see things through to their conclusion.*

Feel—and share—the emotion. "I will never forget when all of us were waiting on the results from this beta test, and suddenly..." These are often pleasant experiences; other times painful. They can be full of humor, of anticipation, or anxiety. How did the emotional experience impact you...change you? *Share this. Feel it. Make the prospect feel it with you. Shared emotions creates bonding, and bonding builds trust. Dare to be human.*

What did you learn? We learn something new everyday. Share what you learned. If the experience uncovered a weakness, be up front about it. *In doing so, you show a prospect that you offer not just what you can do today, but what you will be able to do tomorrow!*

These are important points to remember, because they not only flesh out who you are and your commitment a greater good, but more importantly create the human dynamic that is the seed for long term, prosperous relationships.

> Show a prospect that you offer not just what you can do today, but what you will be able to do tomorrow!

II. Know What to Say Before You Say it!

"So, what do *you* do?"

Imagine you are attending a social event. You encounter a person you haven't seen in years, and strike up a conversation. In the conversation, the inevitable question arises: "What are you doing these days?"

Good question! You've just re-evaluated your value proposition in terms of the *measurable impact* your work brings to others. How does this translate into answering the question: What do you do?

So get your story straight.

In order to make it clear to yourself and the public, it might be helpful to complete the following sentence:

"I am in the business of ...."

a.   selling life insurance

b.   selling building supplies

c. human resource consulting

d. real estate

e. information technology

f. business consulting

Remember: keep it simple! If you cannot describe what you do in a short paragraph, you probably don't understand it yourself.

As a management consultant, my work has often been broadly defined. As a result, I have also struggled with this concept. Many of us have. Now is the time to identify what you do, once and for all. By clarifying your value, you enable yourself to focus on what kind of prospects you are seeking. It's matching your service with the needs of the people!

Before your next meeting with a Center of Influence (COI), consider these steps to develop your message, and a clear description of what you do:

> By clarifying your value, you enable yourself to focus on what kind of prospects you are seeking.

1. Identify your target market

This should be familiar territory by now. Take a good look at the market you are targeting. Who are its members? Who would you like them to be? How broad or how narrow is your target market?

2. Clarify your prospects' wants.

Remember that you must always approach your market from its point of view. Different markets value different things. It's not about what you sell or offer—it's about your market's wants that you can fulfill. What do they want?

3. Articulate the value you deliver in addressing those wants.

Whether you offer one type of service or ten, the objective is to use your succinct marketing message to get the conversation started. Having this information ready will make it much easier for a fellow contact or center of influence to identify and introduce you to prospects that fit in your market. You must make it as easy as possible for them to help you!

Taking it Further: Your COI Talking Points

Perhaps you are still feeling stuck. If so, why not simply try telling your story through a series of **talking points?** For example, when you meet with a relatively new COI, he or she may ask you the following questions (**Note:** this is not intended to be a script of how a realistic conversation would take place, but rather to outline the essential points that you should try to convey):

COI: What do you do?

You: I'm in the business of helping my clients identify, set, and achieve their financial goals.

COI: How do you accomplish this?

You: Through a series of fact-finding sessions with my clients, I gather information pertaining to:

1. their specific financial goals

2. their anticipated timeline for each goal

3. their family values

4. their charitable interests

5. their legacy

I take this information and work with the client to identify financial goals that follow the SMART formula: Sensible, Measurable, Attainable, Realistic, and Time-specific. Through my products and services, I help my clients lay the foundation and create a roadmap for achieving their goals. To this end:

1. I will meet with each client twice per year for review purposes.

2. A staff of five (5) people will properly service my clients.

3. Most importantly, each of my clients will receive WORLD CLASS SERVICE.

For comprehensive service, we work closely with lawyers, accountants, trust officers and fee-only planners to coordinate the over-all financial plan and to make certain there are no loose ends.

COI: What are your qualifications?

Chapter 4

You: I have the following qualifications:

    1. Chartered Life Underwriter (CLU)

    2. Chartered Financial Consultant (ChFC)

    3. Seventeen (17) years professional experience

COI: That's impressive. What companies and products do you represent?

You: I have relationships with the following companies:

    1. ABC Life Insurance Company (service representative)

    2. XYZ Securities (broker dealer)

COI: What are your business goals?

You: I have established the following objectives for my business:

    1. To acquire fifty (50) new clients per year for the next three years, each with a minimum net worth of $400,000.

    2. Including my current clients, my total client base will not exceed 250.

COI: That's ambitious, but not out of reach. How do you believe I can help you?

You: Thank you for asking. I would really appreciate your advice and counsel as I take my business through this exciting transition. [Name of Mutual Friend] suggested that you would be a valuable resource and that I should listen and follow every word you share with me. Apparently, she thinks very highly of you!

> Flattery will get you everywhere, including further discussion about how your services benefit people.

Flattery will get you everywhere, including further discussion about how your services benefit people. If you can back up your claims with real-life stories, that's even better.

Important: *If the COI is a relatively new acquaintance, your initial goal should be to gain his or her confidence—even though you may have acquired the meeting through the positive recommendation from a mutual friend.*

*The following approach should be pursued **only** if your relationship with the contact or COI is "warm" enough, and there is genuine trust and respect. **Note:** if this is a new acquaintance, it may take **more than one meeting** before you can make the following request.*

Sharpen Your Point of Contact

You: Also, I would like you to introduce me to three people you know who may be able to benefit from what I offer...

COI: Actually, our conversation reminds me of a friend who is looking to grow his business here in town. Perhaps it may be a good idea for the two of you to meet!

You: I would love to speak with your friend! Would it be acceptable to call him right now? If you would introduce me to him, then I can set an appointment.

COI: Why not? Let's give it a shot!

Again, this sample conversation with a COI does not realistically reflect how it will go, *but rather the ground you should cover.* In speaking with a COI, it is vitally important to have a game-plan in place, and to have your story *scripted* accurately so that the person you are meeting with can feel confident that you are serious about where you want to go, and what you want to do. He or she will have no interest in wasting time on someone who is just fishing for anything that might bite.

Talking Points: A Step-by-Step Guide

Need to put your talking points together for an upcoming meeting? Use these step-by-step instructions as a guide.

1. Identify your target market.

2. What are this market's primary wants and needs?

3. Describe your products and services, and how they address these needs. This is your value proposition.

4. How do you ensure your client's satisfaction? Be specific.

5. Describe your qualifications.

6. List your business objectives in as much detail as possible. Where do you want to be in three years?

7. How do you plan to reach your objectives? What will be your most important activity?

8. Describe in a single sentence the number one reason people should have a 20-minute conversation with you.

This leads us into the next topic: the vital importance of having a script that is accurate, properly crafted, and delivered *from the heart, not from memory.*

Effective scripting is delivered from the heart, not from memory.

Chapter 4

The Secret to Script Success

We all have attended plays, concerts and movies—whether it was a sell-out show on Broadway or your third grader's stage debut in the school musical. Regardless of the setting, in your child's school or on Broadway, the same principle applies: the performers follow a script, and that script is *rehearsed* repeatedly before the performers go before an audience.

A similar pattern occurs in football and other sports. Many professional football teams have the first 25 to 30 plays of the game scripted before the game begins. Ask any professional football coach, and he will tell you that he knows exactly which plays he will run. He will evaluate how each play worked, and continue to use the most productive ones.

Using a script is not about being manipulative; it is about being prepared.

In the courtroom, defense attorneys will use the same argument that worked to get their clients acquitted in previous, similar cases. Surgeons will follow the same procedure for any given medical operation, and a pilot has a flight plan all mapped out from take-off to landing. You would not want to be in the courtroom, on the operating table or in the plane if the person in charge was not *well scripted*.

The same is true for sales professionals. Many people will argue that having a script is an effort to manipulate the prospect or client into doing something he would not normally do. Nothing could be further from the truth.

Pros are scripted. Amateurs ad-lib, and "wing it." This is laziness—not taking the time and making the effort to prepare.

Using a script, whether it is provided for you by your company, or one you write, is not about being manipulative or superficial. *It is about being prepared.* Scripts get a bad rap sometimes simply because they are not used properly. We have all had times when a sales person is talking with us, and we really feel as though he is talking *at* us. We can spot an amateur quickly.

Don't Memorize Until You Internalize!

Most people think that scripts need to be memorized. In many cases, they must be, especially for Broadway plays. However, actors do much more than recite the words—they perform. To this end, they are not only focused on the words, *but on the message* the words (and actions) are delivering. They have to internalize it—so that the message comes not from the mouth, but from the heart.

When this goal is achieved, the delivery is flawless. The words and the message come out naturally—to the point that the prospect is completely unaware that what he hears is scripted! In the case of a well rehearsed and performed play, the audience *forgets* the fact that what they are seeing is scripted, *and instead becomes captivated by the story.*

To successfully prospect, you must learn to develop and deliver scripts with effectiveness. If you do, there will be no limit to how far you can go. It is a tremendous and valuable investment of your time and energy, because once you know the script, very little will change. Even further, neither will the basic questions, problems, objections, and solutions. Once you learn to effectively cover these areas (and have heard and addressed the same questions over and over), you will be unstoppable!

As you refine and deliver your script (which ultimately communicates your value proposition), you may make modifications. This is appropriate, because in the process, you are internalizing—*you are focused more on the message and spirit of what you are saying, rather than being hung up on the precise words.* The difference between the amateur and the professional in all things in life is the skill and delivery. Anyone can hit a golf ball, but few people can hit it like Tiger Woods. It takes dedication, talent and practice. Woods has perfected his skill with long hard practice. You can do the same with your prospecting.

Sales professionals have perfected their delivery of words and inwardly know their value proposition. They have practiced overcoming objections, and their response to questions. The more practice they get among role players and yes, in the field as well (although you don't start there), the *sharper* their point of contact becomes. On that note...

Rehearsing Your Script

We have established that it takes practice, practice, practice. Does this mean that you simply go in front of the mirror and talk to yourself? Many pros do just that! However, practicing your script with a colleague or friend will offer several additional advantages:

You have the ability to test a conversation. If you are new to your business, conversations and various levels of rapport can go in almost unlimited directions. Practicing with another professional who has been there and can help role play with you will test the effectiveness of your communication.

In the case of a well rehearsed and performed play, the audience forgets the fact that what they are seeing is scripted, and instead becomes captivated by the story.

You uncover objections and learn to handle them BEFORE they occur. We have all been there...we have our message, our delivery rehearsed, and we think we have all the answers...until someone blindsides us! They give us an objection or raise an issue that we have never considered. The more you practice (with more colleagues or friends), the better your chances are of avoiding this painful situation.

You break the conversation down into manageable parts. Your conversation process should have structure—a beginning, middle and end—with a well defined objective. Breaking the process into manageable parts makes the conversation much easier to grasp.

You learn what works and what doesn't work, and share it with other colleagues. This is a crucial element to ensuring a consistent level of quality and reliability among many representatives who serve the same company. This is a great opportunity to form a study group with your peers.

You increase your confidence. As you practice your talk, as you internalize your message and believe in what you are saying, you will see the difference! Internalizing your message will give you confidence in yourself and in what you offer people.

Correct use of scripts and being well rehearsed is vital to proper preparation. You owe it not only to yourself, but also to your prospects, to have the answers available when they ask. If you are not prepared; if you do not have the answers; or if you stumble and stutter as you search your head for the right words to say, you will fail. So much is riding on your delivery—always be prepared.

To this point, we have dealt only with what is spoken. What you verbalize is only half the formula to effective communication. Equally important is what you say *between the lines*—and it had better match your talk. We are referring to the power of *subtext*.

> Subtext is a kind of underlying language that will either add to what is spoken, thus reinforcing and strengthening it; or it may contradict the spoken word, sending confusion and creating mistrust.

III. Speaking Between the Lines: The Power of Subtext

> By ensuring that the messages of your body and gestures match that of your words, you will increase your success in connecting with prospects and building long-term relationships with them as clients.

In any conversation between two people or within a group of people, there are messages being communicated not only through what is being said, but also through the underlying dynamics of what is *not* being said: the **subtext**. Subtext is a kind of underlying language that will either add to what is spoken, thus reinforcing and strengthening it; or it may *contradict* the spoken word, sending confusion and creating mistrust. This mismatch of communication happens all the time:

- ☑ Imagine the couple that has been dating for several months. They are on a romantic walk along the beach. The woman is filled with emotion, she stops and turns, gazing him in the eyes, and says, "I love you!" The man pauses, looks down to the ground, and responds, "I love you, too." His words say love, but his other motions indicate otherwise.

- ☑ The manager is on the phone with his supervisor. It's 4:30, and she wants to know how soon he will have his report on her desk. The manager is cornered—he hasn't even started. He responds, "Uh, I will have it for you first thing tomorrow." His hesitation in responding lets the supervisor know that he is not even close to completing the report!

- ☑ A little boy is running in the living room—something he knows his mother does not want him to do. He is dodging between the furniture when he bumps an end table, toppling a lamp, which comes down on the floor with a crash. The mother hears the sound and enters the room. "What happened?!" she asks her son. The boy's bottom lip is quivering. "I don't know!" he responds in a shaky tone.

We have all had times when we KNOW that we could have been more persuasive, more sure of ourselves, more confident, or better able to connect with another human being. In each of the illustrations above, one party is saying one thing, while his subtext is saying something completely different.

Subtext is a combination of many different elements, which include (but not limited to) body language, posture, hand movements, eye contact, tone of voice, images and gestures of physical contact.

Chapter 4

Most of us unconsciously perceive the subtexts of others with whom we interact. Imagine you are in the office, giving a presentation to a group of your colleagues. Some of them have their eyes fixed on you and continue to nod and respond accordingly. One of them, however, continues to yawn and look at her watch. In such a situation, any one of us would presume that individual is less interested in what we have to say than the others.

Referring back to the previous section, when you recite a script from memory, instead of internalizing it and delivering it from your heart, you send a subtext message that could be one or both of the following:

1. You do not really know what you are talking about.

2. You do not really believe in what you are offering.

Often, subtext signals are less obvious—to the point that although we get the message, we cannot always put our finger on why. Have you ever met a new person who, on the surface, appears friendly and agreeable? Yet, for a reason you cannot fathom, you have a sense of distrust about him...but you cannot articulate why.

> Many of us have different masks for different situations, and they are often necessary for us to live our lives effectively.

While it is important for you to accurately read the subtext messages others send, for our purpose, we are more concerned with helping you learn to control the messages *you send to others*. By ensuring that the messages of your body and gestures match that of your words, you will increase your success in connecting with prospects and building long-term relationships with them *as clients*.

Perception Dictates Reality

You have heard the expression, "You cannot judge a book by its cover." However, all of us do just that every day. *How* we present ourselves to others in our mannerisms, our dress, and our posture all reflect on the image people have of us. These are the things people perceive *first* before we ever open our mouths to speak.

Countless examples can be used to illustrate this point, but perhaps the most convincing is that of the very first televised presidential debate between Richard M. Nixon and John F. Kennedy in 1960. At the time, television was still a new frontier for politicians, and it was evident to most that Kennedy's appearance was much better than Nixon's (whose most noticeable flaw was his five o'clock shadow!). The result: the majority of people who *watched* the debate on TV felt that Kennedy had won; conversely, those who *listened* on the radio thought the winner was Nixon!

What image are you currently projecting? How does this compare to the image you wish to project? Do your prospects and clients see the same person that your spouse, parents and children see?

Many of us are much less guarded when we are among those who are closest to us. However, when we are out in the world, among people who do not know us so intimately, most of us are more guarded. *We wear a mask.*

In much of western society, our masks are, in many ways, what allow us to live and work together—because true feelings, emotions, and personality traits are in control. Many of us have different masks for different situations, and they are often necessary for us to live our lives effectively.

In business, this control is often equated with *professionalism*—a measure of conduct that is refined, confident, and often with conservative expressions of emotion.

For example, take a representative of an IT firm, meeting a new prospect who needs to update her office's computers. The prospect says she is considering letting her teenage nephew do the installation (it's a small company, but still does several million per year).

You might be thinking, to yourself, *This person is risking far more than she could ever hope to gain! Is she nuts?* However, in your conversations, you would not (hopefully) vocalize such thoughts in that manner. Instead, you would advise the client on the facts, using tact, sensitivity, and professionalism. *You would think before you speak.*

Financial service people face this challenge all the time. How often have you heard prospects make the most bogus excuses for poor financial decisions? How often have you found yourself biting your tongue, searching within yourself for the means to stear the prospect or client on the right path, yet doing so with tact and sensitivity?

Of course, we all know people who do just the opposite. (Note: this isn't always bad either. Some people appreciate blunt honesty—yet most do not. It's best to lean on the side of caution, and weighing the dynamics of your relationship with the individual before you choose to tell him that taking "hot stock" tips from a cabby on the way back from the airport is a nutty idea.)

Here are some fundamental guidelines to follow if you want to maintain a proper, professional image for successful prospecting. These guidelines will also help you make sure that your vocal and subtext messages are consistent.

Look people in the eye, speak clearly and with resonance.

We all have encountered people who just will not look us in the eye. Is it shyness? Are they hiding something? Who knows? Regardless of the real reasons, a lack of eye contact sends a subtext message of low confidence, and in some cases, disrespect.

At the same time, your voice also sends a subtext. Typically, a higher pitched voice sends a subtext message of ineffectiveness, regardless of how competent that person may be. It is perceived as lacking confidence and authority. This is true for both men and women (although a certain law of relativity still comes into play).

When you speak, you must speak with authority.

How do you do that? When you speak, or resonate, your voice from the chest, you send a message of strength, confidence, and dependability. On the other hand, when your voice resonates through your head, it sounds higher and more "nasal."

You may read this and respond, "My voice is my voice. There is nothing I can do about it!" Yes, that is true to some extent. But you can control, and in many cases train your voice to carry more authority and resonance.

Study and analyze your voice. Does it reflect the subtext you intend? If not, you must hear yourself as others do. Record your voice with a high fidelity recording device (a common feature these days on most smart phones). Record your scripts. Don't just listen for pitch and resonance, but how many "uhs" and "ums" and "you-knows" fill in the gaps? Work on that also!

Through practice, develop the habit of speaking from your chest. It takes a little more work in the same way that breathing deep takes more effort than breathing shallow (which often leads you to resonate too often through your head). But as with anything else, practice, practice, practice!

Maintain a sharp appearance.

We had to say it, didn't we? The quality of your appearance, through subtext, indicates to others the level of respect you have for yourself and the people with whom you interact. This is the case not only in how you dress but also in your overall physical condition.

Further, when you look sharp, you feel sharp! The payback is immediate!

What to Wear?

For many of us, one of the day's hardest decisions is in the morning when we get dressed. Political correctness aside, generally speaking, women dress to look attractive. Men dress not to make a mistake (i.e. pants pressed, shirt tucked in, belt and shoes match).

In most industries, conservative is the trusted approach. For men, dark colors in suits, a white shirt, and a muted tie. Women must also be conservative in their use of color, although they still have more flexibility than men.

Develop Your Style!

While it is important to adhere to certain standards, it is equally important to develop our own sense of style—one that sends the proper subtext message. We should endeavor to dress in a manner that says something about who we are—our values, our family, our work, our alma mater, whatever we deem important.

Style is not something you just choose one day. It is ultimately something you develop over time, whether it is dress for work, hanging around the house, or going out with your spouse. As your wardrobe evolves, your sense of style will emerge.

Overweight? Always Tired?

For many of us, our metabolisms slow as we get older. We just cannot afford to eat the carefree way we may have when we were in our youth.

When you look sharp, you feel sharp! The payback is immediate!

Chapter 4

Many people, most notably those who do not exercise, complain of always feeling tired. The reason for this is actually very simple. The lifestyle to which today's Americans have grown accustomed is completely out of sync with the way our bodies are programmed to operate and survive.

This programming runs very deep: it is the result of two million years of evolution. Examine your life conditions today, and compare them to those of your very distant ancestors, who walked the earth just a few hundred years ago. Starvation and famines were common, daily life and work were extremely hard and brutal. We have it easy by comparison.

As a result, only those humans whose bodies could conserve and store energy—and regulate its metabolism based on the availability of food—could ever hope to survive and reproduce.

That is why humans walk the earth today. As a race, we owe our existence to the same genetic programming that today, is making many of us overweight and tired.

When you don't exercise, when you spend your day sitting at a desk or driving a car, your body is not getting the physical activity it needs. This lack of activity tells the body that it doesn't need fuel, and stores the calories you take in as fat.

Plus, our eating habits go beyond high-fat foods. We also eat far too many carbohydrates—which is immediate fuel provided it gets burned through rigorous physical activity. If not, more fat!

That's why when you eat so-called "fat-free" food that is high in carbohydrates, it will be turned into fat anyway.

Plus, our habit of binge eating (eating fewer large meals instead of many smaller ones) is actually a signal to our body that a famine is on the horizon, and that it must slow down the fuel-burning rate and store as much fat as possible. Why? Our bodies are programmed to survive long periods without food. If you go even half a day without eating and then pig out at meal time, your body thinks it's your last meal for the foreseeable future. Conserve, conserve, conserve, your body tells itself.

We can't change this programming. Rather, we must work with it. Here are some basic steps, but I highly recommend that you explore the many resources available to you to lay out a detailed program of getting back in shape if this is something upon which you need to focus.

> As a race, we owe our existence to the same genetic programming that today, is making many of us overweight and tired.

1. Eat more sensibly, and eat throughout the day.

Animals graze. So should you. Three normal meals, and three medium snacks (or six small meals). Show restraint—and don't ever stuff yourself. Drink water throughout the day—eight glasses at minimum.

2. With professional guidance, start a resistance (anaerobic) training program.

Exercise with weights. Proper weight training doesn't have to take much time, and it can be extremely relaxing when you are finished. It does take work—you want to work your muscles hard enough that it HURTS! This causes them to grow, heal and change (which in turn burns fuel—even while you sleep!). You become stronger and healthier. Remember, you don't have to go to a gym. You can start work at home with a set of dumbbells.

> In any relationship, you will never always share agreement. But you must always strive to share understanding.

3. Add an aerobic routine.

This means running, biking, joining a class. Do something that you like and is convenient. Alternate your aerobic and anaerobic activity throughout the week.

This process makes you stronger, and gives you more energy! Your metabolism goes up—and the weight goes down.

Listen More Often than You Speak

With as much attention as we have given to speaking, scripting and presentation, one might be surprised to read the above headline. However, you know that God gave us two ears and one mouth for a reason. Yet you would be amazed at how many people are completely lost when it comes to listening.

Listening is one of the most important skills you can ever develop. Listening is the key to mutual understanding, which forms the basis for successful relationships. When sincere understanding and caring are present in any relationship, it transcends that relationship above the daily "transactions" which may occur.

Disagreements and other issues which may end a less stable relationship become almost trivial when two people share an understanding of what lies in the heart and mind of the other.

Chapter 4

In any relationship, you will never always share agreement. But you must always strive to share *understanding*. This is why it is crucial for you to learn to listen to all the people you encounter.

How to Listen

Effective listening is described as a skill, but in reality, it is a simple habit of communication. Like language itself, it becomes second nature. We must strive to reach the point where we do it without thinking of it as a "skill" or "technique" (just as some of us tell our young children, when dealing with strong emotions with another person, to "use words," rather than hitting).

> The first, and perhaps most important step to effective listening:
> Put your personal agenda aside.

But to get to that point, we must make a constant conscious effort to listen. There are three simple steps to effective listening:

1. Put your personal agenda aside.

This is the most common obstacle to effective listening. Have you ever sat through a conversation with another person, and as she was speaking with you, you went "a-huh," and nodded, the entire time thinking how you would respond? Have you ever been so eager to impress another person with your "wisdom" that you completely disregarded anything she had to say?

How can this be avoided? It's very simple. When another person needs your attention, you must consciously command yourself, "Okay, I know I have other things on my mind right now. But this person has something important to share and discuss, and so I will have to come back to those other things a little later."

Once you get the hang of it, it really IS as simple as it sounds. Again, it just takes practice.

2. Maintain undivided attention.

You must make a habit of showing sincerity—indicating that you want to listen and understand. This means maintaining regular eye contact and establishing a clear connection with the other person. Your temperament must be inviting.

Further, give your undivided attention. Don't allow your mind to wander or to fall into the old habit of thinking about what you will say next. If you realize that this is happening and you miss what the other person is saying, simply ask him to back up and repeat it for your clarification.

Sharpen Your Point of Contact

As you hear the other person's point of view, imagine his situation; begin to approach it from their perspective. This is a powerful exercise in gaining a true understanding of another human being—and an important step in making a connection and building relationships.

3. As you listen, feel free to converse.

By all means, converse. But do so with the intent of clarifying your own understanding, rather than attempting to get your own point across. Repeat what the other person is sharing with you, so that you may:

- ☑ Internalize the other's viewpoint in your own mind, thus increasing your own understanding, and
- ☑ Reflect your own understanding of what he or she is sharing with you.

Through this process, you enhance your communication, and reduce misunderstandings. More importantly, you give the other person respect and validation. There is perhaps nothing better to nurture a relationship than a sense of shared understanding.

"So, when do I talk?"

Yes, believe it or not, your viewpoint matters! However, just as others deserve your undivided attention, you deserve to have theirs. When you have demonstrated that you understand the other's position and have shown genuine empathy, other people will be better able to be open to what you have to say, whether it is a point of disagreement, concern, or affirmation.

In fact, your expressed understanding of the other's perspective will actually give more credibility to your own point of view and your advice.

Remember the Names of People You Meet

We have all been there. We are in a social gathering or a public place. Then, out of the blue, we hear our name called out.

"Keith! Hello!"

We turn our head to see the person calling our attention. The face is familiar, but we just can't match a name....

When you remember the names of individuals whom you have met only once, you send a subtext of someone who is polished and professional and who is genuinely concerned about other people.

Chapter 4

"Hey......*you!*" we reply with an exaggerated pointing motion. "How's it going?"

At that instant, *she knows it*—and you know that she knows it. You can't remember her name, or worse, you have no idea who she is! You feel like a heel. What kind of subtext does this send?

I have such little concern for others that I did not even take the time to remember your name when we met.

Perhaps that is a bit too harsh. But it's safe to say that virtually all of us have faced a situation in which we have either forgotten someone's name, or someone else has forgotten ours. As common as it is, this doesn't make it any less embarrassing, and in business—any less excusable.

A person's name is music to her ears, and when you remember the names of individuals whom you have met only once, you send a subtext of someone who is polished and professional and who is genuinely concerned about other people.

Think about the potential value of every person you meet. It is almost unlimited. Given this, does it not make sense to consciously make an effort to improve your retention of the names of people you meet? Of course! Here are some tips on how you can do that:

Make sure you hear it correctly. Some names are more difficult to remember than others. When someone introduces himself to you and tells you his name, repeat it back to him. You can also ask him to repeat their name, if needed.

Ask how to spell it. An additional method of increasing retention is to ask the person how his name is spelled. It also enables you to create a more visual memory of the name, and associate it with the face of your new acquaintance.

Use the name in conversation. When talking with your new acquaintance, use his name just a couple times, to reinforce your own memory. Use some restraint, because evoking the person's name too much can make you appear pretentious.

Use word association. Associating a name or word with something else that is more familiar to you is a trick most of us have employed at one time or another—when forgetting a name or word was simply not an option. Look for something in common—for instance, if a person's name is similar to a favorite writer or actor, you can use that as a means of remembering.

> When talking with your new acquaintance, use his name just a couple times, to reinforce your own memory.

Write it down! This seems obvious, doesn't it? If you carry a small notepad or smartphone with you, taking a moment to jot down the name of a new acquaintance should become a habit. The act of writing itself helps you remember, and you can retrieve it later to make additional notes in case you would like to follow up.

Reciprocate. When introducing yourself, be clear about sharing your name. If it's spelled in an unusual manner or if your name has many "versions," make a habit to clarify that up front. "Hello, my name is Carrie—with a C." It's not egotistical—it's being sensitive. People appreciate it.

Another Strategy with Social Media...

You can also use social media technology to help you attach a name to a face. When you connect with someone new, and enter their contact information into your address book, attach their photo too. How tough is that? When the photo becomes part of the entry, it synchronizes to your smartphone as well.

The steps are very simple.

- Enter your new contact's data into Outlook or Plaxo (or other similar utility).

- Go to your contact's LinkedIn or Facebook profile page. On their profile photo, right-click and choose "Save picture as..."

- In your My Pictures directory, create a sub-directory called "Contacts"

- Re-name the image file for the contact you are recording, and save it.

- In Outlook or Plaxo, double click on the photo box, and assign the photo accordingly.

That's it! You're done. Now, as you routinely go through your address book, be it on your computer or hand-held device, you will see that person's photo with others and be better prepared to match the name to the face!

These are just some of the most essential points you must remember to ensure that the subtext messages you send are consistent with what you are saying. As we indicated earlier, the last thing you want to do in making a first impression is to confuse people. Focus on your presentation, your manners, and skills in listening and in reflecting. Follow these steps and you will find that any barriers you may have previously experienced in building rapport and connecting with others will quickly fade away.

Before you know it, you will be on your way to making new friends and building long-lasting, prosperous relationships!

(Chapter 4 Endnotes)

1 Whiteley, Richard C. *Love the Work You're With*. New York: Henry Holt and Company, 2001.

Chapter Review

1. What is the definition of Value Proposition?

   _____

   _____

   _____

2. Name two approaches to articulating one's value proposition.

   1. _____

   2. _____

3. Do you have any centers of influence? If yes, indicate how many.

   If no, explain why! _____

   _____

   _____

4. What is the value to you in preparing and rehearsing scripts?

   _____

   _____

   _____

   _____

5. What is subtext? How does it affect your message?

_____
_____
_____
_____

7. What did you learn most from Chapter Four?

_____
_____
_____
_____
_____

Chapter 5

Chapter 5:

What Do You Want?

I. No Shortcuts, No Quick Fixes

You have heard it before, and you will hear it again. To get what you want, you must understand that there are no shortcuts around discipline.

Discipline helps us reach our potential and get what we want. It is not enough to *have* the skills and the talent. To succeed, you need the discipline to exercise those skills on a consistent basis.

Three Keys to Strengthening Discipline

If we want to enjoy the freedom of discipline, we need to employ three keys simultaneously. When we use these keys correctly, we get closer to our goals.

Key #1: Delayed Gratification

Delayed gratification acknowledges that life has both pleasure and pain. As author M. Scott Peck, M.D. says, "Life is difficult".

The process of writing a book is a great lesson in delayed gratification. It's like writing a term paper every night for a week, a month, or even a year before you experience the satisfaction of a completed project.

Discipline is key to the role of coaches overseeing a group of athletes. The late Tom Landry, former coach of the Dallas Cowboys, frequently summed up his job as a coach in an interesting way: "I have a job to do that isn't that complicated, but it is often very difficult—to get a group of men to do what they don't want to do so that they can achieve what they've wanted all of their lives."

Delayed gratification helps build the discipline we need to succeed in school, as well as in our careers. It helps us not only to earn more, but also to become more responsible with the money we earn, to plan for the future and live within our means.

Key #2: Making Our Choices before "The Moment of Choice" Arrives

We all know that life is full of choices. We also know that it is the choices we make that determine the outcome of our lives and our careers. **We are responsible.**

To ensure that we make the right choices, we must understand exactly what we want in order to organize our options. We must have a clear understanding of our priorities.

When clear priorities are in place, making the correct choices becomes much easier—our priorities serve as a guideline for our decisions. However, clarifying your priorities requires one very important prerequisite—and that's the third key...

Key #3: Knowing What You Want

We need to have a clear understanding of our priorities.

The third key leads us naturally into the heart of this session. A focused goal answers the question, "Why?" Everything we do must be for a reason.

When approached this way, we see that discipline is not restrictive—indeed it is quite liberating. Furthermore, it is a responsible use of our freedom.

What do we mean when we say this? What is freedom? Many people define freedom as the ability to do *whatever you want, whenever you want*. In essence, it is constantly to make choices that give in to immediate gratification.

> Delayed gratification helps build the discipline we need to succeed.

However, do people who use their freedom this way really achieve happiness? Do they truly get what they want? No. In fact, they end up feeling trapped and frustrated because they *cannot* get what they want. Those who recognize the *true potential* of their freedom to choose set their goals and live disciplined lives. They are the ones who are truly liberated.

Children want to know why discipline is necessary—what's in it for them? The reasons we give must be important. The practiced life of discipline must come from motivations rooted deep within the soul. *It needs to be a passion.* This passion will give you strength in moments when you feel weak.

Hone these keys to discipline, and you will be on your way to experiencing a life of discipline and will discover that you have the power to persevere.

The Power of Perseverance: Hitting the Wall

Discipline will get you going on your way to achieving your goals. But it will take perseverance to get you there.

What is the biggest challenge of running a marathon? Of course, the biggest challenge—for "everyday" runners—*is finishing*. Marathons are long-distance races, and the most notable of them attract the best competitive runners from around the world. However, beyond the *competitive runners* are the everyday people who also compete in these events. The vast majority of them don't expect to come in first, or even 50th! They are there to compete with themselves. *They are there to finish.*

Marathoners have an expression when their strength begins to run out. Many runners consider the marathon two races in one: the first 20 miles and the last 10-K. In the last 10-K, you're exerting the most effort, your legs are complaining, your body has run out of fuel, and your head feels cloudy. The pain is too much. You are ready to quit. This is called *hitting the wall.*

Hitting the wall is when you want to give up. It's when your positive thoughts begin to give way to the desperate realization that you can quit, relieve your pain, and everything will "still be okay," the world won't end.

> Discipline will get you going on your way to achieving your goals. But it will take perseverance to get you there.

Chapter 5

You don't have to be a marathon runner to experience this. Our reaction to hitting any wall is what causes so much *oscillation* in our lives—bouncing back and forth between good habits and bad ones. We get ourselves going, but don't see things through. This is why discipline and perseverance go hand-in-hand. Discipline isn't any good without the wherewithal to stick with it. To see our goals through—to finish—we need to have perseverance.

The Wall takes Many Forms

We encounter many walls throughout our career. They are often the excuses we give ourselves—the reasons we are not doing the things we know we should do—including prospecting. For perseverance, we need to recognize these walls and be ready not to hit them and stop, *but to break through them and continue on our way.*

Here are five ways to adopt a lifelong habit of breaking through walls you may encounter:

1. Know What You Want—Have a Goal.

Daily life is far more tolerable when we are able to keep the "Big Picture" in mind. Perseverance has to have a real, meaningful goal. If we truly believe in what we do and how we serve our clients' interests and improve their lives, we are less inclined to quit.

We need to maintain goals that make sense—goals that enable us to relate our present activity to ultimate and worthy ends. All of the mundane parts of daily life can become meaningless if we aren't vigilant, and we fail to keep the bigger picture in mind.

Important, meaningful goals—for your clients, your family, *and your income*—make for a wonderful finish line. However, since they are often so far away and there are so many excuses that could keep us from getting to them, we need to employ a second step to help us persevere.

2. Break Goals into Manageable Parts.

Marathon runners often run their course one borough at a time, one bridge at a time, or one block at a time. Authors write books one chapter at a time. Similarly, this compares to the answer of the timeless question about how to eat an elephant: *one slice at a time.*

Every area of our lives can be broken into manageable parts. Manageable parts are good for our careers and our relationships. Perse-

> Perseverance has to have a real, meaningful goal.

verance is far more achievable when we run our race through life at a tolerable pace. Shortly, we will examine this concept further in helping you get from where you are today, to where you want to be with your prospecting, sales and income objectives.

3. Make Trials Your Friend.

Do you know anyone who can't handle a crisis? They don't expect the occasional headaches or make allowances for the inevitable setbacks that are an everyday part of life. As a result, obstacles (many of them minor) wipe them out instead of just tripping them up. They hit a wall and shatter into a thousand pieces.

As we mentioned earlier in this session, M. Scott Peck, M.D. nailed it with the opening line to his classic book, *The Road Less Traveled* with the wise words: "LIFE IS DIFFICULT." Once we accept this fact, we can go about the business of getting important things done.

How do you "make trials your friend?" The answer is psychological. Look back to our first session. A big "wall" in prospecting is our fear of rejection. No one likes to be rejected. In chapter one, we challenged you to look at the most common fears in prospecting. Then we challenged you to look at those fears objectively and ask yourself: "What's the worst that could happen?" Let's revisit these questions for a moment:

> If I telephone a person, tell her about my services, and request an appointment, *what's the worst that could happen?*
>
> If I approach an individual at a social gathering, and gently encourage her to open up to me a little in regard to her financial and insurance concerns, *what's the worst that could happen?*
>
> If I send a letter, perhaps enclose a copy of a helpful article on financial planning, and then follow up with a phone call, *what's the worst that could happen?*

Stress is defined (and measured) by the gap that exists between your expectations and reality.

Understanding that these are not near-death experiences will help you to put them in the proper perspective, and reduce *stress*. **Stress is defined (and measured) by the gap that exists between your expectations and reality. Close this gap, expect the challenges,[1] and you will find that your stress is reduced, and your perseverance stays intact.**

4. Stay Objective and Focused on the FACTS.

When we hit the wall, our minds fill with a million excuses and rationalizations for quitting. It is at these critical junctures—when we hit that emotional, intellectual, physical, or spiritual wall—that we need to consciously weigh our options. We need to put emotion aside, and review the facts:

- ☑ I have a goal—I know what I want.

- ☑ I've broken my goal into manageable parts.

- ☑ I expect there will be trials.

- ☑ Difficulties are a part of life and make me stronger.

It is at this point that most people tend to rely too much on positive thinking—at least in the traditional sense. Being objective and focusing on the facts is avoiding the pitfalls of playing positive mind games. Don't pretend that all the pain and hurt and frustration will go away just by thinking positive thoughts. Perseverance requires us to face our obstacles honestly, acknowledge them for what they are, *and crash through them!* Quitting points must be aggressively attacked, fought, and defeated. That's perseverance.

Family, friends, and colleagues close to us can help at this point. They can help us to stay objective. That brings up a final step we need to take to maintain perseverance.

5. Surround Yourself with Conquerors Rather Than Quitters.

Perseverance is a lot easier when it is the standard operating procedure of the people with whom you spend your time. Our behavior is strongly affected by the company we keep. We need to make sure that the significant others in our lives are the types of people who model perseverance. They need to be people with a good track record. They need to be centers of influence!

Imagine playing a game of tennis. When you compete you should always want to play someone who has superior skills. You don't improve when you can easily beat your opponent. You need to play an opponent who makes you work hard, concentrate and maximize strategy. You want your opponent to do his best so you can, in turn, do your best.

Whether it's the game of tennis or selling our services, we all do better when we have a circle of friends who make a habit of

> Our behavior is strongly affected by the company we keep.

perseveringWithout strong, encouraging friends, you're going to have a difficult time breaking through the walls.

Friend, business partner, and client of mine, I. David Cohen, has shared with me his experience in breaking through the walls:

> "My own career had its difficulties that I faced and conquered. Back in 1991, after thirty-three years with one insurance company, that company went into rehabilitation. The result was that all my commission dollars disappeared. My next step was to ally myself with other insurance carriers so that I could continue my career. Not knowing what to do or how to deal with this devastating change, I was referred to a consultant by the name of Tom Wentz in Columbus, Ohio.
>
> My approach going in the door was that I had a problem, and he needed to fix it. To my surprise, Wentz told me that he could not "solve my problems," and neither could I. What I needed to do was to "decide what I wanted."
>
> In our discussions, he passed along a book entitled *The Path of Least Resistance* by Robert Fritz. Later, I attended a four-day workshop with Mr. Fritz. Between Tom Wentz and Robert Fritz, they were able to help me turn a tragedy into a victory."
>
> Over the years, I have integrated much of what they taught me into my own life. I heartily recommend you read the book *The Path of Least Resistance,* as well as Tom Wentz's book, *Leadership and Golf: Swing to Balance."*

The concepts of structure, oscillation, behavior, problem-solving, and creating come from these brilliant consultants. The pages that follow (concepts of Wentz and Fritz) will give you a deeper understanding about getting what you want instead of attempting to "problem-solve" your way into the future.

> *In tennis, you want your opponent to do his best so you can, in turn, do your best.*

Diffusing the Wall: An Introduction to Structure

In any challenge, hitting the wall is a natural part of the process. However, there are things we can do to help diffuse, or weaken, the wall so that we don't find ourselves hitting it again and again—which causes what we call *oscillation*.

As we mentioned earlier, **oscillation** is the cycle of moving back and forth between good habits and bad ones. In sales, many of us face the same struggle when it comes to our prospecting, which results in frustration and "dry seasons"—ultimately leading to attrition:

- ☑ We identify a number of prospects and call on them.
- ☑ We begin the sales cycle focused only on those prospects (i.e. we stop prospecting). We gather facts and information for a solution to our prospects' situations.
- ☑ We conduct sales presentations over the next three months (still, no prospecting).
- ☑ We make sales (but now have no more prospects).
- ☑ We start all over again!

Look at this process over a typical calendar year:

January:	*Prospecting*
February:	Fact finding; case preparation
March:	Presentations and closings
April:	*Prospecting*
May:	Fact finding; case preparation
June:	Presentations and closings
July:	*Prospecting*
August:	Fact finding; case preparation
September:	Presentations and closings
October:	*Prospecting*
November:	Fact finding; case preparation
December:	Presentations and closings

> Oscillation is the cycle of moving back and forth between good habits and bad ones.

At the end of the year, we have no prospects and literally have to start all over again, because we only focused on one project at a time. Every day, we must focus on acquiring new prospects.

The patterns we described represent an attempt to change behavior without changing the underlying *structure*.

The result is oscillation. Ending back where you started. Constantly in turmoil and frustration. For many of us, ours is a life filled with conflict. Ultimately, whether we are attempting to lose weight, prospect for clients, achieve a goal or "solve a problem," we are working within a structure that is not designed to help us achieve our goals. Instead, we lack discipline, moving from one immediate gratification to the next, hoping that they will provide a sense of internal peace and satisfaction with our lives. It doesn't work.

This occurs in most of the struggles we deal with in our lives. As we bounce back and forth, the lag time may be so large that we are unaware of the oscillation even taking place. In a diet or financial matters, it could take a matter of months for us to hit each end of the wall and then bounce back; but for some, it can take years.

What is Structure?

When it comes to discipline, we always hear how undisciplined people lack *willpower*. Willpower is important, but what most people do not understand is a force that is far more powerful. It's called **structure**.

Structure refers to how key elements in your life are arranged in relation to each other. These include such abstract things as ideas, desires, fears, beliefs, aspirations, and values. They also include the very tangible elements of your life, such as current resources like the things you own, where you live and work, what you do, and equally important, your interpersonal relationships.

This approach has been well articulated by Robert Fritz, whose unique "structural" approach to planning and creating has been hailed as revolutionary. Fritz's observations are that people who create results—independent of current problems, obstacles or resources—are the ones who are responsible for the extraordinary advancements of the human race.

In his book, *The Path of Least Resistance,* Fritz states that energy in a system follows a path of least resistance, going where it is easiest to go. Water in streams, electricity in circuits, companies in the marketplace, individuals in daily life, all follow a path laid down by the unseen but evident structure underlying them.

In streams, for example, the stream bed interacts with the rate and volume of water flow to produce changing surface patterns. The surface runs smooth when a stream bed is smooth and/or water flow is high. Standing waves appear when a stream bed is irregular and water flow is moderate.

Similarly, in businesses, key components interrelate to give rise to patterns of behavior. Some structures support desired results. Others lead instead to conflict between elements.

Imagine you work for an investment firm that sells stocks and other investment products. At this company, the official, executive-decreed rule is "Quality service is number one!" However, in the field and on the trading floor, an *unspoken* rule, "Daily commissions are number one!" drives the day-to-day actions—the behavior of the people. Despite the official claim, the structure of advancement, recognition and compensation rewards short-term transactions over long-term client relationships.

Now, in such a structure, is quality service *really* number one?

Of course not! In spite of the *official* rule, the *unspoken* rule takes precedence. This structure—the relationship between formal and informal rules—gives rise to considerable *conflict* within the organization. Quality suffers. Revenues go down. The firm has *commoditized itself* in a highly competitive industry. If something is not done, bankruptcy and foreclosure are inevitable.

What can be done? It depends on how the leaders view their current situation. If they focus on the problem of sales and revenues, and merely cut jobs and costs to maintain as much of the status quo as possible, are they going to be able to create a viable, healthy organization?

Probably not. However, if they look at the real root of the problem, the executives will recognize that they can only create the results they want by creating a hierarchy of values in which *both rules* are acknowledged. *It should be made clear to employees that quality service and long-term prosperous relationships are to take precedence over short-term transactions.*

Reward structures are changed to reflect the emphasis on long-term accounts as the primary goal. The new structure supports both values, yet ensures that quality service drives the behavior and is, in fact, number one! As a result, quality, morale and production all increase significantly. In two years, the company grows. A new future has been created. The company is not simply getting by. It is thriving and growing! Would this have happened had the leaders merely attempted to "fix" a corporate structure that was profoundly flawed?

Sometimes our structure leads us to what we want. Sometimes it leads us away from what we want. Our task is to consciously set up structures that consistently support our highest and truest

> Water in streams, electricity in circuits, companies in the marketplace, individuals in daily life, all follow a path laid down by the unseen but evident structure underlying them.

What Do You Want?

goals. To do so, we must understand the influence of structure on our personal behavior.

Though structure determines almost everything we do, not all structures move toward final results. A table, for example, is rigid, structured for stability. A rocking chair is designed to oscillate, structured to rock back and forth.

> Sometimes our structure leads us to what we want. Sometimes it leads us away from what we want.

In our professional and personal lives, perhaps most structures do NOT direct us toward our goals—because we are living by a structure that we have not designed for ourselves with our goals in mind. What we must learn is that while our lives follow our structures, we also have the power to create *new* structures that direct us toward our goals.

Don't believe it? Experiment with little things to prove to yourself that this will work, because right now, you might be having doubts. You may be thinking about your own situation, your own challenges and thinking to yourself, "Sure, easy for those guys to say. *They're not in my situation.*" Or perhaps you are thinking, "Well, that all seems to make sense, but it's not the right approach for me."

When we talk about structure, we are talking about the laws of nature! To say to yourself that it won't work for you or that somehow it is not going to fit your situation, "that's for other people, not me," is like saying that the law of gravity is not for you either! Indeed, just as you are affected by the law of gravity, so too is your behavior determined by the structure of your life. IT DOES AFFECT YOU, WHETHER YOU LIKE IT OR NOT, WHETHER YOU CHOOSE TO BELIEVE IT OR NOT.

Give yourself a chance to prove it. Do some experiments. Try some little goals first, before focusing on the big goals. Discover it inwardly for yourself, because if you don't GET IT in your own heart and mind, if you don't discover it for yourself, none of what is discussed in this book will make a bit of difference!

A Simple Illustration of Using Structure to Create a New Reality

Years ago, I heard a radio panel discussion about public transportation, and how necessary it is to help lower income people find good jobs. The concerns were that people in poverty did not have cars or easy access to transportation. Nor were there many

Chapter 5

good-paying jobs within walking distance of where they lived. As a result, according to members of the panel, poor people could not work without buses to get them where they needed to go.

While they didn't speak of it in this way, the advocates of public transportation were saying that without buses, poor people would be unable to lift themselves out of poverty. *They would be trapped.*

During this conversation, a caller named Kevin chimed in. Kevin briefly shared his story—how two years ago, he was living on welfare. Today, he is earning $65,000. Two years ago, this was his situation:

- ☑ He was on welfare.

- ☑ He lived in a ratty apartment with roommates who would steal anything of value.

- ☑ He lived in a neighborhood that was NOT close to any meaningful employment.

- ☑ He did not own a car, nor did he have access to a bus (a key point).

Public transportation advocates would see Kevin as a clear example of someone who was trapped! Without public transportation, they asserted, people like Kevin would not be able to get themselves off welfare.

But wait a minute. Remember, Kevin's situation *was in the past.* Today, he has a new reality. He has a successful job that is across town from where he lived before; and he created this new reality *without* relying on the bus. How do you think Kevin did it? The talk show host really wanted to know!

"I managed to save up about $100, and keep it hidden from my roommates," Kevin answered. "I took that money and bought a bicycle—and a GOOD lock."

That bicycle profoundly changed Kevin's structure, and as a result, changed his life. By acquiring it, he created a new reality! The bike gave him transportation to meaningful employment. The point of this story is not about the necessity of public transportation—the point is that Kevin could have viewed his current situation, and concluded "I am stuck."

Instead, he took personal responsibility and changed his structure. As a result, Kevin created his new reality.

> By definition, building a network is building a structure.

What Do You Want?

"Good for Kevin! How Does His Story Help Me Prospect?"

What a great question! Kevin's story illustrates how little things can make a big difference (more on this idea in Chapter Five). All it took was a bike to help him change his life. Now, here's the surprise: we have been talking about structure from the beginning of this book! For example:

Structure determines behavior.

☑ In Chapter One, we talked about the psychological issues in prospecting, which include your self-understanding, your fears, and your practical know-how and abilities. All these factors make up part of your structure.

☑ In Chapter Two, we addressed various marketing structures (wide product base to narrow market, etc.), and your own capacity to identify and begin to reach out to your market. We illustrated structures even further by showing you how to build a network of centers of influence. By definition, building a network is building a structure.

☑ In Chapter Three, you learned the importance of communication in all its forms—starting with a clear understanding of what you offer people, and how to convey it succinctly. To do so effectively requires a script that is *structured* to help you build relationships with prospective clients. From there, you modify your structure to help you stay accountable—by establishing your personal board of advisors.

Structure determines behavior. The structure of your thinking affects your actions, attitudes, and emotions. The structure of your target market and of your network affects with whom you are able to connect and meet. The structure of your communication impacts how successfully you are able to nurture those connections into prospective client relationships. Lastly, the structure of your own board of advisors (and how you manage it) holds you accountable. How's that for determining behavior?

The focus of this chapter is on *goals*. Structure is a means to helping you achieve a goal. In the context of this book, your goal is NOT to learn about prospecting—ultimately your goal should be *increasing your service, and ultimately increasing your income*. Prospecting is simply a very necessary means to that end.

Therefore, prospecting must become part of your structure.

To this end, we must briefly set aside all that we have learned about prospecting. Now, we will direct your attention toward your goal, and work *backwards*. This next step begs the question:

Chapter 5

How much money do you want to earn?

We will be addressing that question shortly.

II. Your Goal is Not to Solve Your Problems

Worthy goals are not about solving problems, or making something *go away*. Problem solving has dominated many peoples' thinking and planning. If this is all you care about, then another problem will simply take its place.

Case in point: years ago, a beginning New York City high school teacher named Steve Mariotti faced his first day on the job at Boys & Girls School. This inner-city high school had become known as the worst in the entire district:

- ☒ Seventy-two teachers preferred unemployment over going to work.

- ☒ The dropout rate was 50 percent.

- ☒ The NYC Board of Regents placed the *entire school* on probation.

Mariotti was a math teacher. His class had 59 students enrolled with 42 seats and 39 books. The students lacked discipline, respect, and didn't even have pencils and paper! Initial diagnostic test scores were dismal at best.

A hopeless situation, isn't it? Just picture it. All those kids in their unstructured lives! Imagine yourself talking to Mariotti on that first day, right after school (for some reason, I keep imagining the scenario in a bar...!). He describes to you his situation—spending most of his time just trying to keep the kids' attention, and the classroom in order (never mind trying to teach math!). *Remember, his job is just to help the kids learn math—and pass a proficiency test (a major part of the educational structure).* After hearing about this hopeless situation, you might ask him, "So, Steve, what are you going to do about it?"

Imagine if he were to respond, "The issue here is more than getting them to learn math. I must help them develop skills and experiences that will profoundly change the direction of their lives, increasing performance in ALL subjects—not just math. They will WANT to go to school and will WANT to learn. They will acquire personal life skills, such as integrity, relationship

> Worthy goals are not about solving problems, or making something go away.

building and communication. Most importantly, they will believe in themselves and will believe that they can accomplish anything to which they set their minds."

"Oh, by the way," Mariotti adds, "They will do it within one school year."

Imagine how a *problem-solver* would respond, if he were to hear this "pipe dream" of an answer:

"Okay, Steve, I think you have had enough..." the problem solver says. "Are you crazy? You can't even get them to listen to you! Give it up! Those kids are gone, and cannot be saved! Transfer to a better neighborhood school, or work with younger children. They are the ones you can save! *Those high school students are hopeless."*

Fortunately, if Mariotti did hear such negative advice, he ignored it. The reality is that Steve Mariotti changed those children's lives and accomplished ALL of his pipe dream objectives—within one school year—by introducing them to **entrepreneurship.**

By teaching high-school students the methods and rewards of starting and owning their own businesses, Steve Mariotti set out to accomplish far more than he would have if he had only focused on math proficiency scores. Every one of those children discovered how they could build their futures, set goals and reach them. They excelled in math and in all other subjects. Several went on to college.

Today, Mariotti's programs are in place, serving low-income youth throughout the country. He is founder and president of the **National Foundation for Teaching Entrepreneurship** (NFTE.com), based in New York City.

What does this story teach us? What does each of us have in common with a novice teacher of undisciplined, inner city youth from New York?

Most of us can become overly fixated on our problems to the point that it limits us in how we set our goals. We look at what we **know** we can do, what our current capacity or structure will allow. With that information, we set our goals.

Rarely does this work, because we have kept ourselves in the same structure that helped create those problems in the first place.

These types of goals are called "fit" goals, and they rarely create significant, lasting results. They are also sneaky and misleading because they *sound* doable. And, they are deadly.

> Most of us can become overly fixated on our problems to the point that it limits us in how we set our goals. We look at what we know we can do, what our current capacity will allow. With that information, we set our goals.

Chapter 5

The Four Fatal Flaws of Fit Goals

There are four fatal flaws in this limited "fit" approach to goal setting:

1. A focus on getting rid of what you don't want rarely results in creating what you truly do want. This problem-solving attitude is tied to a victim's mentality. A common example you may have encountered with clients is their desire to become debt free. How does becoming debt-free allow people to live fulfilling lives? Being debt free, while important, doesn't equal financial strength. One can be broke and still be debt free.

2. Second, incremental goals fail to bring out the highest and best in us. "Make no small goals," the old saying goes, "for they lack the power to stir our souls." They rarely stir us to sustained action, let alone to produce consistently outstanding results. Simply put, it becomes just another thing "we have to do."

3. Third, problem-solving rarely accounts for unpredictable changes. How many of us think of reality, and its inevitable changes, as the enemy rather than a useful force to be harnessed in support of our vision and end results?

4. Fourth, and perhaps most significant, conventional problem solving approaches are based on what we know is feasible *today*. This limits us from the very beginning. It essentially prevents us from stretching for goals for which no conventional approach is currently available.

> Albert Einstein warned that the kind of thinking that gets us into a predicament will not get us out of it..

Albert Einstein warned that the kind of thinking that gets us into a predicament will not get us out of it. To invent real and lasting results, we need a strategy that focuses on *creating*—bringing into being—what most matters to us and to our careers. We need an approach to a strategy that causes us to reach for the highest and best in ourselves, our families, and our clients. As you shall soon learn, this approach requires us to *work backwards*.

Doing the Impossible

Rather than being focused on solving our problems, we must envision what we want out of all proportion to our currently perceived resources and capabilities. In business, this is referred to as a "stretch and leverage" strategy. Businesses set what appear to be impossible goals for their size and capacity. Then, relying on

What Do You Want?

resourcefulness and innovation, by invention, experimentation, copying, borrowing or learning, and calculated risk—they leverage available resources into outstanding results. You must learn to do the same as you prospect for new clients and expand your income base.

> A focus on getting rid of what you don't want rarely results in creating what you truly do want.

Think about Kevin who we discussed earlier, living in a dump, no job, no transportation, and on welfare. If he looked to "fit" his goals only to what his current capacity was, what would be his result? Where would he be today? He would still be stuck.

Fit limits. Stretch liberates.

Stretch goals set up "a chasm between ambition and resources." A chasm! Not a nice, comfortable fit. The challenge is to improve... and to do so radically—not 10 or 20 percent, but 500 or 1000 percent—even higher perhaps!

So, What is it to Create?

Creating is a widely misunderstood concept. Many people think of "being creative" as doing things differently. But being creative is different than actually creating.

Creating is not about fixing what doesn't work, solving problems, or doing old things differently. It's not positive thinking, visualization, or brainstorming. Nor is it a trendy type of strategic planning designed to simply change the way you do things. The creative process is a fundamentally different way of approaching what you do. It is a reliable, step by step process that leads to tangible, recognizable results.

Creating is much less about the process, than it is about the product. It is about bringing into being results that matter.

Too often though, creativity is confused with doing the unusual or unconventional, with eccentricity and bizarre behavior. As you will learn, creativity is not the key to creating.

While the processes creators use may vary greatly, the end results are almost always the same. Novelists end up with novels, painters with paintings. An architect sees a building take shape as it was envisioned. A company creates the quality products and services its customers value.

However, what most people think of as creating is simply old methods done with a different twist. When someone asks "How can I live my life, run my business, or produce my product more creatively?" they miss the point. The question implies that creating is an add-on, a kind of magic pill taken to make things better. Even worse is when people refer to "creative problem-solving." Now there's an oxymoron!

Are there rules for creating? Recipes we can follow? In a word, no.

Creating is, at its root, a learning process in which creators teach themselves how to bridge the chasm between goals and their current capacity. We set our eyes on a goal, even though we don't know how to get there. We teach ourselves. Through learning we extend our capacity to create. Through learning, we create the structure we need to get what we want.

In the process of creating, as in the playing of jazz or the blues, there are no rules, no simple formula for bringing into being what truly matters. There is, however, a set of common practices that guides the efforts of all creators. Creators set up a dynamic framework, a structure, in which they see and hold Vision and Reality simultaneously and through which daily decisions and actions consistently support the realization of desired results.

> Creating is about bringing into being results that matter.

III. How Much Do You Want to Earn?

(The Structure of Creating)

The structure of creating is driven by your vision, rooted in reality, and focused on action that consistently drives you toward this vision. In this structure, you hold your vision—what you want—and your current reality in a dynamic tension that generates energy for action.

Planning is truly strategic and is often crafted in a just-in-time fashion as the creation unfolds. Choices and behavior are aligned with primary values and vision. Small steps lead to success and momentum. Momentum creates a force which makes larger steps easier to take, increasing the capacity to create. An expanded capacity leads to further successes and, eventually, to outstanding results.

Whoa. You may want to read the top two paragraphs over a few more times before moving on.

Step 1: How Much Do You Want to Earn? (Your Vision)

Start with a clear, compelling picture of what you want, a vision. Decide now how much you *want* to earn.

Caution: If you are answering this question based upon what you think you can earn, you are falling into the trap of a "fit" goal. You must not limit your income goal to what you perceive as your present earning capacity.

This is no small matter. Uncovering what you want is the most radical, the most painful and the most creative act of life.

Unfortunately, most individuals and organizations are surprisingly vague about what they want—even those with elaborate mission and vision statements. Too many mission statements are full of generic, easy-to-agree-with statements like "to excel" or "to be the best in our industry." On the other hand, too many people and organizations focus on what they don't want or on what they can reasonably expect. *Most are unwilling to specify what they truly want because, given current capacity, they don't believe it can be achieved.*

If you don't get past this hurdle, you are not going to get anywhere!

Do you regard yourself as a **realist**? Do you keep your dreams and plans within the realm of what you consider possible?

> You must not limit your income goal to what you perceive as your present earning capacity.

Visionaries are opposed by realists and vice versa. Unwilling, or afraid, to stretch for what they truly want, realists compromise, settling for reasonable, doable goals. "Doable goals" serve a valuable purpose: as action steps to higher goals! However, modest goals rarely stir anyone to sustained action.

You MUST separate what you want from what you believe to be possible. Creating is about learning and inventing. You must decide on the "what" and not be too concerned about the "how." You just need to know you want to produce it. You'll learn to create it as you go. The possibility is discovered by doing. As the old saying goes, "Where there's a will, there's a way."

John F. Kennedy's 1961 challenge to put a man on the moon by the end of the decade had far more power than if he'd said, "It would be nice to go the moon someday."

Vision isn't just words on paper. Kennedy's moon speech was a vision. Martin Luther King's "I have a dream" speech was a vision. When Grumman Aerospace was awarded the contract to

Chapter 5

build NASA's Lunar Excursion Module, the landing craft that would take the first human beings to the surface of the moon, the company put up a sixty foot flag of the moon in their cafeteria with an arrow pointing at the landing site and a caption saying "We are going here!"

For the purpose of our lesson here, let's assume that you set a goal to earn $100,000. For building our structure to reach this goal, we have to start at the end and work backwards.

Step 2: Assess Your Current Reality

If a friend were to call you on the telephone and ask you for the best way to drive to Cleveland, you may initially find that an easy question to answer. After all, if you live in Columbus, everyone knows that the quickest route is to take Interstate 71 north. It takes you right to Cleveland.

As a result, you respond, "That's easy! Just take 71 north!"

Your friend pauses for a moment. "Mmmmm," he responds. "That may not work for me. You see, I am in St. Louis."

To begin to move toward your goal, you must clearly know where you are today, and have a clear understanding of what you have or don't have in the way of resources and capacity.

This may be scary for some people, because sometimes this process forces people to confront issues that they have ignored for far too long. They have to face reality! But reality is not to be feared. You must look at it objectively. Furthermore, your current situation should only be assessed after your vision is clearly defined.

It is vitally important to identify goals that reach beyond what you deem possible or feasible. To dwell on your current status first only reinforces in your mind what you believe you "can't" do, not what you can. Why make one of the biggest challenges of goal setting even more difficult? Assessing your "stretch" goals first ensures that problems, crises, shortages, and limitations in capacity do not hinder the vision-building process. *Clarifying vision first ensures a stretch strategy, not a compromising fit.*

For our example, you can assess your current situation by addressing the following questions (with sample answers provided):

> **How much income do you want to earn?** Again, we will assume that you have chosen to earn $100,000.

> Most are unwilling to specify what they truly want because, given current capacity, they don't believe it can be achieved.

What Do You Want?

What is your time frame (one month, one year, two years…) Your time frame is over the next calendar year.

What is the average value of each sale? Based on your current income and production level, you determine that your average value of each sale is $2,000. **Note:** if you are new to the business and do not have enough practical experience and track record to make an accurate determination of this figure, consult with your sales manager.

How many sales will be required to reach your income goal? This is a question of simple math—at a rate of $2,000 per sale, you will need to close 50 sales to earn $100,000.

What is your rate of *initial interviews* to sales? This interview is typically the first personal "official" meeting in the sales cycle. The goal of this meeting is to keep the dialog going, and to set a "closing meeting," as described previously. For our example, we will assume that your ratio of initial interviews to sales is **six** to **one**.

How many prospects will be required to arrange an initial interview? Continuing with the backwards approach, this question assesses how many prospects you must contact in order to get the initial interview. We will assume that you identified and contacted **ten** prospects, and acquired initial interviews with **six** of them.

What is your rate of prospects to sales? On this track, we continue to the closing interview, and the final sale. For our example: 1) With your **six** initial interviews, you arrange **three** closing interviews. 2) Of those **three**, **one** makes a purchase. Therefore…Your ratio of prospects to final sales is ten to one. Averages dictate that you must identify and contact ten prospects to close one sale.

Why must we go through this laborious procedure? Fundamentally, the process is no different than any other objective, regardless of how simple or complex. For example:

1. If you are having a cookout and the main course is hamburgers, and you have invited ten people, and you assume that each person will eat two hamburgers, you know that you must be prepared to cook 20 hamburgers.

2. If you invite 20 people to go to the movies, you know you must buy 20 tickets, and have transportation for twenty people. If it's four people to a car, you will need five cars.

John F. Kennedy's 1961 challenge to put a man on the moon by the end of the decade had far more power than if he'd said, "It would be nice to go the moon someday."

Chapter 5

In our profession, we must have a clear understanding of how many prospects we must identify and contact to ultimately reach our financial goal. If you are new to the business, you will be able to reach out to your managers and your peers to help you "fill in the gaps" that you may be unable to do on your own.

We will also acknowledge up front, that this process is *easy to understand, but difficult to implement!* But so is eating an elephant, remember? How do you do that? One slice at a time!

With this in mind, let's "slice" our business plan:

1	Financial goal	$100,000
2	Time frame	1 year
3	Average value of each sale	$2,000
4	Sales required to reach goal	50
5	Ratio of closing interviews to sales	1 in 3
6	Ratio of initial interviews to sales	6 to 1
7	Ratio of prospects to sales	10 to 1

The bottom line:

500 Prospects	100%
300 show interest	60%
150 agree to a presentation	30%
50 will buy from you	10%

In our example, based on a 50-week year, your first obligation is to:

SECURE 10 QUALIFIED PROSPECTS PER WEEK!

The structure described above is full of variables, many of which you can control. For example:

- ☑ You decide how much you want to earn.

- ☑ The market you target and the products and services you offer determine the amount of the commission you earn per sale.

Suppose your average commission per sale was $4,000, and you continued to acquire ten new prospects on a weekly basis. What

> In our profession, we must have a clear understanding of how many prospects we must identify and contact to ultimately reach our financial goal.

would happen next? Your income would double!

On the other hand, if your average sale doubles, the number of prospects required to achieve your initial income goal of $100,000 would be cut in half.

While most seasoned sales professionals will tell you that the law of averages is inescapable, it is still in your power to make sure that your own success rate in setting appointments and closing sales falls in the high-end of the bell curve. In other words, even if *most* professionals must identify ten prospects just to set six interviews, your own approach, research and discretion has a bearing on how closely you come to this mark. Refine your prospecting skills, your presentation and your knowledge of the market, and you may find yourself setting *seven* or *eight* appointments for every ten prospects identified!

On the other hand, if you are lazy and don't do your homework, you may find yourself only getting *three* or *four* appointments for every ten prospects. It works both ways!

Please remember: **structure determines behavior.** Once you have established your goal, the next step is to determine where you are in relation to where you want to be. *In almost every case, the missing link is lack of prospects, not a lack of product knowledge or selling skills.*

As a positive career move, please sit down and:

1. Determine what you want.

2. Discover where you are relative to what you want.

3. Develop a structure to implement your game plan.

4. Decide a constant review and analysis strategy to make certain you are heading toward your goal.

The factors we outlined are highly predictable. However, they are based on the law of large numbers—no different than an actuarial table. You shouldn't make any true value judgments for at least one year.

If all else fails, and you don't want to implement "everything" we suggest then simply do one thing: *acquire ten new prospects each week.*

> You decide how much you want to earn.

Chapter 5

Step 3: Prepare for "Creative Tension"

During the process of creating there will always be a discrepancy, a gap, between vision and reality. This is not stress, which we defined as the gap between *expectation* and reality. Vision and expectation are two separate animals.

This "creative tension" is a real, tangible force and is recognized by many experts. Earl Nightingale referred to this tension as "constructive discontent." It's a clear, objective view of where you are as opposed to where you want to be. If you don't like your job, for example, you decide that you want the flexibility of having your own business.

You may be reading this material because there is some level of dissatisfaction with where you are in your career. Perhaps things are going well, and you just do not wish to become complacent. Or, perhaps business is slow, or you are just starting, and you want to breathe some new life into your career.

Now, while other people may take this discontent and sit around and whine and complain, you choose to channel your energy more positively. "Earn $200,000?" your problem-solving friend says when you mention your goal to him. "You can't do that! You know how much hustling that would take? You need more customers! You have a family! You'll just be setting yourself up for disappointment."

You want to increase your income. Your current situation is that you need to identify ten prospects per week and you are beginning to wonder how you will achieve this based on your current relationships.

This is creative tension! This is what gives great music its dynamic impetus. This is what draws us into great art. It pulls us along through the complex plot of a well-written novel. It sets up a dynamic structural-tendency to move. Action within this structure can move toward vision or reality. There are three ways a creator can resolve this creative, structural tension:

1. **Give up.** Let go of your vision completely and let reality drive the action. Most of us do this.

2. **Compromise.** Fit your vision to what seems possible. Many of us do this, much to our dismay.

3. **Create.** Stretch for the vision, then change reality until it is realized. Few of us do this.

> During the process of creating there will always be a discrepancy, a gap, between vision and reality. This is not stress, which is the gap between expectation and reality. Vision and expectation are two separate animals.

What Do You Want?

Only the last strategy consistently produces real and lasting results. The key to success is holding structural tension, not just a vision. It's being constructively discontented. IN THE PROCESS, YOU ARE CONSTANTLY CHANGING YOUR CURRENT REALITY.

Your current state shifts in response to both successes and failures as well as to outside events and issues beyond your control. New assessments of reality pinpoint your current position. Course corrections are made immediately. You think about starting a business in the context of where you are. Then if someone were to ask you, what are your steps? Would you have a detailed plan?

Well, business planning is important, but you can't obsess over the "next 500 steps." **FOCUS ON WHAT YOU WILL DO NEXT.** THE PLAN EMERGES OUT OF THE DOING.

How do you write a book? You do it one chapter at a time.

Creating is more like sailing a boat than taking a train. On a train you know not only where you start and end, but all the stops in between. There is almost no flexibility to deviate from the pre-established route to accommodate shifts in current status. Suppose you're on the train, and the current situation changes: a large tree falls down across the track as the train is approaching. Does the train have the power to adjust, or change reality? Can it move the large tree, or move itself out of the way and continue its course? Of course not!

You want to increase your income. You need to identify ten prospects per week and you are beginning to wonder how you will achieve this based on your current relationships.

This is creative tension.

However, on a sailing trip, all you know for sure is where you're starting and where you want to end. The route you sail is not predictable. It is affected by external forces like winds, tides, currents, and storms.

You make up the route as you go.

Sailors and creators both use the forces they encounter to their own advantage. They incorporate the energy of change into their own systems. When blown off course, sailors simply establish their new position, then revise their course as needed.

Compare this to what happens when a train goes off the track!

Operating within the framework of structural tension allows sailors and creators to invent innovative, often elegant, paths that leverage limited resources into expansive results.

Chapter 5

Step 4: Use Feedback and Adjustment

Earlier we discussed the importance of having your own board of advisors. This board will provide the valuable feedback, that will allow you to constantly update your situation, amplify successful actions and stop doing or change those actions that don't consistently produce useful results.

Feedback leads to learning, increased capacity, effectiveness, and most of all, momentum. Momentum is a powerful force which can be used to sustain action in the face of adversity, problems and setbacks.

As the creative process closes in on results, much of the creative tension that was generating energy has been resolved. Therefore it is key to build and maintain momentum as a force that enables you to follow through fully, to complete the necessary action steps and produce the final results.

Creative Tension and Hitting Your Goal: Beware!

When we define creative tension as the gap between your vision and reality, this naturally leads to the next question: What happens to this tension when you reach your goal?

> Creating is more like sailing a boat than taking a train.

This is what some might call "the success trap." While we walk you through the steps of reaching a quantifiable goal, some experts will warn against this because it causes some people to short-change themselves ("So you say you want to earn $100,000? Why would you not want $150,000, $200,000, or more?").

Whatever your goal may be for the next twelve months, keep it in perspective. No goal is an "absolute" end in itself—it is simply a means to something greater. If you decide you want to earn $100,000 this year, go for it—but next year you must set your sights higher still. *It may not all have to do with money.* For example, you may wish to structure your business and client base so that you can earn a determined income level, but from a smaller, more select group of clients. Working with this smaller group will enable you to give them more attention, which you find rewarding beyond the monthly paycheck.

Ultimately, your goals will be tied to your quality of life. If you choose $200,000—again we ask, "Why?" What will that bring you that you do not presently have?

I. David Cohen recalled the story of meeting the son of a highly respected and well-loved attorney in our community. Unfortunately, David met this man at his father's funeral. Knowing that he was also practicing law, David approached him and said, "I can imagine what a legacy your father has left to your profession, and how proud you must feel to be his son."

The young man looked at David and responded quite bluntly, "He may have been a great attorney, but he was no father. His priorities were all about his work. His clients came before us *every day*. I loved him, but I never knew him. I probably will not miss him."

Wow.

To say that hearing this young man's response was a paradigm shift is an understatement. While David had no less regard for his father, it was an eye opening experience. As sales professionals, we must remember: *Money is a means to an end—you can't take it with you.*

Conclusion

You may realize after reviewing this chapter that this material will not only apply to your career, but also to all aspects of your life. With this in mind, remember the age-old saying: *Be careful what you wish for…you may get it!*

As you work to build a successful career, give equal consideration and planning to how that success will positively impact other areas of your life—namely your relationships with family and friends. As you move forward, maintain a balance.

Feedback leads to learning, increased capacity, effectiveness, and most of all, momentum.

Chapter Review

1. What are the three keys to strengthening discipline?

    1. _____

    2. _____

    3. _____

Chapter 5

2. What are the five ways to adopt a lifelong habit of breaking through the wall?

   a. _____

   b. _____

   c. _____

   d. _____

   e. _____

3. Explain what is meant by the expression structure determines behavior.

   _____

   _____

   _____

   _____

4. Why must we prospect for new clients every day?

   _____

   _____

   _____

   _____

   _____

   _____

> Money is a means to an end—you can't take it with you.

5. What are the four fatal flaws of "fit goals?"

   a. _____

   b. _____

   c. _____

   d. _____

6. You have three choices to resolve structural tension. What are they?

   1. _____
   2. _____
   3. _____

7. What does it mean to "create?"

   _____
   _____
   _____
   _____
   _____
   _____

8. What did you learn most from Chapter Five?

   _____
   _____
   _____
   _____
   _____

Chapter 6:

Your Moment of Truth

I. Service and Prospecting

Some of you may remember the good old days when milk was delivered to your home or doctors actually made house calls—I do not but I often hear of them. That was the heyday for customer service, some will say—a time filled with customer loyalty and satisfaction. However, these days, with the reduced level of service we seem to be getting from business, it is more likely that we will hear complaints rather than compliments from customers. So, what has happened to sincere customer service, and how does it affect our roles as sales professionals?

> Too many sales professionals are focused too much on selling the customer, rather than servicing them.

All of us know that customer service is on the decline in the United States. If you walk into any fast food restaurant, fly on most domestic airlines or shop at a mass merchant you are likely have a negative (or at least, a forgettable) experience. Of the more than 30 industries tracked by the American Customer Satisfaction Index, airlines, banks, fast food restaurants and hospitals have recently posted some of the lowest scores.

Most experts agree cost-cutting in corporate America is the primary reason for the decline in customer service. From the company's point of view, good service is expensive because it requires educating staff. Ironically, in a competitive, price-driven environment such as ours, some companies have a difficult time seeing how they can strengthen their competitive edge by enhancing client service and creating *loyalty*.

But that's no excuse for us—regardless of what our company's policy may be. Many representatives in the financial services industry—especially those whose incomes are derived primarily from commission-based sales—are overly focused on *selling* the client, rather than *servicing* them. Once the check has cleared, the client does not hear from the representative—until he or she has something else to sell.

As professionals, it is our job to serve our clients, not sell them. People don't like to be sold—but they do like to be served.

"I agree," you may respond. "But what does client service have to do with prospecting for *new clients?*"

It has everything to do with it! Think back to a time when you ate in a great restaurant, or discovered a new store and you received what we will call OUTSTANDING SERVICE:

- ☑ The people went above and beyond what you would normally expect—*just to please you.*

- ☑ The people were polite, respectful, and you could tell *that they cared.*

- ☑ The service was outstanding, delivering what you wanted, and then some.

- ☑ In addition, the products were top quality.

It is the overall decline in customer service that makes these positive experiences really stand out in our minds. We hope that you can recall positive service experiences amidst the enormous collection of bad experiences we have all had. When you have had a positive experience, how did you react?

You probably told someone. You recommended the store or restaurant to your friends. You became that business' advocate. You became its salesperson, and you weren't even on the payroll.

That is why providing outstanding service is more than just doing the right thing by your clients. Providing outstanding service is crucial to building client loyalty—and client loyalty is absolutely necessary for introductions to new prospects.

> Client loyalty is absolutely necessary for introductions to new prospects.

Your Moment of Truth

How Would You Rate YOUR Service?

Take a moment and imagine you are your own client. Would *you* hire *you?*

Think about this and decide how you would rate your service. Place yourself in the position of your client. Are you providing the kind of service that you would want to receive? Are you fulfilling the "Golden Rule"? This is a tough question for some of us—and we need to answer it inwardly and honestly.

Let us explore this issue further with some specific questions:

Do I recognize the Total Lifetime Value of my client?

In commission-driven industries, this question may seem rather preposterous. Of course, we know from where our paycheck comes. However, are we focused only on the current paycheck, or are we keeping in mind the total lifetime value of each client? This value can be determined not only from what the individual client buys, but also from all the additional new clients that the individual sends our way.

With this knowledge in hand, do I make my clients feel as important as they truly are?

Most of us have either heard and/or used the expression "You are my only client!"—which indicates to our client that she is the most important person to us. It is one thing to say it—but do our actions back it up, or are we just paying lip service to the idea?

Do I know WHY my clients buy?

Everyone has his own personal reasons for the choices he makes, and those reasons will never have anything to do with our needs. You may want your prospect to buy because you need to pay your mortgage, but your reasons do not matter. The only things that matter to the prospect are his reasons and concerns. This is his opportunity to be self-centered and self-absorbed.

Am I enthusiastic, friendly and pleasant?

This is another common-sense question. However, we all have days when we feel less pleasant, and this can affect how we relate to others. If you have client meetings on a day when you do not feel very friendly, you had better "suck it up" and put on a friend-

> The Total Lifetime Value can be determined not only from what the individual client buys, but also from all the additional new clients that the individual sends our way.

ly face. You will also find that changing your posture and your physical disposition will also make you feel better! Remember what we covered in our discussion about subtext. What you do not say speaks volumes and sometimes belies what you are trying to say.

Do I truly care about my clients?

True professionals take a very close and almost intimate view of their clients; because it is through these people that the professional carries out a big part of his "life's mission." Just as each of us value our relationships with our families, so too must our clients become near and dear to us. In many cases, our clients will function to assist us in our careers far more than our families are able to do.

Do I deliver what I promise, and then go beyond expectations?

We have discussed this before, so it should come as no surprise. Not only is it vitally important to follow through on your word, but it is crucial to go above and beyond the call—to surprise your clients—by doing more than is expected.

Do I base my choices on the interest of my clients, or on what is most convenient for me?

Here is a very personal question, one which you can only answer in your heart. Your choices and actions must be driven by the consideration of what is in the best interest of your client, and not by what is easiest for you.

Do I take responsibility for my client's happiness with our products and services?

The choice that we make reveals the truth that lies within us: the truth of how deeply we care about our clients.

If you represent a larger company, it is likely that you will not be the only person with whom your client interacts; however, you are the primary representative. You are the face that has been put on what is normally considered a faceless bureaucracy. This means that if there is any problem, regardless of who is at fault, it is your responsibility to resolve it and ensure that your client's needs are satisfied. If a client calls with a concern or a complaint, your response is not about whose fault it is. Rather, it must be

> Your choices and actions must be driven by the consideration of what is in the best interest of your client, and not by what is "easiest" for you.

Your Moment of Truth

about what must be done to resolve the problem. This is another example of accountability and how important it is to our success.

These are just a few of the questions that you can explore in evaluating your own level of commitment to serving your clients. As we have said before, in order to decide where you want to go and how you will get there, it is important to first determine where you are. By inwardly and honestly examining your own actions, attitudes and priorities as they relate to your clients, you will be in a stronger position to identify and correct weaknesses. You will begin to open new opportunities to go beyond the expected.

> The paradigm of customer "satisfaction" is too low of a standard upon which to measure our effectiveness in customer service.

Client Satisfaction vs. Client Loyalty: Which Would You Prefer?

In his best-selling book, *Customer Satisfaction is WORTHLESS; Customer Loyalty is PRICELESS,* author Jeffrey Gitomer defines the key differences between satisfied customers and loyal customers.

In essence, the paradigm of customer "satisfaction" is too low of a standard upon which to measure our effectiveness in customer service. After all, we all know that it is far more cost-effective to keep a client than to find a new one. Yet, this concept still has not sunk into the fabric of American business. If customers are satisfied, that is good enough.

What follows below is a summary of how Gitomer defines the various "levels" of customer service:[1]

When Your Customer is...	Tells Others	Refers Others	Buys Again
Loyal	Everyone, all the time	At every opportunity	Always, for ever and ever
Very Satisfied	Some people	If they are in the mood	Yes, maybe (but open to other offers)
Satisfied	If asked	If asked	If convenient
Apathetic	No	No	Maybe, maybe not
Unhappy	10 people	No	Maybe, after several years
Wronged	25 people	Never	Never
Angry	Everyone, all the time	Never	Need we ask?

Chapter 6

The middle shaded row is considered the benchmark: customer *satisfaction*. In his book, Gitomer actually adds a lower level, beneath "Angry," if you can believe it. He calls it **LAWSUIT!** Guess how many people are told at this level? *The whole city!*

Have you ever been so upset with a business that you cannot help but spread the word about your lousy experience? It's called giving "reverse referrals," and the dynamics that can do wonders for spreading the good news about your service can work against you as well. So, beware!

The Moment of Truth

> The choice that we make reveals the truth that lies within us: the truth of how deeply we truly care about our clients

In customer service, I use an expression: "the moment of truth." This is defined as a time of client contact, during which the representative is confronted with a situation for which he or she must make a choice.

You may wonder: why is it called a moment of truth, and not a moment of choice? One way to explain it is that at these various moments, the choice that we make reveals the truth that lies within us: the truth of how deeply we care about our clients.

In the client relationship cycle, there are many different moments of truth. Each of these moments—and their outcomes—can be divided into three parts:

1. The moment (the stimulus)

2. The choice (our response)

3. The truth revealed (the message we send to the client-- what I also refer to as showing your true colors)

Let's look at some examples of Moments of Truth from this perspective.

Moment of Truth:
A prospective client calls for the first time.

Have you ever called a business, inquiring about its service, only to get brushed off? Imagine that you want to have your kitchen remodeled, so you call four companies that focus on kitchen remodeling.

You call **Company A**, and a polite representative answers the phone. You indicate your need for an estimate to have your kitchen remodeled. The receptionist puts you through to a sales representative, who schedules a time to come that afternoon, to take some measurements, and to ask a few questions. He arrives on time, is very polite, listens to your concerns, and asks intelligent questions. He even gives you a complimentary tape measure before he leaves!

He assures he will have a detailed estimate for you by noon the next day. As promised, a fully typed estimate arrives in email the next morning at 10:45.

You call **Company B.** The experience is similar to your previous one, except the sales rep on the phone begins to ask questions about your budget—as though he wants to know how much money you plan to spend before he will schedule an appointment. You don't surrender a number, but to get the conversation moving you make it clear to him that you are interested in quality—and you know that costs money. "The soonest I can fit you in is next Monday," he responds. Obviously, he's pretty busy! Good for him!

You call **Company C** and get an answering machine. You leave your inquiry on the machine. No one calls back for five days.

You call **Company D,** and the owner answers the phone. The conversation goes well, and he is very polite and interested in what you have to say. He asks if tomorrow afternoon is okay to meet, and that's fine with you. He arrives on time, takes notes, asks questions, and agrees he will get an estimate to you in a day or two. It arrives three days later, hand-written on a blank sheet of paper.

Four companies, four moments, four choices, four truths. Based on the choices that were made in each of these examples, *what truth does each company reveal about its attitude toward you, the prospect?* What *unconscious* message do you, as the prospect receive based on the behaviors of the people you call?

The Truth of Company A: "You are important to me, and I value your business. I will do whatever it takes to earn your business, your loyalty, and your trust."

The Truth of Company B: "How important you are depends on how much money you want to spend in the next thirty days ("Lifetime value? What's that?"). I am busy enough *today* that I can live without your business."

The Truth of Company C: "We are not home. Leave a message—we'll call back when we get around to it."

The Truth of Company D: "When I say I will get something to you, I am really not sure. It depends upon how other things play out. It depends upon whether or not you are getting me on a good day."

You may notice that in all of the above examples, the *amount* of the quote was irrelevant. Based upon these experiences, the initial responsiveness has a big impact on how prospective customers choose to buy. If they do not like you or if your actions and attitudes reveal a truth that says you do not value them, you have seriously impacted your chances of acquiring a client, let alone building a relationship.

> If your actions and attitudes reveal a "truth" to the prospect that says you do not value them, you have seriously impacted your chances of building a relationship.

Opportunities are missed all the time. I recently visited a clothing store to buy a pair of jeans. I walk in, the store is empty. I see the clerk behind the counter. I say, "Hello," and he responds in kind. I say, "I am looking for some Dockers and a couple of belts."

He responds, "What do you want to see first?"

"The belts," I respond.

He points to a corner. "Over there."

I go to the corner while he continues to kick back. He never budged from his obviously comfortable position. He could have provided more personal service. We can all relate to receiving poor service. Ask yourself, "Do I behave in a similar manner?"

Moment of Truth:
A client is upset, angry or has a complaint.

When a client feels as though there is a problem or feels that a mistake has been made, it can cause tremendous stress and anxiety. After all, many of us are providing services of a very personal and important nature.

There will always be times when problems arise. If a client calls you (or one of your colleagues or an assistant) and is obviously distraught or even angry, how you respond at that very moment will impact your ability to resolve the situation.

Veteran life insurance agent, I. David Cohen, recalls this story when addressing the complaint of a client:

Your Moment of Truth

Years ago, I received a call from one of my clients because the company I represented made a mistake by withdrawing the incorrect amount from her checking account. When I answered the phone, I could tell she was upset. I needed to understand fully what had happened.

Even though I was not directly involved, I apologized. "We screwed up". "No, I know you weren't..." my client began to respond. "No," I interjected, "We screwed up, and I apologize. I will correct the situation immediately. How soon can we meet for lunch so that we can discuss the issue to make sure that your needs are being met?"

The fact was, I wasn't directly involved, and it wasn't my mistake. But it was still a reflection on me. I am her representative. To her, I am the company. Now, I'll find out what went wrong, and make sure it doesn't happen again. I will tell the company how it affected my client and thus how it affected me.

However, doing that does not involve my client, and she will not know anything about those conversations. It does not help her to listen to my petty excuses or defensiveness. What my client wants to hear is that the problem is being resolved and that it is my top priority. No excuses are necessary. Just fix it and move ahead.

> "What my client wants to hear is that the problem is being resolved and that it is my top priority. No excuses are necessary. Just fix it and move ahead."
> —I. David Cohen

When such a situation occurs, even if the client is particularly irate or even hostile, you have two choices:

1. You can become defensive.

2. You can empathize and seek greater understanding.

Which response will create results that are more positive? Let's consider this further: what truth does the client glean from each of these options?

Becoming defensive reveals a truth of selfishness. "You have a problem, but my first concern is with protecting myself, regardless of any level of *direct* responsibility I may have for the situation, or for how it hurts you." Shifting the blame for mistakes never works!

Empathy and understanding sends the message that you are caring, responsible, and professional—even in situations where the client may be angry or even hostile. Because one person loses his cool does not give you the excuse to do likewise. The truth revealed: "I care about you. My priority is to make certain that your issue is resolved and that we can move forward with a positive relationship. I am equally responsible for what goes wrong and for what goes right."

Chapter 6

**Moment of Truth:
A mistake is made, and you discover it first.**

When I worked as a creative director, I had a client that was in a hospital in a town five-and-a-half hours away. I had recently finished producing a fund-raising campaign video, and the client needed the final copies in her office by a certain date. I monitored the progress with the tape duplication company. My client needed her video by Thursday evening for an important board meeting (which only occurs four or five times per year, given the busy schedules of all its members). I confirmed that the vendor, the tape duplicating company, was scheduled to ship their tapes via overnight mail on Wednesday, for a Thursday morning delivery (This was in the days before YouTube or transferring large digital files over the internet.). I felt confident that my client would receive it Thursday morning—in time for the board meeting that night.

Thursday morning arrived, and around 11 a.m. I called my client to confirm that she has received the package. She indicated that it has not yet arrived. I contacted the tape duplicator to confirm that the package was sent. The manager there looks up the tracking number and discovers that a clerk in the office mistakenly sent the package out for *ground* delivery! As a result, my client will not receive her package until Friday afternoon, or even the following week. By then it will be too late.

I prepared to contact the client with the bad news. Even though the mistake was not my fault, I was still responsible. Therefor, I could not just call the client with the problem ("There you have it. I'm sorry—I wish I could do more."). *I needed a solution ready before I picked up the phone.*

> Becoming defensive reveals a truth of selfishness.

I did have a few extra copies of the final video already on hand. I had no choice: the client needed it for a meeting that night, at seven o'clock.

The moment of truth was upon me: I was getting in my car and delivering the package myself. By 11:30 I was on the road, and I called the client:

"Hello?" she answers.

"Trudy?" you respond. "This is Keith. I have the information concerning your videos. You will have them by 5:30."

"That's pretty tight," she responds. "What happened?"

Your Moment of Truth

"Despite yesterday's confirmation with them to the contrary, the duplication company failed to send the tapes out correctly," I explained. "Chances are the original package will actually not arrive until next week. That is why I am bringing some tapes to you personally. I am on my way now and should arrive by 5:30. I am extremely sorry for this mistake."

Trudy realizes that it is more than five hours *each way* for the trip. "You're driving it to me?" she responded. "I am so sorry! Are you sure that is the only solution?"

> You should not call your client with the problem ("There you have it. I'm sorry—I wish I could do more."). You must have a solution ready before you pick up the phone.

"Trudy, you have no reason to apologize. The mistake was made on our end, and given the fact that your board members are expecting to see this video, it's the only solution. The possibility of you *not having* what you require for tonight is simply not acceptable. I'm just glad your close enough to get there in a couple hours!"

"I look forward to seeing you!" Trudy responds, her emotions understandably mixed. "Thank you, Keith. You are right—this is very important and I appreciate your efforts."

In my moment of truth, I could not respond with excuses or by blaming others. I had to evaluate the situation in terms of what was in my client's best interest, and I acted accordingly.

In the wake of someone else's mistake, I also rose to the occasion to win even more trust with my client.

How will Trudy feel? Colleagues told me that she continued to share the story about how I drove nearly twelve hours just to deliver an important package to her. That's service. *That's something to talk about!*

II. How to Provide Outstanding Service

We already know that the concept of valued service gets a lot of "lip-service," but few representatives actually deliver. We have all heard slogans such as "service is our middle name," but what we hear is rarely what we receive. In fact, service is a sore point for most consumers today—and it seems to be getting worse.

Examine the definition of service according to *Webster's Ninth New Collegiate Dictionary*:

> service — contributing to the welfare of others.

Chapter 6

How do sales professionals serve their customer? Let's look at some examples:

Investment Representatives

These professionals talk with people about various investment strategies based upon the client's goals and risk tolerance. If the client never implements the recommendations, has the representative provided any real service?

Understanding their financial goals and risk tolerance without implementation and follow through is not service...it is busy work.

> In the wake of someone else's mistake, you can rise to the occasion for what will be one of your finest hours.

Attorneys

Estate planning lawyers prepare wills, trusts, business agreements, contracts, and advice which are the basic tools involved in every estate plan. If the client never executes the legal agreements or takes the advice the attorney provides, has the attorney provided any service?

In this capacity, the more involved the attorney is in advice, implementation and follow through, the more valuable his service becomes.

Certified Public Accountants

Accountants are the ultimate bean counters. From a historical perspective, they can tell exactly what happened with their client's money, how much the client owes in taxes and strategies about how to save on taxes in the future. If the client doesn't take the advice but only signs the tax return, how much service does the client receive?

The more involved we are in our clients' lives, the less our service becomes reduced to a commodity.

Real Estate Agents

A very successful real estate agent once described to me two kinds of agents: The first is the one who truly cares about the interests of his client; the other is the one who *lists* as many properties as he can, resting his income in the law of averages rather than in the quality of his service.

Real Estate Agents who are truly committed to service shine. People buying and selling a home are often going through a stressful time--they need the empathy and the expertise of a professional that cares about the needs of her client.

Product Distribution Representatives

These professionals are found in virtually every industry, selling anything from apples to zippers. The dynamics of business relationships vary as widely as do the products they represent. What makes the best in the business so successful: Extraordinary Service. The best in the business know that they don't sell products—they provide for the needs of their customers. Products are only one means to that end. They know that good customers value the product knowledge and expertise the sales professional possesses. The sales professional isn't as concerned about short term sales as he is about the long-term relationship.

In highly competitive markets and fields, it's the quality of service that will rise above price.

Let's explore some ideas you may want to consider when thinking about service.

Transport to the Airport

One salesperson I know always offers to transport their clients to the airport—especially for early morning flights. You really can't trust that a cab will show up on time! The agent claims that he receives more referrals from this group of clients than he has from any other group.

> Service is a sore point for most consumers today—and it seems to be getting worse.

Birthday Cards

Instead of a normal birthday card, why not create your own? Use a calligrapher to print your client's name and date on a card that indicates that they are a great person. The card invites him to call you so that you can buy him the beverage of his choice. Make the card bright yellow or red. Eventually he will know it's from you before they open it. It's unique—it becomes your "trademark."

Newspaper Articles

You should copy anything you read in any publication that would be of interest to one of your clients and mail it to her with a personal note that simply says, "I was thinking of you when I came

Chapter 6

across this article." This is another example of how being a good detective will pay off for you. Keen observation skills and an awareness of what is going on around you will make this an easier task to handle. If it's an article you read online, don't just email it...print it out and mail it with a personal note!

This approach to client relationship building is so important, that *Business First of Columbus* actually has seminars open to the public on how to do just that! They see it as increasing service to their subscribers...by teaching them how to leverage their newspaper subscriptions for all their worth!

Client Appreciation Get Togethers

The sky is the limit. You can have a formal dinner party or a picnic. It's up to you. The sole purpose is to thank your clients for their business and make them feel important.

One client of mine has now made a habit of having regular lunches with his clients, as one-on-one sessions. Another does a series of ongoing events that are open not just to clients, but to all friends and people within the community and circles of influence. They don't just sponsor these events...they plan, organize and host them.

Members of Armed Services

If your clients have sons or daughters serving in the military—especially overseas—send care packages. Cookies, cakes or anything else from home will endear them to you. It's also a great morale builder for people who are serving all of us, and are far from home.

> In highly competitive markets and fields, it's the quality of service that will rise above price.

Tickets to Sporting Events

Most people enjoy seeing a football, basketball, baseball, or soccer game. Purchase tickets and ask if your clients would like to attend. With a proper fact gathering process, you will learn more about their interests and be able to provide appropriate tickets.

Educational Meetings and Seminars

Assume you have a client who loves gardening. You read in the newspaper about a three-day symposium on gardening and landscaping. You give your client a call and ask him if he would like to attend. You provide the ticket and you almost guarantee a call telling you about what he learned. It makes a great opportunity to talk about referrals.

Magazine or Newspaper Subscriptions

Knowing your clients' interests can direct you to send an annual subscription to their favorite hobby magazine or to the book-of-the-month club! For clients who have lost their sight or simply have trouble reading—audio books are terrific and make outstanding and thoughtful gifts.

My suggestion is that you study your client list to determine what you could do to provide outstanding service to each of your clients. This was just a sampling of ideas. You can think of many more!

III. The Eight Rules of Outstanding Service

In summary, let us review what we call the Eight Rules of Outstanding Service. Together, they make up your "compass" that helps you determine the most effective ways to serve your clients, stand out, and create enthusiastic introductions.

Rule #1: Serve for the Joy of It

We have emphasized from the very beginning that you must internalize and inwardly understand the true value your services provide. You must see yourself first as a servant.

Think back to a time when you came to someone's rescue. Hopefully, it was not too long ago. How did that make you feel? It most likely gave you a sense of euphoria, of joy in helping someone.

It is not something you do just for the money. If it is, you will burn out far too fast. I can honestly say that one of my first joys of helping others was when I was ten years old delivering newspapers. It was fun getting to know my route customers (I delivered the evening newspaper), and to actually become part of their lives. There were times when some customers faced health challenges, and I would visit them in the hospital, or leave something "extra" with the paper (like a box of candy). Did I do it for the tips? No...I did it because I cared—*because I wanted to*. Of course, the tips didn't hurt, either.

Rule #2: Never Substitute Your Convenience for Customer Service.

Remember the example of the "moment of truth" when the client's package was shipped out incorrectly? In this situation, the proper response was getting in the car and making the ten-hour round-trip drive. Forget any prior plans. Forget the convenience.

Any sales professional who is unwilling to be inconvenienced for the sake of his client's needs, does not deserve his commission. Too many people on the "customer service frontline"—especially those who work for companies that do not reward great service, make customers feel like a bother. "I'll get to you when I get around to it," is the timeless, yet far-too-common message. Serving should NEVER be an inconvenience—it should always be an HONOR and a PRIVILEGE.

> Any sales professional who is unwilling to be inconvenienced for the sake of his client's needs, does not deserve his commission.

Rule #3: Every Complaint is a Cry for Service

You have heard that other people's problems are your opportunities. When a customer expresses a problem or a concern, it is a request for service made at point-blank range. In many cases, it is the ultimate Moment of Truth, because the test of your commitment and your character is revealed in the difficult times, not the easy ones.

"What about those pesky clients who are *always* complaining?" If you have a client who is always finding something to gripe about, then that person is most likely attempting to fill a void in his or her life. *It is still a request for service.* Your reaction should be to stop looking at that person as a "heckler," and start seeing them as a human being who has needs. Be proactive, and schedule some extra time to listen and understand, and you may discover that the frequent complaining is merely a symptom of some deeper issues. Help your client uncover the issues, and you have begun the process of creating a new reality for your client and deepened the bonds of loyalty.

Rule #4: Seek Out Moments of Truth, and Become Legendary

Earlier we illustrated some examples of Moments of Truth. They are everywhere! Focusing on the negative causes too many people to *avoid* such situations. *We say, seek them out and embrace them.*

Moments of Truth are more than just responding to complaints or when a mistake is made. You find Moments of Truth when:

A client (or prospect) has a special need or request. The more you can customize your service to meet the specific needs of your client, the more you will distinguish yourself amongst your colleagues. Go the extra mile, take the road less traveled, and become legendary!

A prospect cannot make up his or her mind. Many prospects do not know what they need, and many of them do not even know what they want! This is common among many service industries. If you run into such a situation, do not put them off or tell them to call you when they are ready. Instead, evaluate their situation and the results they wish to create, and leverage your own knowledge (and that of your colleagues) to provide choices and possible solutions. If they are stuck, you need to be proactive and get their mental gears going.

A prospect is resistant to buying. Various levels of investments are often met with corresponding levels of resistance or hesitation. If a prospect has objections, listen and understand them. Reflect your own understanding of their particular situation, and educate your prospect *from their perspective.* This is not manipulation—in fact, major financial decisions should *not* be made without considering other factors that may be involved. Walk your prospect through each concern, and address it. Doing so confirms their commitment to their purchase—and their loyalty to you as their rep.

The prospect is ready to buy. In his classic book, *How to Win Customers and Keep them for Life,* author Michael LeBoeuf, Ph.D. "retells" an experience from Samuel Clemens (aka Mark Twain), who listened in awe to a preacher at a mission gathering. Clemens was so inspired by the speaker, he was ready to contribute five dollars to the collection plate—up from his usual one dollar donation. However, *the preacher continued talking,* apparently enjoying the sound of his own voice. Clemens' inspiration soon gave way to frustration; when the collection plate came by, he kept his five dollars, and instead removed a dime! What do we learn from this story? We should be looking for signals of when the prospect is ready to purchase, or agree to an interview. We need to know when to stop "selling" and ask for the order (aka close the deal).

The prospect buys! Is this the time to relax? Never! Once the client buys, then the real service begins. As we discussed earlier, now is your opportunity to give your client what they *don't* expect. Al-

> The test of your commitment and your character is revealed in the difficult times, not the easy ones.

Chapter 6

ways send signals that you are thinking of them, that you appreciate them and that you value them and their business.

The prospect refuses to buy. If you do not make the sale today, is that the time to quit? Is it time to remove that prospect from your list? Some of the best people in our business will openly tell you that among their best clients were the longest and toughest acquisitions. I know an insurance wholesaler who pursued a prospect for three years, without ever getting an interview! It was not until the prospect heard her speak at a professional meeting that he agreed to meet with her. Today, he is one of her best clients.

Rule #5: Remember Who You Serve

Supervisors and sales managers play a specific role in the client-rep relationship. The good ones will be the first to state: You do not work for me: you work for your client. But you *report* to me!

Some experts observe two models that exist officially or unofficially in many work and service environments. They are the *Inerted Pyramid* and the *Chain of Command*.

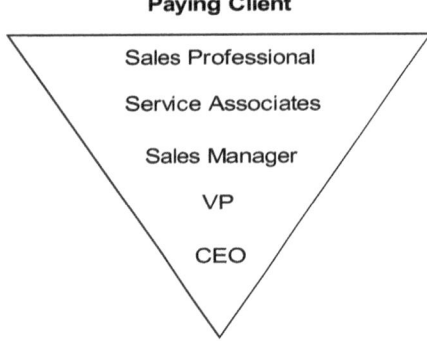

In the Inverted Pyramid, the client is on top.

In the **Inverted Pyramid,** the client is on top. Everything else flows downward. In this model, everyone works for the client, and this thinking is what drives every-day actions and decisions. It's a healthier and more accurate way of looking at business. You will notice that the higher up in the "corporate structur" the lower the person is in the pyramid!

Your Moment of Truth

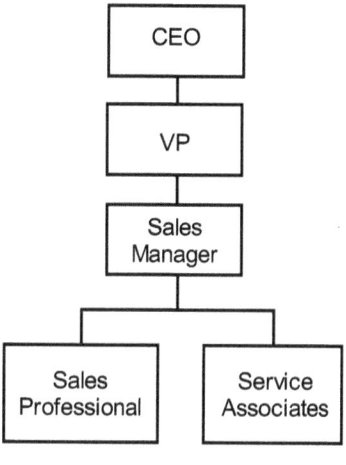

The more antiquated yet all-to-common model is the **Chain of Command**. In this situation, the focus of the people is not on what the client wants, but *what the boss wants*. Keep the boss happy, and you keep your job. If you're lucky, you won't have any pesky clients to get in your way.

As you can see, the client is at the bottom—even though the client is paying the money that covers everyone's salary! The staff, and in some cases even the boss, *just doesn't get it.*

If you find yourself in a chain of command, seek out opportunities to create change that directs all actions and focus to the needs of the client.

Rule #6: No One is an Island

In both models, you will see that the primary representative, although he or she may be the lifeline to the client, is still part of a greater team. In many cases, you may find yourself managing a team of associates that help you serve the needs and interests of your clients.

In essence, your clients are their clients—that is the way they should see it. When they assist you in getting a job well done, it is your responsibility to provide positive reinforcement that will ensure that their quality help and assistance continues.

That is why we strongly recommend that every skill, every courtesy, and every measure of respect that you show to your prospects and clients, you must also be shown to your colleagues and associates. Make them happy, and they will help you make your clients happy. It's that simple.

Chapter 6

Rule #7: Serve More, Sell More

Your goal is to serve first. Selling is a *means* to this end. It is service to sell a product or insurance policy to a client who really needs it and can understand the benefits that they receive. Is it service to oversell someone, or get them to buy something they do not need, just so you can get the commission? Of course not! That's not service. It is exploitation and it is unethical.

To serve is to care. To serve is to ensure—to the best of your ability—that your clients are receiving the benefits of what you provide. As we all know, people do not buy products or services—they want benefits. Focus on the benefits, and you will succeed and become more valuable to your clients.

> What does Outstanding service have to do with prospecting?

Rule #8: What Goes Around, Comes Around

All through this chapter we have said very little about the various steps that you must take to prospect successfully. In the beginning of this session, we posed the question: *What does Outstanding service have to do with prospecting?*

Our answer: "Rule #8. What Goes Around, Comes Around."

Rules one through seven have all been focused *outward*—directing you to keep your attentions on your prospects and clients. We have said very little about what they do for you—it has all been about what you can do for them.

Now, rule number eight is all about you. You focus on serving, and you allow yourself to be served. You offer and deliver help—you ask for and receive help in return.

Case in point: When asking a client for introductions, what is your first question to him? Is it for names of their friends?

No. You first ask your client to acknowledge that you have provided outstanding service.

With that achieved, you then ask your client if he feels that your services would be equally (if not more) beneficial to others.

When he concurs on your second point, you ask him for referrals and introductions.

Conclusion

Service is about giving, and most people who have really given service from the heart will tell you that the benefits are plentiful. You will also find that when you know you have served from your heart, and your clients have acknowledged it, any fear or hesitation you may have felt about seeking referrals and introductions will be swept away.

Use the *Golden Rule:* treat and serve people as you would want them to treat and serve you.

(Chapter Endnotes)

[1] Remember our points from Chapter 3: this can occur when your verbal language and subtext messages conflict as well.

Chapter Review

1. What is the importance of Outstanding Service to prospecting?

   _____
   _____
   _____

2. How do you evaluate your own service to others?

   a)_____
   b)_____
   c)_____
   d)_____
   e)_____
   f)_____
   g)_____
   h)_____

Chapter 6

3. Define Outstanding Service.

   _____
   _____
   _____
   _____

4. What is a Moment of Truth?

   _____
   _____
   _____
   _____

6. Name four ways YOU can provide Outstanding Service.

   a. _____
   b. _____
   c. _____
   d. _____

7. What are the Eight Rules of Outstanding Service?

   1) _____
   2) _____
   3) _____
   4) _____
   5) _____
   6) _____
   7) _____
   8) _____

8. What did you learn most from Chapter Six?

_____
_____
_____
_____
_____

Chapter 7

Chapter 7:

Prospect and Flourish Everyday

I. What Next?

Each of us has different values, objectives, and motivations. Why do some people become successful while others languish and die? Have you ever attended a seminar, workshop, or convention and listened to the main platform speaker discuss how she became successful? After hearing and digesting the speaker's thoughts you come to the conclusion: if she accomplished what she accomplished with her skills then I should be a multi-millionaire.

Conclusion: it's not (just) about skills. I believe the so-called missing link is what the speaker may have left out: *internal fortitude*. It's more exciting and entertaining for us to learn how she implemented a huge sale or how a prospect walked into her office and placed a huge order.

It's even more exciting to hear that the speaker credits her success to the fact that she loves people. When speakers start down that road, I begin to have my doubts: Is that the secret? You must be a people-lover?

Unfortunately, there is no secret. If there was, everyone would have discovered it years ago. The view this whole process as merely a "formula" or tactic is to completely miss the point. Throughout this book, you have been bombarded with tactics and "formulas" that you may or may not choose to adopt. Does this mean that everyone who reads this book will reach unparalleled success over the next twelve or twenty-four months? I certainly hope so.

Knowing what to do is important—but it takes internal fortitude to stay disciplined and focused on creating the results that you want.

What is fortitude? Merriam-Webster defines it as "strength of mind that enables a person to encounter danger or bear pain or adversity with courage." The same source also describes fortitude as "a quality of character combining courage and staying power."

I think of it as being able to keep pushing after you have "hit the wall." And hit it, you will.

Fortitude in Action

By calling your attention to fortitude, we are basically repeating one simple truth that you have heard time and again: If you really want to succeed, *then don't give up*. Here's another story I. David Cohen has to share, this one about fortitude:

Back in 1986 I interviewed an Israeli who wanted to sell life insurance. I'll call him Sam. The manager of our office asked for my opinion regarding Sam's ability to become successful. I had a problem—he barely spoke English and I felt that he could never effectively communicate with English-speaking individuals. I suggested to our office manager that he should not hire Sam.

As you might guess, the manager did appoint Sam as an agent and his career commenced. Sam had a very simple sales talk: "You need insurance. You are going to die."

How could anyone survive in our business with such a sales talk? One day Sam related to me an incident that had recently happened. A businessman apparently agreed to purchase a large life insurance policy and completed all the necessary paperwork. The policy was delivered to Sam and now he had to contact the proposed insured and collect the money and deliver the policy. The annual premium was $10,000. The proposed insured would not return any of Sam's telephone calls. My reaction: I suggested to Sam that the individual may have reconsidered his decision, and decided not to purchase the insurance.

Obviously, this was not what Sam wanted to hear. He quarreled with me. He stated the proposed insured wanted the policy, and that the problem was simply getting in touch with him, someway, somehow.

What do you think was Sam's solution? He decided to phone the prospective client at home at 2:30 in the morning! Startled out of his sleep, the prospect agreed to drop off a check at the agent's office in the morning.

Knowing what to do is important—but it takes internal fortitude to stay disciplined and focused on creating the results that you want.

To every one's surprise, at 10:00 a.m. the prospect delivered a check for $10,000, signed the necessary papers, and departed with his policy.

He arrived as a prospect. He departed as a client! Now that's fortitude!

You don't tell stories like that from the main platform. It's too unbelievable and it doesn't relate to anything most of us would consider. How many of us would have "gotten the message" and given up?

But it happened to Sam, and he didn't give up. He did what most of us wouldn't have done, but it worked for him. Today, Sam is one of the most prominent sales representatives in the United States.

> Many of us enter our professions without realizing the price that must be paid.

Freedom Has its Price

One of the very reasons we are attracted to the sales profession is the freedom to manage our careers how we choose.

However, this so-called freedom is also one of the major reasons so many leave; many of us enter the profession without realizing the price that must be paid. Successful sales professionals work in many different styles and modes. What works for them may not work for you. It's for you to make your way, *your way!*

Unfortunately, many newer sales people simply want to emulate what they believe the veteran is doing! What they want to copy is the glamorous ride, not the day-to-day unimaginative, routine, boring aspects of our profession.

However, as we all know, without the pain, there can be no gain. The successful pros paid the price. So must you.

II. A Quick Recap

Everyone in business today has the task of effective prospecting. Great sales professionals do it well—the average ones do it poorly. In each and every case, without mastering the art and science of prospecting the future becomes very bleak. As we stated before, the number one reason people fail is lack of prospects.

No matter how good looking you are or how intelligent you may be, without someone to tell your story to, there is a 100 percent chance for failure.

You have been given dozens of great ideas and concepts about how to explore for and qualify new people to meet and talk with

Chapter 7

about your business. Let's review some of the fundamentals that we have learned from each of the previous chapters.

Chapter 1: The Prospecting Enigma

Prospecting is defined as the continuous activity of exploring for and qualifying new people to meet and talk with concerning your business.

Prospecting is an enigma. The number one reason people fail is lack of prospects.

There are five hurdles to overcome in prospecting:

1. You don't understand the value of what you sell.

2. A common fear of rejection. You must overcome fear by simply asking yourself: "What's the worst that could happen?"

3. Not knowing exactly what to do or how to do it. We briefly reviewed many approaches to meeting new people, from cold calling to volunteering in your community.

4. Laziness. We all feel lazy from time to time. To avoid laziness becoming habitual, you must adopt habits of action. You need to become a doer.

5. Overcoming the difficulty. Most new things are difficult at first. Like riding a bike, habits associated with successful prospecting must be practiced, practiced, and practiced until they become second nature.

The number one reason people will buy from you is they like you. As elementary as it sounds, it is also true. To this end, you must focus on:

1. Being punctual.

2. Being honest.

3. Being polite.

4. Being responsive.

Prospect and Flourish Everyday

Chapter 2: Not Everyone is a Prospect

A **natural market** is a group of people with whom you have a natural *affinity*, or *access* because of similar values, lifestyles, experiences and attitudes.

- When you have an *affinity* with a certain group, you have something in common.

- When you have greater *access*—those people to whom you can reach with greater ease, other than direct personal knowledge and acquaintance.

Niche markets are groups of people defined by certain criteria. These groups are large enough so that you never run out of names and small enough so that the members connect with each other to the point that your reputation can precede you.

Niche markets can be defined by:

1. Occupation
2. Demographics
3. Geographics
4. Psychographics

Chapter 3: Building Prosperous Relationships through Networking

Networking is receiving advice, assistance and new acquaintances from people you know. It is not selling anything or manipulation of other people. Networking is a crucial process to one's career. There are **two faces of networking**: building contacts (focus on quantity) and building relationships (focus on quality).

A **referral** is when a friend gives you a prospect's name to call. An **introduction** is when your friend calls the prospect for you.

Influential and often dynamic individuals are called **"Centers of Influence (COI)."** They represent the key to effective networking—and successful prospecting.

A **mentor** is a center of influence who takes a personal interest in guiding you in your career.

Social mobility is vital to successful networking. These activities allow others to see you in the community, be it in the business community, in the schools or on other fronts. People know who you are and where to find you.

Networking events are often sponsored by open groups that will host events in their respective communities on a regular basis. Some groups require paid membership; many do not.

Referral groups are highly structured groups of independent professionals who meet on a regular basis to trade referrals and network. They will almost always require a membership fee.

A **personal board of advisors** is a group of three to five (or more) centers of influence who share your vision and want to see you succeed. They provide:

1. Advice
2. Counseling
3. Encouragement
4. Pressure to follow through on your commitments

Chapter 4: Sharpen Your Point of Contact

Do you know how you would respond if asked, "What business are you in?" It is extremely important not only to be able to articulate what your business is and what you do, but also to approach it from how your work benefits others.

It is amazing how many people in business do not realize what their own **Value Proposition** is. This is the reason why a prospect should want to give up 20 minutes of their time to have a conversation with you.

The value proposition is best described in measurable terms. That is, the measurable benefit you can deliver—such as money or time saved, or revenue's increased. Further, how those benefits make your clients *feel* is equally important.

A value proposition can easily be articulated in two ways:

1. **Before and After** — in which you express what your client's situation was like before your involvement; and what it was like after.

2. **Story Telling** — where you articulate the scenario of the impact you made, with perhaps more emphasis on how you arrived at the desired results.

Before meeting with new centers of influence, you should:

1. Identify your target market.
2. Remember that ad-libs are for amateurs.
3. Define the value you offer.
4. Articulate all of the above succinctly.

You can leverage the above information into greater detail by creating a COI **Talking Points**—a "personal script" you can use to help you become better prepared.

Scripting is important because it is a key part of being prepared. Being prepared is vital to strong customer service and clear communication.

Scripts should not be memorized. Rather, they must be internalized. When you internalize something, you first communicate the message to yourself to make sure that you have a clear understanding. When this is accomplished, you are much more able to deliver your message from the heart (and you will be much more reliable "on your toes!").

Scripts should be practiced. Practice helps you fine tune your delivery; decide (with help from peers and colleagues) what works and what doesn't.

In any conversation between two people or within a group of people, there are messages being communicated not only through what is being said, but also through the underlying dynamics of what is *not* being said: the **subtext**. Subtext is a kind of underlying language that will either add to what is spoken, thus reinforcing and strengthening it; or it may *contradict* the spoken word, sending confusion and creating mistrust.

Chapter 5: What Do You Want?

Discipline helps us reach our potential and get what we want. It is not enough to have the skills and the talent. To succeed, you also need the discipline to exercise those skills on a consistent basis. You can strengthen your discipline with three keys:

1. Delaying gratification.
2. Making your choice before the moment of choice arrives.
3. Knowing what you want.

Hitting the wall is when you want to give up. There are five ways to avoid this situation or to overcome it.

1. Have a meaningful goal.
2. Break your goals into manageable parts.
3. Make trials your friend.
4. Stay objective and focused on the facts.
5. Surround yourself with conquerors rather than quitters.

Structure refers to how key elements in your life are arranged in relation to each other. In nature, structure determines behavior. This applies to our lives as much as it applies to water in streams. When we understand this concept, we can design our structure to create the behavior we want.

There are two kinds of goals: Fit goals and stretch goals. The flaws of **fit goals** are:

1. Getting rid of something does not create positive results.
2. Small, "realistic" goals do not bring out the best in us.
3. Problem solving does not account for the unpredictable.
4. Fit goals are limited to *today's capacities* and do not consider the potential for growth.

Stretch goals are ambitious and drive us to create results that we never thought possible. Stretch goals drive us to decide first what we want, and then to redesign and rebuild our structure to help us reach our goals.

Chapter 6: Your Moment of Truth

Providing Outstanding service is more than just doing the right thing by your clients. Providing Outstanding service is *crucial* to building client loyalty, and client loyalty is absolutely necessary for *introductions to new prospects.* You can evaluate your own service to others by answering the following questions:

1. Do I recognize the total lifetime value of my client?
2. With this knowledge in hand, do I make my clients feel as important as they truly are?
3. Am I enthusiastic, friendly, and pleasant?
4. Do I truly care about my clients?
5. Do I deliver what I promise, and then go beyond expectations?
6. Do I base my choices on the interest of my clients, or on what is most convenient for me?
7. Do I take responsibility for my client's happiness with our products and services?

Client loyalty is far more important than client satisfaction. **Loyal clients** will never leave you and will always go out of their way to tell others about you.

Your **Moment of Truth** arrives at a time of client contact, during which you are confronted with a situation in which you must *make a choice*. That choice will reveal how deeply you are committed to your clients.

To service your prospects to the greatest potential, **you must sell them.** You must make them clients.

There are **Eight Rules of Outstanding Service:**

1. Serve for the Joy of It
2. Never Substitute Convenience for Service
3. Every Complaint Is a Cry for Service
4. Seek Out Moments of Truth, and Become Legendary
5. Remember Who You Serve
6. No One is an Island
7. Serve More, Sell More
8. What Goes Around, Comes Around

These are just some of the key points we covered, and you would be wise to review this book often. There is a great deal to absorb, although much of it comes down to common sense.

Chapter 7

This leads us to what many of you may be thinking: how do I fit all of this into my already hectic schedule? We have three answers: green, red, and yellow.

III. Green, Red, and Yellow

"Great!" you must be thinking. "Just what I need: another time management system!"

Actually, we are not recommending a new system for you to manage your time and priorities. You may have already adopted the very simple habit of making to-do lists, while others may have each hour of the day carefully planned and scheduled. Whatever extent through which you manage your time, the following suggestions should adapt easily into your normal routine.

None of this is new. It's been around and presented in many different forms over the years. For the sake of simplicity, I will present it here as **Green, Red and Yellow**. Through this system, you divide your activities into the following three Time/Activity Zones. Each zone is color coded.

> None of this is new. It's been around and presented in many different forms over the years.

Time	Mon	Tue	Wed	Thur	Fri	Sat	Sun
6 AM							
7 AM							
8 AM		Green					
9 AM							
10 AM							
11 AM							
NOON							
1 PM							
2 PM		Red					
3 PM							
4 PM							
5 PM							
6 PM							
7 PM				Yellow			
8 PM							
9 PM							
10 PM							

Green Zone (Offense)

In the Green Zone, which we also call Offense, you need to be proactive about acquiring new business and finding new prospects.

Prospecting. Each and every day your antenna must be up so that you will have a steady flow of qualified people who need and want your services.

Case Study. After carefully listening to your clients' goals and objectives, you prepare solutions that fit perfectly with their monetary budgets.

Presentations. You package your solutions in a format that serves your prospect/clients' needs.

Red Zone (Defense)

In the Red Zone, which we also call Defense, you need to hone your sales and service skills. This is ongoing client service activity and the feeding of existing relationships. *In the Red Zone you are investing time and energy from which you will reap the benefits when you are in the Green Zone.*

Call backs. A prompt reply to phone calls, emails or faxes will endear you in the eyes of your prospects and clients. It shows you care.

Sales skills. Understand your prospect's personality and alter your sales techniques accordingly. Don't sell—let him buy!

Product knowledge. You can never know too much about your products. Continue your quest for product perfection. People love to deal with knowledgeable and articulate service representatives.

The most common mistake about the Red Zone is that people spend too much time here. Yes, it can include busy work, and if you are doing too much of that, you may need to consider getting some help. Your time and energies must be leveraged to doing that which *only you* can do. Farm out the remainder (such as clerical assistance).

> In the Red Zone you are investing time and energy from which you will reap the benefits when you are in the Green Zone.

Chapter 7

Yellow Zone (Neutral)

The Neutral Zone suggests activities not necessarily directed toward your business, but gives your life a sense of "balance." As we have said all along: it's not always about the money. Family and community are what give us purpose. They are the things we value most and what we work to nurture and protect.

Family time. This time is as important as work time. The enrichment your family provides for you enables you to recharge your batteries and become a better person.

Socializing. To really learn what makes people tick, meet with them in social situations. Whether it is a game of bridge or a garden club meeting, it's your opportunity to view people in a non-work environment.

Board service or volunteering. This is about giving back (not to mention creating social mobility). Who hasn't considered serving others? To really feel good make volunteering one of your top priorities.

You can graphically sort out the "zones" in your calendar, in whatever proportions work best for you.

> The Neutral Zone suggests activities not necessarily directed toward your business, but gives your life a sense of "balance."

What Does Green, Red & Yellow Provide?

With amazing simplicity, this system (which you can incorporate into any of your current weekly planning practices) allows you to:

Build structure. As we said, structure determines behavior. If your days are structured so that if you are prospecting in the mornings, do nothing but prospect in the morning. Do not take phone calls (unless they are prospecting related) and do not deviate from your regimented activity. Do not pass go; do not collect $200.

Stay focused. By not allowing other types of activities to intrude during the various time zones of the day, you are not allowing yourself to lose focus. You do not allow yourself to be "yanked in a million places at once." You also prevent yourself from becoming a slave to the "urgent." If something must be done, there will be a time later to attend to it.

Maintain balance. We all strive for balance—and ultimately, something gives. Remember the accomplished attorney who spent all his time on his work, and not with his family? That man didn't keep balance. He allowed one "zone" to consume his entire schedule—like a parasite!

As it is said in the book of *Ecclesiastes*, "There is a time for everything, and a season for every activity under heaven..." (Ecclesiastes 3:1 NIV).

Conclusion

We have given you the tools, and the shared knowledge that is the accumulation of hundreds of combined years of experience. In this last Chapter, we conclude with greater emphasis on mapping out what specific results you want to achieve, maintaining fortitude, focus, and keeping your life and your tasks in balance.

There are no shortcuts. This takes work. Remember that you must break big jobs into smaller tasks. If you lose balance, you will create a void in your business as well as your personal life.

Bonus Section I:

Serve Your Prospects BEFORE They're Customers!

Marketing tools play an important role in the sales cycle. For those producers who face the challenge of having to create their own marketing materials, I have added this bonus section that addresses essential points so that you can learn to get the most out of your customer communication efforts.

Part I. Define Your Message

It's the Message, Not the Media

Too many people still think more about *how* they want to say something, rather than *what* they want to say. Indeed, the quality not only of our service, our business, but of ALL aspects of our lives—our relationships with customers, as well as loved ones—often comes down to how effectively we communicate. This starts with having the right message.

Communication is not just about being able to write and speak. It's about how we conduct ourselves, how we dress, act—the subtext messages we send out. Of course, it's not just about **how** (the media), what it first comes down to is about **what** (the message). What message are we sending out to the world—both consciously and unconsciously?

Bonus Section I

Part I of this bonus section deals with the first issue to be addressed in revolutionizing your customer communication: your message (which communicates your value proposition). You must have one. It must be compelling, engaging, and to a certain extent, unique. Get your message down, have your people burn it into their hearts (i.e. scripted) and you are on your way.

Often I hear colleagues, prospects and clients approach me and say, "We need a brochure," or "We need a video," or "We need a website." WRONG! What you need first is a message—a true value proposition that will illustrate why a prospect should want to sit down and have a 20-minute conversation with you. Too many people still think more about how they want to say something, rather than what they want to say (Remember what we said earlier about scripting?).

> What message are we sending out to the world— both consciously and unconsciously?

So, with that in mind, let's move forward in revolutionizing your customer communication. However, just as in Chapter Four, before we get into style (in this case, the media), we must revisit substance, and that and we will start with your message.

First, What Value Do You Offer?

This reflects on the point we emphasized earlier on: do you understand your value? Anyone who knows the first thing about marketing will tell you that the most common mistake people make in their customer communication is to confuse product features with client benefits. The second most common mistake people make is less known—and that is a lack of clarity in how that benefit is communicated.

Take into account how many messages you are hounded with each day. Compare this number of today with twenty years ago, or even ten years ago. We live in a media-driven, fast-paced world in which we have less than a second to capture someone's attention. In this kind of environment, you can no longer be subtle. Customer benefits cannot be implied—they must be stated up front and in clear-cut language. But the benefits must be real—whether they are tangible or intangible.

For example, ask yourself, "What's my business?" I asked this of a recent client, a stock broker. He said that he specialized in selling stocks in a particular industry. Actually, he couldn't articulate it in one or two sentences. We considered this question further; taking into account his product, the competition, the nature of his ideal customer. With further analysis, we concluded that he helped these companies enhance the liquidity of their "obscure" stocks, by helping them to identify second- or third-generation stock holders and setting up buy-back programs. His target prospects were both these small companies, as well as their stockholders. But each group required a different value proposition.

His business was more than just brokering specific stocks. It was, in fact, helping small companies identify and match themselves with more desirable stock holder relationships, thus increasing the value of the stock itself (and thereby the company) by increasing its liquidity (i.e. services of valuation and buy-back).

Second, Build Credibility to Build Trust by Delivering Value—by Serving

Many people are hesitant to be too aggressive in pushing customer benefits because they are afraid that it will make prospects wary and skeptical, and push them away. They feel to do so is risky. That can happen, if you fail to back up your claim. This is why establishing credibility and trust with your prospect, literally in the same breath that you claim the benefit, is vitally important.

In other words, you cannot just blindly claim that you will provide said benefit, you must also tell the prospect *how* you will do so. Doing this will, as I initially coined in a publication I wrote many years ago, turn wary prospects into trusting customers.

Why is this important? It is because customer confidence is, by its very nature, very low. People raise their guard when presented with a message that they perceive to be created to serve mainly the interests of the messenger.

Every relationship has a "trust account." In marriage, for example, when one does good things, one makes a deposit into the bank account. When one betrays the trust or does something that's bad, one makes a withdrawal.

In business, it's the same way. When you are focused on the little things as much as the big things, when you deliver what you say, when you say you will, when you exceed customer expectations, you make deposits into the emotional bank account you have with your customers.

When you do not deliver on your claims, when you fail to meet expectations, you make withdrawals. As you can imagine, your average withdrawal is much bigger than the average deposit.

Every relationship has a "trust account."

Further, when you are new and starting out in a new customer relationship, it's safe to assume that your balance is in the red.

Credibility and trust is established through clear and direct customer communication, backed up by people who are friendly, honest and straightforward in how they conduct business and represent your organization.

So, how do you back up your claim?

The answer is simple. You tell the truth. No hype. No BS. Simple, plain, honest and straightforward.

Of course, beyond simply telling customers how you will work to deliver on what you promise, there are also many additional approaches that can have a tremendous impact on building credibility and trust with your prospects and customers.

Happy Customers

We all know how powerful customer testimonials can be, when done correctly. Getting past or existing customers to give testimony to how you helped them, and to do so openly with full attribution, is a necessity of effective marketing. Indeed, it allows you to get the most leverage out of your work. Through your service, you are not just creating a loyal customer, you are creating an independent advocate for your message.

Testimonials can be collected through a simple telephone interview and used in print or on your company website. However, an even more powerful way to leverage customer testimonials is on camera—sitting your customer down and having them share from the heart the benefits you have delivered. Assemble a collection of these video testimonials and before you know it, you have built your own customer showcase.

> Through your service, you are not just creating a loyal customer, you are creating an independent advocate for your message.

A portfolio of happy customers is the ultimate means of delivering the sizzle and the steak, all wrapped up in one neat package. When prospects see the satisfaction in the eyes and tone-of-voice of your happy customers, they become green with envy. They will want what your customers have. Who do you think they will call?

Testimonials...If They Write It, It Won't Come

Testimonials are powerful because they give you credibility and they show you have a successful track record. Most importantly they reflect the feelings that your clients have when you have served them with success.

Further, when you state your value proposition in your elevator speech or marketing materials, it is important to have testimonials to back up your claims. If you don't have compelling testimonials, get them!

Often when I pass on this advice to others, they will indicate that there are several past clients or associates whom they believe will give them a testimonial.

The mistake is made in how they attempt to get it.

Don't call your associate and ask them to write a testimonial for you. When you ask, you may say that you are simply updating some of your marketing communications and indicate that you would love to cite them as a happy past client and ask them to share just a little of their story.

"Sure!" they will respond. "I would be happy to."

And then you wait. Odds are you will keep on waiting, because the testimonial will never come.

The point here is not to give your colleague something to do. They have enough on their plate. The reason the testimonial won't come is not because they aren't happy—they are just too busy. After all, it is not their job to do your job. Instead:

1. List out your top five or six colleagues, and invite them for a cup of coffee and a conversation. Then, your job is to find out what they have valued in your service, why, and use that as a foundation for the testimonial that you write.

2. Use the meeting and the conversation not just to learn what they value, but also to uncover opportunities for improvement on your part. And ask them this question: "Given your happiness with what we have done, who else should I speak with? Who else may benefit just as you have?" This is perhaps when you may want to have a printout handy of their LinkedIn connections, and highlight contacts with whom you would welcome an introduction.

3. When you arrive back at your desk, write up just a few sentences that summarize, in their words, what they value. You write the testimonial—not them.

4. You then send it back to them via email, for their approval. Most of the time, they will sign off on it as is—or they will return it to you with a little embellishment and thus sounding even better.

Serve Your Prospects

As discussed earlier, when most of us encounter a message that we perceive is purely self-promotional, our guard goes up. Our attitude is, "All right, what are they trying to sell me this time?"

But when we are presented with a book, CD or DVD, well packaged and professionally produced, with a title that empathetically conveys a benefit to us, with no strings attached, we tend to lower our defenses.

What would you think if you were handed a booklet entitled, *Ten Ways to Tell if You are Over-Insured*?

Chances are your perception would shift from "What are they trying to get from me?" to "What can I get from them?"

Delivering information carries a lesser perception of being self-serving, even though most members of your audience fully understand that the messenger has something further to offer—for a price. But what's important is that beneficial information serves the reader, viewer or listener (i.e. the prospect). It gives them the first taste of what you offer: information, help, and most of all, value!

Begin delivering value in the form of tangible benefits; even if it is in the form of greater knowledge, you begin building the relationship. Where relationships are in place, there is credibility and trust. These days, it is also what many refer to as Content Marketing. But the principal has been around for decades.

Goettler Associates, a Columbus, Ohio-based fund raising consulting firm, serves nonprofit organizations all across the country. When the firm started in 1965, there were but a handful of such organizations in the entire country.

Today, there are hundreds of such firms serving a growing industry, and many more independent consultants with whom Goettler Associates must compete on one level or another.

The founders of the company realized this many years ago. They knew that building and maintaining credibility and trust was

Serve Your Prospects

vital, as they served an industry and profession that often experiences highs and lows in the trust arena.

To position themselves above the competition, Goettler Associates created what has become the flagship of their marketing, and of "serving their prospects,"—they call it *The Goettler Series.*

This family of short publications now exceeds twelve volumes, each providing valuable insights and helpful information on various aspects of capital fundraising for nonprofit organizations. Each volume focuses on a specific subject. Together, *The Goettler Series* can be seen as a comprehensive manual on fundraising success.

To be sure, it's out there, and Goettler Associates continues to use it to serve their prospects. As company president John Goettler freely admits, "Calls come in all the time from people who have used our publications, relied on them, and even taken them along to various positions. They use them for years. So, when the time comes and they know they need counsel, we are the ones they will call—because they feel as though they know us."

How's that for credibility and trust?

> In a world where everything that can be said has been said...how can anyone or anything be unique?

Before the advent of the content marketing model (which has prevailed in the wake of low-cost digital distribution), organizations that could afford it engaged in "custom publishing." This was the production of books and magazines not by traditional publishers, but by companies as an offspring to their overall advertising and marketing campaigns.

These publications would, and in many cases still do, have the look and feel of traditional magazines, but have a much more targeted audience. Some even accepted advertising, with editorial standards as high as other top commercial publications. But their main differences lie within two factors:

- First, they have a highly-targeted and well-managed database of readers. In other words, they literally know personally who they're talking to.

- Secondly, they provide methods of feedback, such as a response card, website and a toll-free number.

This encourages an on-going dialog—or relationship—between the reader (the prospect) and publisher (the seller). This relationship exists as a direct result of the business taking the first step in customer communication. The soul purpose was not to sell, but to serve the needs of the prospect, by simply offering complimentary information that would benefit them in some way, regardless of whomever the prospect eventually chose to do business.

In a world where everything that can be said has been said, and everything that humanly can be done has been done (although this realm does grow each year), how can anyone or anything be unique?

The reality is, we are all the same. The other side is, we are all unique. Each statement contradicts the other, and yet each statement is true.

In business, uniqueness can be determined in some way by the level of your competition. Where do you stand on the Commodity-Monopoly Scale? If you are on the far commodity side, you are selling on price (and had better have low costs, or be able to handle slim margins). On the monopoly side, you own the market, because the benefits you provide can be obtained nowhere else (at least that's the perception).

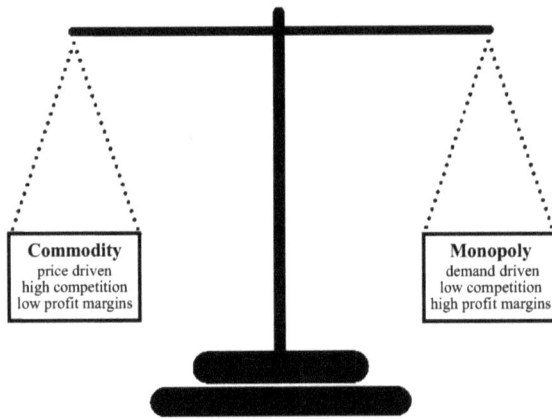

So, this begs the question: how do you make yourself stand out? How can you create a message that is different from what everyone else is saying, especially in a competitive marketplace?

Well, what is everyone else saying? "Top quality" and "great service" are expressions that have become tiresome and overused—to the point that they have little meaning. It's time to start examining your marketplace more closely, and talking to your customers. Seek out the gap.

A true value proposition can take time to develop, and it can be one of your biggest challenges. Indeed, the challenge may not be

Serve Your Prospects

as much to your creativity, as it can become to your own capacities. Standing behind a guarantee, for example, is a challenge that might scare off many people. The point that many business people forget is that guarantees are typically implied if not overtly stated—so one might as well capitalize on it and benefit themselves in the long run.

Developing Your Message: The Final Stretch

So, we have gone over the basics of developing your marketing message in an age of information overload...

1. We've addressed the importance of a value proposition that stresses benefits to the customer versus getting lost in product features. Further, in light of the message overload everyone of us faces, we have established the importance of being upfront and compelling in telling prospects just what they can get from us.

2. We've established the growing necessity to substantiate our claims, because people are naturally skeptical. Getting their attention will do you no good if you cannot keep it. Thus, building credibility and trust, by showing off happy customers and serving your prospects with truly beneficial information is vital to keeping the attention of your prospect.

3. Finally, the biggest challenge is the uniqueness of our message and how we offer our product or service. In today's crowded message arena, "me, too" messages don't cut it.

Let's say we have these elements in place and written down. How do we take these three main components and craft them into a cohesive value proposition that will serve as the foundation for all customer communication (and indeed, customer relationships) to follow?

Simple. The procedure is pretty fundamental—essentially the same as writing any basic business proposal or media release. Using the information you have collected thus far, consider the following points:

1. Identify your customer. Knowing your customer, his or her concerns, fears, needs and wants is the first step in revolutionizing your customer communication.

You must be able to differentiate yourself from the competition, even if it is simply making a claim that a competitor could also make, but you are beating them to the punch.

2. Identify your customer's unmet want or key problem. This is all coming from the perspective of your customer. What is the problem? Further, what is the consequence of this problem remaining unaddressed (this accentuates the pain—which is why we want rid of the problem in the first place)?

3. State in upfront and very clear terms, your solution to the problem (i.e. the benefit you provide). Here is were we position how we will benefit the customer, and make the pain go away, or help the customer get whatever it is that they want.

4. Indicate HOW you will implement your solution, and back it up further with previous success stories (i.e. build credibility and trust). Again, if this were a news release, the editor or journalist would expect your claim to be backed up—indeed the previous successes are the root of the actual story. Otherwise, it's full of hot air.

5. State clearly how you are different from others in your field. Again, looking at this as a news story, an editor is going to want to know what makes this so-called news story "new." You must be able to differentiate yourself from the competition, even if it is simply making a claim that a competitor could also make, but you are beating them to the punch.

The Next Step

With the essence of your message in place, you can then move forward to the next part: the tools which your people will use to deliver your message to the world.

Part 2: Leverage Your Media

With Your Message Down, You Need a Strategy to Deliver It

In the beginning we talked about how too many people first approach their marketing from the standpoint of the tools—the brochures, the website, the video—without first considering the importance of a message. Now that we have gone through the basics of determining a meaningful, compelling message to attract your prospects and keep their attention, we can now spend some time discussing the strategies and tools that your people (the communicators) will use in the ever-dynamic and important process of customer communication.

Earlier in this section, we discussed key issues to consider in evaluating where you are in your customer communication, in relation to where you want to be. Now, you need to revisit these items, and use this information to create a Marketing Action Plan (MAP). This does not need to be a long, drawn out process. However, you can't make effective choices on marketing materials unless you have a strategy on how to utilize them.

Let's quickly review these items from earlier. However, instead of examining them from the standpoint of where we are, we will use them to consider where we want to go, and reorder them accordingly:

Issue 1 — Your Sales and Marketing Goals

What results do you want to create? How can you be more specific? Do you want raise overall sales by 50 or 100 percent? Perhaps it's 500 percent? Perhaps you want to break into a new market altogether. In addition, let's be sure it's reasonable and time specific. This is where you may need to pull out the calendar, or project management software.

> One way or another, your people are the connection. They are your communicators.

Issue 2 — Your Market and Competition

Much of this information may not change (however some basic market research may reveal factors of which you may not have been previously aware).

Issue 3 — Your Customer

Again, know your customer. What do they want? How would they get it? What would attract their attention, and motivate them to act?

Issue 4 — Your Niche

Serving a specific niche is an excellent starting point if your potential market appears too big or overwhelming to attempt as a whole. Different sub-markets must be approached in different ways.

Issue 5 — Your Message

Now that you have a message down, it's one your people can become excited about and carry on with them through every step of the customer communication process.

Issue 6 — Your Marketing Media

Begin here to outline specific strategies that may be successful in reaching and serving your prospective customers. What channels of communication are at your disposal?

Issue 7 — Your People

One way or another, your people are the connection. They are the communicators. They must be in an environment that supports and nurtures strong skills in both sales, customer service, leadership and management.

Issue 8 — Your Budget

You will want to start with a general number for now, and can fill in the blank as you decide what you need to do in your program. In this regard, bear in mind that the most common reason business concerns fail is under-capitalization. Be realistic about what you are prepared to invest.

Problem: Low Consistency in Communication Media

A common problem experienced by organizations of all sizes is not just a lack of a cohesive message, but a lack of consistency in how they deliver that message. I've seen many companies that operate different divisions or branches, and each division is responsible for its own marketing. There is no real unification in how their materials are produced, and therefore there is no "cross-benefit" that leverages the media investment for all its worth.

Often, it is simply a failure of management to see the big picture. Instead of marketing materials being produced as part of an overall strategy, they are piece mealed together as the need or urge presents itself. Each project is approached almost as though it were from scratch. When we speak of materials, we mean all forms—brochures, websites, and audio-video tools.

> There is no real unification in how their materials are produced, and therefore there is no "cross-benefit" that leverages the media investment for all its worth.

Serve Your Prospects

Why is this so important? It comes back to the idea of cross benefit. One piece should reinforce the other, and all your materials must not only follow a consistent graphic scheme, they must reinforce your overall message. Without these requirements in place, you will not be able to leverage your media for the maximum payback on your investment.

The Solution: Total Media Integration

As you can imagine, when your people learn to deliver a single message through a variety of communication media, consistency means going beyond just using the same logo.

Many people think of their marketing materials and other visible aspects as reflective on their image—at least that's the term that gets used most often. I prefer to use the term *identity*, because with that conveys a single consistent theme—not only in appearance, but in the message. Your message, the graphics you choose, all come to bear on the identity you put out there for your organization, and your mission.

This approach also delivers the cross benefit we talked about. When you design your company brochure or catalog, stationery, AV materials and your website all with a unified look, feel and message, each reinforces the impact of the other. Copy and elements created for one, can also be slightly retooled for the other, preventing duplication of work and saving valuable time and costs in conceptualization, writing and design.

Don't Try to Sell—Attempt to Serve

In my many years in capital fund raising for nonprofit organizations, I have often come across clients who, when electing to produce a fund-raising video, want the video program itself to "make the ask," so to speak. Their expectation is to produce an eight-minute documentary style program that concludes with a narrator or person on-screen literally asking the viewer to make a gift to the campaign. This comes from a natural fear or avoidance that many people have to directly ask for a sale (or even make human contact).

Similarly, people often make the same mistake with their customer communication materials. Their hope is that the brochure, website or video itself will be enough to get the customer to want to buy. While this is possible (let's face it, that's the sole purpose of infomercials, right?), it's not always practical or entirely realis-

> When your people learn to deliver a single message through a variety of communication media, consistency means going beyond just using the same logo.

tic in a situation where you want to build long-term prosperous relationships with your customers. Materials are key to getting the prospect's attention and perhaps even getting them to pick up the phone, but from then on the responsibility lies with you and your people.

Serve Your Prospects (again!) in Four Steps

When you channel your resources to serve your prospects by delivering value upfront, you not only deliver your message in a compelling manner, you build credibility and trust, and in many ways will make yourself stand out among the competition. You lay the foundation for the first sale, and many more to come.

Step One: REFLECT Your Understanding of what Your Prospects Really Want (benefit)

Empathy is vital to effective communication—starting first with the importance of listening to people with the true intent to place oneself in their own situation—to understand what the other person wants and needs. For our purpose, this is just a recap of what we talked about earlier: the importance of having proper and accurate research on your market, and the various dynamics involved in appealing to its needs. Either way, there is a popular saying in the professional speaking industry that applies equally to sales and marketing: (your prospects) won't care about what you have to say until they know how much you care.

Step Two: RELATE to Your Prospects, Lowering Their Guard and Nurturing Trust

Step two exists on many planes, in personal contact as well as in marketing communications. On a personal level, part of listening is giving objective feedback: you must reflect back to the individual what they just shared with you, without any commentary or perception of a desire to influence. All that is necessary is that the other person feels understood, acknowledged, and respected. Agreement is not important. Only understanding. Only when the other feels understood will they be open to hear what you have to say. This what we refer to when we talk about lowering their guard.

When we listen, we acquire new information. But that new information won't do us any good if we don't know how to use it. We must now use our new understanding of our prospects not to make a sale, but to establish a relationship. A mere transaction

> We must now use our new understanding of our prospects not to make a sale, but to establish a relationship.

Serve Your Prospects

is not what you want. What you want is to evaluate what they have shared with you, matched it against your own resources (and perhaps those of other people you know), to determine how you can meet that person's needs. Is it tied directly to what you have to offer? Maybe, maybe not. But if you are in the insurance business and encounter an individual who shares a legal issue that must first be addressed (which is likely on the forefront of your prospect's mind), you are best to explore your own resources to help that person address those issues before they are going to be interested in anything else.

> Think about what you offer. There is information that is tied to it.

We must put ourselves in the other's position, and speak to them from their point of view. We address their problem, need or desire from their perspective (as though we were just like them) and then begin to introduce them to a solution. Is it your product or service? Not necessarily. However, we begin to take them, mentally and emotionally, from where they are now, to where they want to be.

Step Three: Deliver Value

This is where the proper leveraging of media tools can really pay off. Think about what you offer. There is information that is tied to it. You have information, either among your resources or in your own head, that your prospect can benefit from right now. How can you get this information to them, at little cost for maximum benefit?

In many cases, this is where most business proposals miss the golden opportunity. If you review most proposals, they are often drab, boring reads. In fact, for so many companies, proposals are created from boilerplates, with little changed beyond the name of the prospective customer, along with some numbers and fees. They often contain language that spell out features or services, with implied benefits they will bring to the customer.

In fact, the business proposal should be a dynamic document, that is more written specifically with the prospect's situation in mind. Indeed, before making any recommendations or effort to make a sale, a proposal should FIRST spell out your understanding of the prospect's dilemma, again, getting past their guard and making them welcome whatever suggestions you may offer.

Next, the proposal should GIVE ADVICE, free of charge, on what your recommendations are, based on the understanding which you just explained. Here is where you really begin to serve your prospect. You want to help them, and ask nothing in return. This is true sincerity, true understanding. Most importantly, it BUILDS TRUST—a level of trust that is often lacking in American business today.

Lastly, with the recommendations on how the prospect will get what they want, you must make your proposal! "First, here is how I understand your situation," you say. "Second, here is how I see your need being met. Third, let me meet your need, and here is how much it will cost."

Step Four: Allow Your Prospects to POSITION You above the Competition (uniqueness)

Let's quickly look back at our Commodity-Monopoly scale. When we have a monopoly, customers see us as the only resource to provide the true benefit they desire. When we offer a commodity, customers do not see any difference between what they can get from us, versus anyone else. Therein lies the difference. By reflecting a true understanding of the prospect's needs, concerns, and situation, we will place ourselves on a higher plain (position) in the prospect's mind. By delivering immediate value—by taking a step that the competition may not be taking—the prospect positions us in a league all our own.

This is where we hit the difference between generating mere sales transactions and building relationships. Are true, sincere relationships a commodity? Of course not! Consider the lifetime value of a single customer—one who comes back to your business every week, month or even once a year, and you will know what I mean.

Now, we are not saying that in building sincere relationships with your prospects and clients, you will be so far above any competition that you can charge whatever you want. But most people want to be cared about, to be loved, to be accepted, and to have friends. When mutual understanding, respect and service are the foundation for a business relationship, it's more important than the price.

Further, when your employees adopt this same attitude and make serving not just customers, but everyone, inherent to their daily routine and mission, the benefits to your organization's bottom line will flourish.

> By reflecting a true understanding of the prospect's needs, concerns, and situation, we will place ourselves on a higher plain (position) in the prospect's mind.

Serve With Print

When one thinks of marketing communications, or marketing media, one often thinks first about brochures and advertising. In revisiting the list from part one, the possibilities of implementing print media are endless:

- ☑ Brochures
- ☑ Newspaper ads
- ☑ Magazine ads
- ☑ Directory ads
- ☑ Transit ads
- ☑ Billboards
- ☑ Postcards
- ☑ Direct-mail letters
- ☑ Catalogs
- ☑ Newsletters
- ☑ Publication articles
- ☑ News articles and interviews
- ☑ Signs/banners/posters
- ☑ Floor displays
- ☑ Books
- ☑ Training publications
- ☑ Fax blasts
- ☑ News releases
- ☑ Monogrammed products

Looking through this list, which is certainly not complete, you will see that each approach exists at a different level of complexity from the other. Simple fliers and advertisements are much easier to plan out and produce than full-length books or catalogs.

...effectively produced and distributed print materials can become your constant presence in your prospect's world...

Bonus Section I

Some Advantages and Disadvantages of Print

Of all forms of recorded communication, print materials have been around the longest in one way or another. Some of the best advantages of utilizing print materials are:

They're tangible. Printed sales and information pieces are useful "tools" that can be passed out in many ways. The nicer the presentation, and more engaging the information, the less likely the piece will be discarded. Even if it is not acted upon immediately, it can be "filed away" and pulled out for later reference. In other words, effectively produced and distributed print materials can become your constant presence in your prospect's world, whether it's on their desk at the office, or in the take-out menu drawer in the kitchen.

They're flexible. Printed communications come in all shapes, forms and sizes. From a simple business card to a 300-page catalog, there is very little you cannot produce.

They're more affordable. Four-color printing is much more affordable than it used to be—much to the point that there is no excuse to produce nothing that is short of first-class in its presentation. Technology has made great strides in the last twenty years to make short-run printing of all kinds much more practical—and smart, given the rate at which printed information can become quickly outdated (more on that later).

They're convenient. People can receive your materials and review the information on their schedule, at their convenience. They don't need a computer or CD player. All they need is a good set of eyes and the ability to read and comprehend.

They can deliver more detailed information. We are talking about delivering information, and different means of communication suits different levels of detail in that information. A brochure will most likely present customer benefits, backed up by messages of credibility and a unique competitive offering—while a newsletter, report or even a full-length book will dive much deeper in details, for the two-fold purpose of customer education (content marketing) and the cultivating of longer-term prosperous relationships.

Print materials, as do every other media form, do have some disadvantages as well...

> ...the kind of communication to which your prospective customers are drawn is something you will need to consider.

They're costly. A direct contradiction to what we said above, right? Even while printing technology have really brought costs down, printing a large quantity of materials to reach a large audience is still indeed a significant investment. That raises the risk that must be weighed against the possible payback.

They're final. Any printer or designer will be the first to tell you: their worst nightmare is pulling a single piece off the stack of a just-completed 50,000-piece print run and find a glaring mistake right on the front (or anywhere else, for that matter). Once printed, it's done, mistakes and all. There is no going back, except to eat the cost and shell out the money for another printing.

They're quickly outdated. Obviously, this depends on the content and the nature of the piece. However, keeping marketing materials up to date can be a challenge for some organizations. And while it helps to have materials that are "ever-present" in the lives of your prospects, it doesn't help if pertinent information (especially contact information) is outdated or incorrect.

"They're boring." Let's face it: in a time of information overload, and all kinds of dynamic media hitting us from every direction, some people may be less drawn to printed materials. To each his own—but the kind of communication to which your prospective customers are drawn is something you will need to consider.

This last point leads us into a summary of just a few of the most basic and common forms of printed communication.

Brochures

Among the most common form, brochures are most effective when viewed as an "executive summary" of your compelling message: Open with strong benefits, without beating around the bush. Back it up with how you deliver those benefits, and/or how you have done it for others, and close with a unique competitive offering with a strong call to action. A pushy sales piece? Not necessarily. However, does it serve the customer's interests? If done correctly, you bet it does. Remember, the purpose is not to close the sale. It is to pique the prospect's interest with your value proposition, and get them to want to have a 20-minute conversation with you.

Postcards

Postcards are a popular and economical means of generating leads and initiating dialog with prospects and customers—when done

---
Many organizations that put out newsletters make the mistake of filling space instead of feeding a relationship with their prospects and customers.

correctly. Because you have less space with which to work, you must become even more focused on a specific compelling message that is designed to evoke a specific action on the part of the reader. Most likely, that action is to simply visit a website or pick up the phone to request more information—preferably an information product that delivers value up front asking for nothing in return (again, it serves as part of a content marketing campaign).

Newsletters

Newsletters are another popular form of content marketing, and can be extremely effective when done correctly.

However, many organizations that put out newsletters make the mistake of filling space instead of feeding a relationship with their prospects and customers. People aren't interested in news that doesn't concern or benefit them in some way, so when crafting a newsletter, forget the birthdays and bowling league photos. It's not about you—it's about them. How can you serve them? What value can you deliver on an ongoing basis (at least quarterly) that will:

- ☑ Be timely enough that your prospect will want to review the newsletter as soon as they receive it, and

- ☑ Be timeless enough that your prospect will keep the newsletter forever.

This will include articles that offer how-to information. It may include headlines from industry related news that can have a real impact on the lives of your customers and prospects (indeed, when sharing such news, specify this impact in your content and share why the news is important).

Books

"Books?" you may ask. Yes, books. You are reading one right now. Since when are books used for the purpose of marketing? It happens more often than you think. In the last twenty years, the growth of small presses and independent publishing has enabled literally tens of thousands of professionals and experts to package their knowledge, experience and expertise into the form of printed, bound books. The resulting product, when correctly produced, is not only something that delivers value to the reader—it promotes the author. It's win-win, all around. Writing a nonfiction book, especially one that pertains to your own profession,

> The growth of small presses and independent publishing has enabled literally tens of thousands of professionals and experts to "package" their knowledge, experience and expertise into the form of printed, bound books.

can be one of the most positive steps you can take for your career and your business.

Everyone wants to write a book. It is one of the most common, yet elusive, goals anyone can strive for. Beyond the challenge of just writing a book is the even greater task of getting it published. It is said that for every book published there are perhaps hundreds, if not thousands, of unpublished manuscripts.

Once you have a manuscript that is complete and of which you are proud, you have only finished the first step. From here, you have two options:

1. Begin searching for a publisher. Bear in mind that we are not talking about agents. Contrary to popular belief, literary agents are more involved in negotiating a sale rather than trying to make a sale to begin with. It is a detailed process of researching publishers who would be interested in your topic, and then writing a business proposal to go out and sell it. In fact, most publishers—and agents as well—will not even look at a manuscript until they have seen a solid book proposal.

2. Publish it yourself. This is your next option, and can be a lucrative one at that if your topic is right and you adopt the appropriate strategy. Further, with today's advanced media technology, you can actually publish yourself in several ways at once, and at a fraction of what it used to cost: in print, electronic and audio-video form.

3. Do nothing. You have finished your book and you are satisfied. Now, you can leave your manuscript on your shelf and in your computer with the pride and knowledge of a job well done (or, just done). Too bad that no one will read it, though...

A book can be a powerful marketing product, and indeed can be the ultimate way in which you can serve your prospects. They also retain a longer shelf-life, and can play a highly important role in helping you build additional credibility and trust with your prospective customers. Further, a book can be a lucrative means of attracting media attention and further establishing you and your organization as a trusted resource in your field.

Serve with Audio-Video

Audio-video takes many forms: from short YouTube videos to 30-second commercials aired during the Super Bowl, to full length infomercials or documentaries:

☑ Radio spots

☑ TV spots

☑ Documentaries

☑ Customer profiles /testimonials

☑ Education and Training videos

☑ Video-based seminars and webinars

☑ Spoken word audio programs

☑ Broadcast interviews (radio/TV)

☑ Slide shows/Powerpoint presentations

☑ Video news releases

> While the cost of production tools have come down—tools used for photography, editing and production—talent, on the other hand, is still the driving factor in quality.

Some Advantages and Disadvantages of Audio-Video

As with print media, audio-video does have its advantages and disadvantages. Let's first review some of the advantages of audio-video:

It's tangible. Just like printed materials, AV tools can be tangible products to be distributed. Packaging is very important, of course, and content is still king. People are much less likely to toss out a DVD—thus it may have a longer shelf life.

It's flexible. This applies differently than to print. Print forms vary greatly. However, when we say that AV can be flexible, I have to say this applies more to DVD video, and in some cases, audio CD. Audio and video cassettes, which have virtually vanished, did not offer flexibility in how the customer accessed the information. Tapes are *linear*, and thus if a customer wants to access a certain part of the material, they must sit through the whole thing or speed the tape back and forth and hope to get lucky.

Digital media, that being Audio CD, Video CD, and DVD, are *nonlinear*, and thus offer us random access. We can zip through chapters and tracks, and if we want a certain segment, we can find it in just a few moments.

It's more affordable. Just like printing has come down in costs in so many ways, so has the costs for the production tools of AV materials. But don't misunderstand my point: the cost of production

Serve Your Prospects

tools have come down—the tools used for photography, editing and production. *Quality still makes a difference, however.*

Video, specifically, can help your prospects and customers visualize what you can do for them. You see this example in television commercials every day. The young woman in the shiny new car; the couple strolling down a beach in paradise; the man who's twenty pounds lighter than ninety days before. If your business offers a substantial benefit to a group of people, or solves a particular problem, then this is the groundwork upon which to build your visual images.

Video can also do a better job of introducing the viewers to you and your organization. This is especially helpful when you are separated from your customers by a substantial distance, with limited or no face-to-face contact between the two of you.

In this case, video puts friendly and smiling human faces behind the business name. When we do business, most of us prefer to think in terms of working with people, not corporate entities. We want to work with people who will treat us the same way we would like to be treated.

Video does a great job of capturing the trust of the prospect, by introducing them to other satisfied customers who will testify to the quality and service provided by your business. You will not only see this in normal television commercials, but in great depth in the infomercials found so often on late-night television. This allows viewers to hear firsthand stories of how others have benefited from your company. It also gives them someone to relate to, when the satisfied customer describes a particular problem or situation similar to that of the viewer.

Some disadvantages include:

It can be costly. Again, a direct contradiction to what we said above. Shooting a video, or orchestrating a recording session can be a costly project, if you choose to do it right. It's an investment that must be weighed against the possible payback.

It's final. Just like a brochure coming off the press, once a disc is burned and distributed, it's out there for what it is, mistakes and all. Not the case of course, for a video distributed over the internet. A YouTube spot can be updated almost as easily as a web page.

It's pithy. Video is a fast-moving medium, designed to cater to short attention spans. This is what most of us are conditioned to

---

Video is a fast-moving medium, designed to cater to short attention spans.

unless we are really drawn into a subject. But when it comes to communicating complex and specific facts and figures efficiently, in a way that people will remember, you are best to put your information on paper. You can review general statistics through video, through the use of computer graphics, but the more complex they become, the less advisable it is to do so.

Video's Powerful Leverage: Showcasing the Happy Customer through Testimonials

As indicated earlier, happy customers are great for getting new ones. Video is a powerful tool in doing this, by creating a customer showcase of video testimonials.

> Happy customers are the finest representation of benefits you can have.

Note my reference to a "customer" showcase over a product showcase. Products are features. Happy customers are the finest representation of benefits you can have. It's great to have the exuberant customer (whose full names are always disclosed unless we are asked to do otherwise) who tells us, on camera:

☑ how you made their life or business less stressful and more enjoyable

☑ what their situation was like before you intervened, and what it is like now

☑ why when asked who to call for similar help, they would think of none other your company

It's one thing to have written testimonials. It's another thing to use on-camera testimonials to visually and emotionally capture the attention of your prospects. Offering steak is easy. But with the help of your customers, your prospects will see, hear and feel the sizzle. With video, you are selling the emotion, the satisfaction, and pride that comes from being your customer! This will only reinforce your Unique Selling Proposition.

To this end, for each happy customer you should:

☑ Conduct a brief on-camera video interview with the customer, preferably in their everyday environment.

☑ With that material (which can be shot in less than a couple hours on site), you script and edit a 30-60 second video spot, taking the happy customer's positive sound bites (brief on-camera testimonials), overlaying parts with key-framed photographs, or supporting video of the customer enjoying the benefits that you provide. The emotional impact can be further enhanced by dramatic dissolves and flowing music.

Each customer spot can be a stand-alone mini-production. The Customer Showcase is simply a collection of these spots. They can be streamed off your website, or distributed via DVD. Of course, the same content can be used to create spots for television or radio. That's the beauty of digital video—the ability to cost-effectively distribute across a wide range of media distribution channels, yet deliver a consistent message using high production standards. Further, since the Showcase is just a collection of spots, it can be easily updated and modified simply by removing old spots and/or adding new ones (much like pages in a portfolio binder).

Other Applications of Audio-Video

Radio/TV spots are perhaps the most common forms associated with this media. These are utilized by companies that are aimed at a large demographic. Some are done quite well, while many are done quite badly.

Education programs/seminars. If you or a key person from your company is in position where they occasionally speak or teach, professionally capturing these events on video allows you to gain additional leverage from these events—especially if you are sponsoring the event yourself. Distributing the program via the internet or DVD adds a value that rivals that of a book or other high quality publication.

Spoken word audio programs, much like videotaped seminars, have equal value. Audio books have been popular for more than 20 years, and what used to be distributed on audio cassette is now done via audio CD.

Podcasts also fall under this category. These are audio programs that are produced on a regular basis (think of it as an audio-newsletter). Typically 15 to 60 minutes in length, they are distributed online via many channels, primarily iTunes (they began as programs that would be downloaded to one's iPod for later listening).

Broadcast interviews (radio/TV) will be a tremendous area of opportunity, especially if you write a book, or have an otherwise compelling message to share with the world. Is your story newsworthy? Becoming a known expert for broadcast interviews is a powerful means of generating media attention.

SlideShare/Powerpoint presentations may not be the first on people's minds when it comes to Audio-Video tools, but they may indeed be the most economical to produce. Presentations have been around for years, originating with traditional slide shows and "transparency" presentations—now evolving into more dynamic computer-driven presentations, which often feature animations, text and video content. SlideShare is the online source of choice for hosting this content.

Video news releases have also long been a common tool for publicity. Many of the news stories you see on TV are either completely or partially edited by public relations people, advancing a newsworthy message that is tied to a product or market offering of the organization cited in the story as the primary news source.

Further Service Over the Internet

We all know that the internet media has revolutionized the way we do business in so many ways (that is, once the bubble burst and all the hot air settled). At the same time, if you consider how we now communicate with the internet, there are a great many possibilities:

- ☑ Spam email (not well accepted)

- ☑ Permission-based email (more acceptable)

- ☑ Pop-up web ads (not well accepted)

- ☑ Banner web ads (more acceptable though less popular)

- ☑ Web applications (i.e. Catalogs, Resources, Customer reference)

- ☑ Web-based newsletters & magazines

- ☑ On-line "pull" distribution of all content produced for both print and audio-video via Really Simple Syndication (RSS) protocol (podcasting).

The expression *multimedia* is fitting in how the web has allowed us to bring the fundamentals of virtually all other forms of media together. For example:

- ↪ Any brochure, book, or other print item that we would have mass produced by the thousand for wide physical distribution, we can now make available as a downloadable Portable Document Format (PDF) file from a website—instantaneously accessible to anyone in the world who has a computer, internet connection and appropriate "reader" software (which is freely distributed). This PDF format—pioneered by Adobe Systems—allows us to maintain the integrity of both the content and the design. Prospects and customers can now open and review our materials on-line, or print them out to go for review at their convenience.

⊃ As the bandwidth has increased for both residential and office connections (the vast majority of workplaces have broadband internet connections of some form, and homes have quickly followed suit), so does the speed at which data can be sent from computer to computer. This means that audio and video content that would have been cumbersome to access via a 56k phone connection can now be tapped into almost instantaneously through cable, DSL, and T1 connections.

⊃ The paradigm of a website—typically defined as a set of static HTML web pages of "brochure-ware"—has shifted to that of the web application—with a more dynamic and interactive structure, and thus more capable of enabling companies of all sizes to deliver value to their prospects over the internet.

The internet has brought the dynamic of immediate gratification to a whole new level.

What does all this mean? It means that in virtually every example I described in the previous sections of print and audio-video communication, the same content can be delivered instantaneously to your prospects. The internet has brought the dynamic of immediate gratification to a whole new level.

Examples of Web Applications

Web applications have been used by companies to serve their prospects for years. Take Progressive Insurance, for example. They want you to come to their website not just to get their rate quote, but quotes from their competitors. Will Progressive's price always be the lowest? Not always, and they are up front with that. They know that they can serve everyone's interests, including their own, by finding the right prospects that fit their market, by allowing those prospects who wouldn't fit their company to screen themselves out. Ingenious!

Major movie theater chains also use the web to serve their prospects and customers. I remember when we had to listen to a phone recording or squint at tiny newspaper print to get show times, only to then wait in line to catch a movie. Today, you go on-line, check the times, view a trailer and read some reviews, and make your choice. From there, you can even buy the tickets

Bonus Section I

in advance on-line—something that might cost a little extra but in cases of long lines or sellout engagements, is worth the extra price.

The Internet and the "People" Equation

All this fuss about e-commerce and buying things on-line begs the question: does it reduce the value and importance of customer service and interpersonal communication?

There is no question that for many, if not most of us, if we can buy our movie tickets faster on-line or at a kiosk, or pump our gas and pay with a credit card with out ever having to leave our vehicle, it's the better way to go. It's fast. It's more efficient and often times more effective to helping us get what we want.

At the same time, let's turn it around. How many of us, when we call our bank, insurance company or any other organization (especially when we have an important concern), find ourselves cursing under our breath in our endless quest to just get to a human being? And when we finally do reach a person, we want that individual to be totally interested and committed to helping us get what we want.

In fact, how many of us have dealt with a "customer service" person over the phone or even face-to-face, and we knew that they really didn't care about our needs or concerns?

Further, even in situations where your people may have less personal contact with your customers, in most cases, your people are the ones who are still serving the customers. One could also argue that because interpersonal contact has in many cases been reduced, it is even more important than it has ever been. We'll get into this topic in much greater detail in Bonus Section III.

> One could also argue that because interpersonal contact has in many cases been reduced, it is even more important than it has ever been.

The Bottom Line

As you can see, when organizing any effort of customer communication, the use of some forms of communication media will come into play. Whatever strategy is chosen will still result in a substantial investment, even with the advances of media technology. However, what can sometimes do more harm than good is when an organization, in an effort to "cut corners" on its investment, chooses a course that produces results that fall below acceptable standards.

The question is, who determines these standards? The truth is that we all do. We just don't know it. During your normal routine, how often do you read a magazine, newsletter, or browse the web? How often do you review a brochure or advertisement for a product or service that interests you? How often do you watch television or listen to the radio?

Because of your constant exposure to communication media, you already have an unconscious standard of quality. Anytime you turn on the TV or open a brochure, you unknowingly compare what you are seeing to that to which you are already accustomed. If it meets this comparison, your attention is immediately directed to the content... the message of the communication.

But what if the quality of your brochure or video falls below standards to which your audience is accustomed? Low quality refers to awkward writing, unprofessional design, or sloppy printing. For video, it can pertain to disjointed writing and organization, or shooting and editing standards that are below those to which people are accustomed.

If your audience encounters poor quality in your communication, your message will go unnoticed. Your audience will not get their attention past your message's flawed delivery. Your effort to effectively communicate will fail.

The Best Quality Goes Unnoticed

In communication media, the best quality is that which goes unnoticed by its audience. In other words, if audiences view a quality video presentation, they will not notice how well the video is done. Instead, their minds and hearts will focus on your message.

If your audience misses your message because it is distracted by poor quality in media, they will not only think less of your method of communication, but they will think less of your organization (thus hindering opportunity for prosperous relationships). This is why we adamantly state that if you choose to invest in communication media, invest wisely and in quality, or don't invest at all.

Bonus Section II:

To Get Your Foot in the Door, Use a Wedge™.

> We all will face situations when we would like to get into the doors of an organization, and yet, we just don't have that connection.

When it comes to business-to-business (B2B) prospecting, we all know that ideally, the best way to connect with new, qualified people with whom we can discuss our business is through a common relationship—a personal introduction.

Yet we all will face situations when we would like "knock on the door" of an organization, and yet, we just don't have that connection. At times like these, how do you reach the decision maker in an organization when you CANNOT contact them on a favorable basis? (**Note:** "favorable basis" is most often defined as a common or preexisting relationship of some kind.)

That is the dilemma we are here to address. And the answer is: **Use a wedge™.**

One of the fundamental tenets of successful prospecting is that meeting new prospects (outside of cold-calling) requires the involvement of a common connection. However, when no connection exists, there is another strategy that can be far more effective. We call it "the Wedge"...and you can use it to open new doors.

The Wedge is a step-by-step approach that is best applied toward a limited number of targeted, business prospects at a time. It is *not* a mass marketing strategy. Rather, it is a highly effective method of securing appointments with key decision-makers—and can be used to penetrate companies of all sizes.

The Typical Obstacles

What keeps us from getting our foot in the door of a company where we have no prior connection? There are plenty of obstacles.

> A "wedge" it is a metaphor for creating influence through value.

Obstacle #1: No Connection or Previous Relationship.

As we already indicated, a common connection is what most people seek when attempting to penetrate an organization. Isn't it so much easier when you know someone whose name you can use when making that first contact, or even have a source of an introduction? Most of the time it is...but sometimes it isn't. I will explain why shortly. Quite often, a wedge is better than a connection.

Obstacle #2: Not Knowing Who to Contact.

If you have no prior connection or "inside information," you most often can identify decision makers by position or title. But the real power of decision often depends upon the given size and political situation in any organization. In many companies, "silent vetoes" abound. Further, what do you do when your "presumed" contact just doesn't want to be bothered?

Obstacle #3: The Actual Prospect.

The actual prospect (the key decision maker, whether you know her identity or not) is often the obstacle herself. Consider how many people are calling on her throughout the day. Voice messages pile up during meetings and during other phone conversations. Send a pre-approach letter? She may get it; she may not. It's just one of perhaps dozens of pieces that arrives on her desk each day.

Obstacle #4: Administrative Staff.

Not only does the loyal administrative assistant and gatekeeper open mail (and occasionally tosses stuff he deems unimportant), he will intercept your call. It is his job to insulate your prospect from outside intruders or distractions (That's you!). So if you are unknown to the prospect or the gatekeeper, then you are in for an uphill battle of getting the audience you seek and deserve.

Obstacle #5: The Current Economic Climate.

The media is always full of bad news, isn't it? Well, there is no doubt that our economy is going through a major adjustment. So many companies, individuals, and families have felt it—myself included. But it has also put too many of us at a heightened level of defensiveness and fear. Layoffs and budget cuts create thoughts of survival and scarcity—not growth and affluence. The objection we hear: "We are on a hiring freeze," or "Our budgets are frozen."

Using the Wedge: An Eight-Step Strategy

A "wedge" is a metaphor for creating influence through value. The steps to follow will be fairly consistent regardless of what your profession or industry may be; however the nuances and human dynamics in your industry and your prospect's organization will also play a role. In other words, deploy these steps using your own judgment and street smarts. For example, a marketing executive may employ this strategy one way when approaching an engineering firm, and another way when getting his foot into the door of a manufacturer.

> You don't determine your value. Your clients do.

This process is fairly simple—but not always easy. If you encounter difficulty, it will likely either be on the first step or the last. You will understand why soon enough. So let's jump in.

Step 1: Identify Your Value Proposition

We have referred to the value proposition in other parts of this book. Nevertheless, when using the Wedge to get your foot in the door, the first question you must ask yourself is: "Why should someone else *want* to have a 20-minute conversation with me?"

Take this first step seriously, otherwise all the steps to follow will be a waste of time.

So let's revisit what the value proposition is all about. Remember, it is not a reason for someone to buy...rather it is simply a reason for someone to take an interest. To this end, you will need to explain how your product or service will do one or more of the following:

- Reduce expenses thus save money.
- Increase efficiency/effectiveness thus reducing waste and saving time and money.
- Increase sales and/or revenues.
- Grow profits.
- Grow stakeholder value.

In the context above, "stakeholders" are all those individuals who have a vested interest in the success of the organization. These include employees, the owners, and yes, even their clients.

If you and/or your product/service can demonstrate at least one of these points in measurable terms, that is the basis of your value proposition in the B-to-B setting. Mind you that there are plenty of ways to reach these conclusions...and it is amazing to me how many businesses have not boiled their product or service down to these terms.

Step 2: Build Your List.

In other words, research the companies that are in your market. Let's say you want to reach out to wholesale distributors of durable goods with twenty to 250 employees, headquartered in your county and three counties adjacent. How would you find them? Perhaps your company subscribes to one of the many list research services out there, such as InfoGroup or Hoovers.

There are plenty of other research tools available on the internet, but I strongly recommend that the first place you check out is your metropolitan library. One of the best library resources is *ReferenceUSA* (the library division of InfoGroup). This is a database on millions of businesses and households which includes information on census, lifestyle, home values, industry codes and even D&B credit scores. It is access to the same data available commercially through what you may know as Sales Genie, minus the monthly subscription fee. Find out if your library offers it, and if not, find one that does.

> Your value proposition is your prospect's REASON to WANT to have a conversation with you.

To Get Your Foot in the Door, Use a Wedge.

Further, you will often be able to access this and other resources online from work or home with your library card. You may not need to make a trip to the library.

Back to our example, the *ReferenceUSA* database can produce a list of wholesale distributors of durable goods with twenty to 250 employees, headquartered in your county and three counties adjacent. You can narrow your search even further by any number of parameters (each record has data in up to 221 fields—we are talking detailed!). It all depends on what you are seeking.

Find out if your library offers ReferenceUSA. If not, find one that does.

This first step is unlocking a gold mine...and I am constantly surprised at how many sales professionals and business people I encounter in my own community who are completely unaware of this resource.

Let's suppose your research yields 28 companies. From there you prioritize.

Which ones will you contact first? Will you start with the companies with the most employees, or the fewest? Will you further qualify by reported gross revenues or credit rating? Perhaps you want to start in your own county first, and expand outward.

The reason for prioritization will become clear shortly. Remember, this isn't mass marketing. This is a highly targeted, value-based outreach.

Starting with your top five to ten priority companies, begin researching the key decision makers. Depending on the size of the company, the data in *ReferenceUSA* will give you either just the owner or the entire executive staff and even the board of directors (It even identifies gender—quite helpful when targeting people with gender-neutral names!).

Whatever you find, it is just a start. Their data is well researched and updated, but it is NEVER one-hundred percent accurate. To further identify who's calling the shots, you can check out additional data sources (Hoovers for one). The company's website may give you all that information up front, and may even include biographical information on each person.

ReferenceUSA will even highlight stories in some media sources related to each company record, and even identify competitors. For further research, check out *BizJournals* online—the media company that publishes business weeklies in the nation's top metropolitan areas and business markets. In your research, you are seeking any information that may prove relevant to your approach.

Step 3: Identify the Influence Circle.

This process is very important. For each company, you will identify at least three to five individuals who may want to speak with you. This group of people is called the "influence circle."* You will identify the positions of these prospects, and you will next confirm the names and exact titles of those positions by phone. For example, let's say that I'm in the IT industry, and I last worked with a company called Rainmaker Technologies, which offered comprehensive expertise in helping businesses leverage their information technology to better serve their customers and make money.

> Bear in mind that the titles used on ReferenceUSA are typically generic.

Plus, I have also had particular success in helping business clients increase their sales revenues. I accomplished this not just by deploying IT/commerce solutions; through proactive support and hands-on guidance, I actually get the outside sales people to *use it*—and do so successfully! This is an important, distinguishing claim which many of my competitors can not—or do not—make. I also have the client testimonials to back up my claim.

In my research, I uncover Unicorn Distribution, Inc., a wholesaler of building materials and HVAC equipment. They have 670 employees and warehouses in seven states.

My initial *ReferenceUSA* research uncovers the following names and titles:

Position	Name	Gender
President	Ron Callebro	Male
Chief Financial Officer	Lisa Hershey	Female
Sales Executive	Bruce Johnson	Male
IT Executive	Terry Jones	Female
Human Resources Exec	Lynn Harris	Female
Vice President	Jim Berry	Male
Vice President	Gloria Smith	Female
Vice President	Lisa Hershey	Female

To Get Your Foot in the Door, Use a Wedge.

Obviously, I want to contact Terry Jones, the person involved in IT—because even though she may have expertise (and even a staff), there may be a need. Perhaps she isn't that much of an expert, and was promoted from within because she knew more than everyone else. I just don't know.

However, in addition to Ms. Jones, I will want to consider reaching out to the CFO and the president, and perhaps Bruce Johnson (labeled "Sales Executive"). Chances are they have a team of outside sales people who rely on a fleet of laptops to communicate and submit orders. And that happens to be relevant to what I offer.

Bear in mind that the titles used on *ReferenceUSA* are typically generic, and you will need to confirm exact titles when you call the company receptionist to confirm the people occupying these positions.

Which takes us to the next step...

Step 4: Verify!

Verification is most crucial, and this MUST be done with the phone. You can also achieve this by checking the company website, but many do not list all that you need to know. Plus, some company websites are not updated as quickly as they should be when personnel changes occur.

When engaging company receptionists, you will have different experiences and levels of guardedness. Much of it depends upon how you handle yourself over the phone—be polite and show respect and appreciation. Here is how such a conversation should go:

You dial the phone. If an automated attendant answers, press "0" for the operator. Nine out of ten times that will get you to a human being without navigating phone options for 45 minutes. If zero does not get you to a human being, you are dealing with a company that truly does not want to talk to people.

> Receptionist: *Thank you for calling Unicorn Distribution, this is Loretta. How may I help you?**
>
> Sales Professional: *Good morning, Loretta, my name is Keith Luscher. I'm updating some records and calling simply to confirm the names of some of your executives. Do you have a moment to help me, or perhaps connect me with someone who can?*

If zero does not get you to a human being, you are dealing with a company that truly does not want to talk to people.

Bonus Section II

Receptionist: *Sure, I can help you. Who do you need to confirm?*

Sales Professional: *Well, for starters I have Ron Callebro as President. Is that correct, and is that his complete title?*

Receptionist: *Yes, it is. Actually, he's the president and chief executive officer.*

Sales Professional: *Okay, great. His name is spelled c-a-l-l-e-b-r-o?*

Receptionist: *You got it!*

Sales Professional: *Alright. I also have a Ms. Terry Jones as your IT executive. Is that still correct? Am I right on gender, and what would her precise title be?*

Receptionist: *Well, actually, she is the IT Manager—she's not really an executive.*

Sales Professional: *Okay...so she reports directly to the President or...?*

Receptionist: *...Actually, she reports to Gloria Smith, our Vice President of Human Resources.*

Sales Professional: *That's very helpful. Thank you. Just two more if I may...*

Receptionist: *Go ahead, you're fine.*

Sales Professional: *I also have Lisa Hershey as your Chief Financial Officer and Bruce Johnson as a sales executive. Are those correct?*

Receptionist: *Lisa is correct, but Bruce is no longer with us. That position is now held by Sam Edwards, and his title is Vice President of Sales.*

Sales Professional: *Okay...great. Speaking of sales, I understand you are in several states. Do you have any idea about how many outside sales people you have?*

Receptionist: *Mmmm...I'm not sure exactly how many...I would say at least fifty.*

Sales Professional: *Alright. Loretta, I think I have everything I need. You have been extremely helpful. Thank you very much for your time and your assistance. I hope you have a great day!*

Receptionist: *My pleasure. I hope you have a great day also. Good bye.*

While not all calls will go this smoothly, the good news is that many—if not most—should.

To Get Your Foot in the Door, Use a Wedge.

You say your goodbyes and hang up. A few additional tips:

- ☑ The "script" you just read was that of a fairly *ideal* call. While they might not all go that smoothly, the good news is that many—if not most—should. Most people *want* to be helpful to others, especially if they feel appreciated and respected. The tone (which I hope you detected) and words from the sales representative are *genuine.* Why? What is the *value* of the service this receptionist is giving to him?

- ☑ When calling another person over the phone, ALWAYS make sure they have a minute to take your call. Note the language in the beginning of the conversation.

- ☑ Suppose during the conversation, while this person is being so graciously helpful to you and your business, you hear what may be another line ringing in the background. If so, offer to be placed on hold while he or she gets that, and can thus continue to help you in a minute or two without feeling rushed or distracted. What kind of respect does that show?

- ☑ Notice how the call was to *confirm* names and titles? Suppose you call asking for names and positions out of the blue. This makes you come off as lazy, unprofessional, and asking the receptionist to do *your* job! Once a rapport is established, it doesn't hurt to ask the person to help you fill in some blanks. You may even get a better insight on who answers to whom, as indicated in the example above. But it's important to present yourself as someone who is already "in the know" to a certain extent.

- ☑ Also note that Gloria Smith, one of the people you did not even highlight as one of your key contacts, turns out not just to be a vice president (generically labeled in the research), but a vice president of operations—and the direct report of Terry Jones, the IT manager. This is a key piece of intel that could have cost you a meeting had you proceeded under previous assumptions.

Let's say you make the calls and for our example, have some changes to make from your additional research. So now, for Unicorn Distribution, we have an influence circle:

1. Ron Callebro, President & CEO

2. Lisa Hershey, Chief Financial Officer

3. Gloria Smith, Vice President of Operations

When calling another person over the phone, ALWAYS make sure they have a minute to take your call.

Bonus Section II

4. Terry Jones, IT Manager

5. Sam Edwards, Vice President of Sales

Great job. Now, with your value proposition already determined, it's time to do some writing. Which leads us to our next step:

Step 5: Craft Your Letter.

At this point you are going to craft a single letter that will go out to each of your prospects at the company. This is where keen writing skills are essential. Yes, it's a basic pre-approach letter—a letter your prospect will receive to warm them up for your call.

The heart of your letter will be the value proposition—the reason your prospect should want to sit down and have a conversation with you. In this case, you have a proven track record of helping previous employers leverage their field-based technology to increase revenues—and the individual production numbers of their sales people. What makes you different: you not only have the expertise, but a successful track record in getting those in the field *to actually use the tools they're given at a great investment of their employer* (which is not an uncommon problem, even today)!

> Mr. Ron Callebro
> President
> Unicorn Distribution, Inc.
> 189 Main St.
> Columbus, OH 43215
>
> Dear Mr. Callebro,
>
> I am writing to you, Lisa Hershey, Gloria Smith, Terry Jones and Sam Edwards. My purpose is to identify the right person with whom I should discuss Unicorn Distribution's opportunity to help its outside sales force increase their production numbers by as much as 75 percent.
>
> Even today, so many companies struggle with their outside sales people in getting them to fully utilize the high-tech tools given to them. As a result, those companies fail to yield the maximum return on their technological investment.
>
> For the past 15 years, that has been my specialty: helping business and outside sales people gain the most from their technological investments. My work and interventions have resulted in higher profits and record-breaking commissions.

To Get Your Foot in the Door, Use a Wedge.

[A bold statement, yes, but in this example, it would ideally be backed up with the testimonials to prove it. Don't have compelling client testimonials? Get them! If you can't do it, hire someone objective and outside who can.]

I would welcome 20 minutes of your time to sit down and have a conversation, so I may learn a little bit more about the challenges your organization faces, so we may both learn about if and how I may be able to help you resolve them. <u>I will be calling you next Thursday, July 18, at 9:37 a.m., to schedule a visit.</u>

Sincerely Yours,

Keith F. Luscher

Note: stories and anecdotes are powerful tools in further developing your value proposition (Reminder: this is the reason your prospect will want to have a 20 minute conversation with you.)

Your letter will define this problem; even cite testimonials, if possible. But such testimonials must be attributable to be credible.

Don't go on much further than this, however. State your value proposition, and your purpose for writing. Remember, you are not trying to sell. *You only want to secure a meeting.* That is all. One simple task. State your peace.

> The heart of your letter will be the value proposition—the reason your prospect should want to sit down and have a conversation with you.

Very important: Don't just tell them you will be calling—state specifically when ("I will be calling you next Thursday morning at 9:37, to schedule a visit.") Then close out, keeping it to one page.

Step 6: Create Your Value Package

If creating your value proposition was tough (and maybe it wasn't...if so good for you!) then this might be an even greater challenge. It's up to you. It may require some bold use of the imagination. At the same time, I also want to strongly warn you against resorting to gimmicks.

A compelling, value-added package does not mean just something to get their attention. For example, I used this strategy in approaching sales managers and often my letter was enclosed in a thin, black, stationery-sized box (3/4 inch deep) wrapped with gold twine or ribbon. On first glance, one might think it was a box of chocolates.

But I guarantee you, had it been a box of chocolates and not a copy of *Prospect & Flourish,* it would have not been nearly as effective in opening doors. They may have enjoyed the candy, but would have not appreciated the attempt to be played. "Thanks for the chocolates," they would respond, "No thanks for a meeting."

One colleague who was in the process of utilizing this strategy is a marketing director for a resort that is attempting to grow their penetration in the business meeting and travel market.

"We have a great facility with tremendous amenities," she shared with me. This included a top restaurant and bakery, which is known for its variety of breads. "Might I put my letter into a gift basket with some of this bread?" she asked.

My gut response was probably not. "It may not get the reaction you want," I told her. "When opening the package of goodies, their initial reaction may be that you are hoping for them to place basket orders for Christmas." The fact was, while compelling, such a bread basket did not accurately represent the value she was attempting to communicate.

Now if that special bread could be delivered in such a way that it becomes a metaphor for higher profits, then we might be on to something! It is not a gimmick to communicate a substantial, sincere message with creativity.

Another option she may consider would be to turn the letter into a personal invitation to stay at the resort for one or two nights and experience it first hand...but it would all be in the presentation.

> A compelling, value-added package does not mean just something to get their attention.

For your situation and approaching an organization, what kind of value-added package or presentation might be assembled? It can be something as simple as a printed, fact-based report on results you created in previous engagements. (Yet, it must also communicate the relevance to your prospect.)

Back in 1994, I wrote and self-published a 50-page booklet called *Promotional Publishing: Turn Wary Prospects into Trusting Clients by Packaging Your Knowledge, Experience, and Expertise*. While it is no longer in print, the premise of the publication was fairly straight forward, as the title indicated: if you want to convert prospects into clients, you need to serve them.

From a marketing communications standpoint, this is not achieved through traditional sales materials, but by leveraging *beneficial* information and packaging it in the form of books, audio-video products and other tangible items, including newsletters. In essence, it was (then) an introduction to what is most commonly referred to today as **content marketing.**

We have already discussed content marketing at length in this book. By delivering high-quality, relevant and valuable information to prospects, you forge relationships that fuel profitable consumer action. *You engage your prospects by delivering value.*

In other words, you serve your prospects.

An effective content marketing strategy (in addition to the *Wedge* strategy) enables you to cultivate relationships with prospective customers on their time table, so that when they are ready to pull the trigger, you are typically the first on the list to be called.

> You engage your prospects by delivering value.

There is nothing new about this principle, and certainly what has changed the most about content marketing in the years since I first wrote about it lie in the forms of delivery. You may note that I originally described *packaging* your expertise in forms that were tangible: you had to create information products that you could feel and touch. Today, online delivery has trumped this rule, which has led to what many experts call a fundamental change in the marketing landscape. After content creation (conceptualization, writing, design and final production), the cost for digital distribution is often next to nothing (which makes the "creation" investment even more valuable). Indeed, the format in which you are reading these words is just another example of cost-effective content delivery.

Content marketing is what building relationships through value is all about. Do you have information that can be re-packaged into a small book, report, white paper or audio-visual presentation? Can you take stories of previous clients who faced problems similar to those of your prospect's and retell those stories so there is a lesson learned? Anything can go here—as long as it's sincere, serves and/or communicates.

Anyone can hand out a business card or a brochure. But if you really want to introduce yourself with a strong impression, forget about making an impression at all. Rather, *aim higher* to positively *engage* and *influence* your prospect. Share insight and knowledge that will serve your prospect by helping them make more informed decisions that will bring them closer to their goals. Hence, content marketing strategies are key to creating powerful networking and prospecting tools. Let your book (or whatever it is you create) become your calling card.

Step 7: Hand-deliver.

No need to go into too much detail here, let's address a few additional points that relate to delivering your package.

- First, even if it is all printed materials, do NOT fold it all into a number ten envelope! Your letter and anything else that goes with it should be, at least, sealed into a flat envelope, and you may combine the elements into a pocket folder as well. Use your imagination, and give your communication the respect that it is due. If using flat envelopes, I would even suggest avoiding plain white or dingy brownish-yellow and invest in a supply of bright, primary colored ones that are visually consistent with your brand and identity. Check out http://www.Envelopes.com for a great selection at affordable prices.

- If you can, have all packages hand-delivered. This may even prove more cost effective, since several identical packages are going to each location. Just have them delivered to the receptionist, and ask that they be sent directly to each recipient.

- Handwrite the addressee on each package, and mark HAND DELIVERED. Do something to communicate that this package was assembled and delivered with plenty of TLC.

Step 8: Follow Up.

Who should you call first? The answer is simple: Start at the top. If the president/CEO is on your hit list, then call him or her first. It will not be uncommon for them to have an interest in your value proposition, but perhaps not just ready to meet you personally (often a good sign that they are not a micro-manager). They will defer you to the operations VP...in which case, you're in!

Don't be surprised if you leave a voice message for the CEO, only to have that person forward your message to a key exec who then gives you a call! Again, you're in!

Step 8A: Follow up until...

Here's the thing: when you call and leave a message for each person (often getting some people on the phone is a real trick), chances are people will NOT call you back. They seldom do.

They have just too much on their plate. But eighty percent of the time sales professionals—even those with a strong value proposition—don't get the appointment because they give up too quickly.

In other words, follow up using what I call "gentle persistence." Don't call every day, but once or twice per week. Doing so tactfully will show you are serious about your conviction in the value you offer. You are doing your job, and gentle persistence shows that you are doing it well. That leaves an impression.

A hint about impressions: the stronger your value package (i.e. more tangible, valuable and thus more shelf life) the longer your package will likely stay on the desk and not get buried.

Upon sharing the first draft of this report with a colleague, she asked me, "So how long is 'until?'"

Good question. I say, until you get an answer from a real decision maker. You seek CLOSURE.

Why the Wedge Does and WILL Work...

So, what is the point of all this work? Why not just send a letter to one person and keep calling until you get an appointment? Here are just a few reasons why this carefully planned and executed, value-based approach is so effective.

It is a better return and exposure for your time and effort. Think about it: you go to all the trouble to research your company, craft your letter, assemble a package, and deliver it. Doesn't it make sense to multiply your odds by the number of people there who might have an interest in having a conversation with you? And without going into specific numbers, these factors can often be exponential.

The process forces you to ask yourself: Why should my prospect want to give up twenty minutes of their time to meet with me? As I indicated before, this can present a challenge for many of us. Often, it reaches to the core of what we do, and how well we do it. The process also encourages us to listen more closely to our existing clients, which itself can open up many more opportunities for service, and referrals.

It gets your prospects talking amongst each other. If your package and message was compelling enough and offers real value, it WILL get them talking among each other. Perhaps it will be in the form of a two-way discussion at a weekly meeting; it can also be as simple as the president sending a VP an email to give you a call and set something up. Either way, you're in!

You are far less likely to be ignored. Suppose you just sent a letter and value package to one person, and that person just happens to be the type that doesn't want to be bothered. Or perhaps you are just getting them on a bad day. How does that affect your odds of getting in? They can ignore your calls, toss your stuff, and tell you to buzz off if you finally get them on the phone. Now consider this: how simply can that be done, if this person knows you are also contacting his or her colleagues? You know the answer...

Where Do You Go from Here?

Quite simply, "wedging" your foot in the door is a strategy that challenges you to put your best suit on, and to question your own quality of service with a spirit that reaches for improvement and greater customer value. But more than that, it is a value-based approach strategy that leverages internal politics in your favor. How many business-to-business sales professionals have lost work, deals or contracts due to internal politics out of their control? This turns the tables around, for the benefit of everyone.

This strategy, when executed with prudence and care, WILL multiply your success rate of getting into the doors of prospective clients many times over. I not only say this with confidence; I guarantee it.

But don't take my word for it. Review this strategy. Study it. Internalize it. Ask yourself: Does this strategy make sense to *you*?

You must first see for yourself that it makes perfect sense, both in logic and simplicity.

> Don't be surprised if you leave a voice message for the CEO, only to have that person forward your message to a key exec who then gives you call!

To Get Your Foot in the Door, Use a Wedge.

Some Questions...

To determine your next steps, first consider some key questions:

- Are you getting your foot into the doors of new prospective clients at the rate you would like to be?

- Are you truly clear on your value proposition? If so, how well is it articulated? Is it pithy? Is it crafted in such a way that it gives a prospect a reason to *want* to have a 20 minute conversation with you?

- Do you have compelling client testimonials?

- Do you have a content marketing strategy in place, not just to fuel your Wedge outreach efforts, but for your ongoing "drip" marketing efforts as well?

If your answers to the questions above are "Yes!" then you should be about ready to go.

If your package and message was compelling enough and offers real value, it WILL get them talking among each other.

Bonus Section III:

From Screen-2-Screen to Face-2-Face:

Leveraging Social Media to Identify, Qualify and (Yes!) MEET New People

> Prospecting is the continuous activity of exploring for, identifying and qualifying new people to meet and talk with concerning your business.

Oh, the buzz about social media. As a teacher and author on prospecting and networking, one of the most common questions I hear these days is on how to best use social media and networking sites. Sometimes people will ask about which site is best.

Indeed, I believe the questions beg back to the definition of prospecting:

Prospecting is the continuous activity of exploring for, identifying and qualifying new people to meet and talk with concerning your business.

Consider for yourself: who you are, what you do and the kind of people you seek—and how this definition applies to you in your situation. Remember: *everybody prospects.*

In reality, I observe that many people who look to the internet first in their attempt to prospect are doing so in hopes to avoid the phone (and I'm included in that group). The good news is that in many circumstances, it helps. Yet no one can deny that the emergence of social media has created powerful channels through which people meet, become friends, and stay connected. Indeed, it is as much as much a marketing media as is broadcast and print.

Bonus Section III

It goes much further than that, however. Social media channels are a means of two-way communication. Not only can you talk, but you can also listen, and engage in dialog. It really has permanently altered the marketing landscape, while fueling the growth of content marketing.

I also believe that the exponential growth in the popularity of social media in business have also been fueled by the turbulent times in which we live. For example, in the old days the first piece of advice you would hear upon losing your job was, "Better update your resume."

> Many who look to the internet first in their attempt to prospect are doing so in hopes to avoid the phone.

Now, you will hear, "Get on LinkedIn!"

As I indicated earlier in this book, the economic recession is also what has led to the explosion of networking groups and activities everywhere, which I also believe has created many positive results. As business professionals are forced to reach out and prospect for new accounts and displaced professionals are forced to prospect for new jobs, this cloud has a silver lining.

At the risk of sounding corny, we are all literally "joining hands" to carry each other through economic difficulty...and the tools of online social media are helping to make this happen. In this case, technology is not isolating us; *it is bringing us closer.*

I believe this dynamic is genuine—not superficial as some people might observe. Indeed, social media are just another form of communication. They allow us to stay in touch with each other as actively or as passively as we wish...*but we still stay in touch!*

This leads to the "trickle" fueling of personal relationships—which has always fueled business. In my opinion, this explosion of social media is also transcending business to a higher level... business is becoming more human.

"How?" you may ask. Simple. To succeed, one must not only talk and be heard. Rather, one must talk, be heard and understood, and in turn, listen. Remember the definition of prospecting? You are "talking with" your prospects. Indeed, you are *engaging* them in a conversation.

For many of us, the explosion of social media can be overwhelming. We see people on their laptops in coffee shops; we see others fiddling with their smart phones. In the early days of Facebook, we heard expressions such as "poking" and wonder what the heck "LMAO" means. In print, on television and on the radio, we are exposed to new, yet well-established brands such as LinkedIn,

Facebook and Twitter almost everywhere we go.

So, this begs the question...

How Can Social Media Help Us Prospect?

If we are a business professional or a new job seeker, we wonder what role this media can play in helping us be more effective in what we do. Here are a few suggestions.

Social media helps us increase our social mobility. This begs back to one of the most traditional forms of prospecting. Where else do you go to meet new people by getting out and becoming visible? This media creates virtual communities, which bring together real people who relate to one another by a common interest, that allow you to make new contacts that you may otherwise not have the opportunity meet.

Social media are great for shy people. How many of us, when entering a big room full of a lot of strangers, suddenly want to withdraw and become wall flowers? It happens to me all the time! Social networks allow us to overcome our sense of shyness by, in a sense, getting in at the shallow end of the pool. It facilitates and warms the connection for one person to call the other for a meeting. We can choose how much of ourselves we want to reveal; we can decide how vulnerable we want to become.

Social media helps us make new connections. There is no such thing as cold calling, if you are making calls to people with whom you are connected in some capacity with others online. For example, the spirit of LinkedIn is very much to enable human connections--and most people fundamentally see it that way. Yet, I have many LinkedIn connections whom I have not met...not yet anyways.

The Number One Rule...and the Biggest Mistake to Avoid

In business, you will still see that many people are out there to close a deal or make a sale. They want to rush the relationship process-whether they are building a business or seeking a new job. This is what leads many people to the single biggest and most common mistake in leveraging social media: attempting to sell without forging a relationship.

*Be a giver.
Serve your prospect.*

The most important rule to follow in building relationships online is the same as building relationships face-to-face: I have preached it throughout this book: You build relationships by adding value. Be a giver. Serve your prospect.

We all have to prospect, whether we are seeking our next client or our next job. That's a given. And there are many things that job seekers and sales professionals may learn from each other. When I am out talking about prospecting or other topics to members of various groups, I encounter people in both situations.

Yet, the challenges remain very similar. Just one example lies in a very important lesson that job seekers are most keenly aware, yet sales professional can sometimes forget. It's a point that author Harry Beckwith states so succinctly in his recent book *You, Inc.*: "The first thing you sell is yourself."

This was a lesson I learned from my own manager when I was with Principal Financial Group. Principal is a household name brand; a FORTUNE 500 company that was founded in 1879; is a 401(k) leader, and remains financially strong even in these turbulent times.

"Those points are all good and important," I recall him saying to me, "but it won't matter unless the prospect knows and likes you first." Indeed, business is about relationships, and if you cannot get another person to like you, they certainly won't hire you—or buy from you. Ultimately, the decision to buy (or hire) is typically driven by feelings. Without feelings, the world would be an empty place.

So people must feel good *about* you, and they must feel good *around* you. Effective job seekers and sales professionals know this. They are all about selling themselves and building relationships—and they do this through value. They give of themselves—both their time and their expertise. *Most importantly, they do it from the heart.*

> "The first thing you sell is yourself."
> —Harry Beckwith

Quite simply: to sell yourself, you must give of yourself. I am not saying you must give away the store; nor am I saying that you give so much that it diminish the perception of your value. You give of yourself when:

- You are socially mobile, volunteering and contributing to your community

- You seek opportunities to help others, such as facilitating introductions between colleagues and friends (online or in person)

- You exercise empathic listening, with genuine interest in the needs of others.

- You play a key role in helping another person create a positive outcome in their life, while expecting nothing in return.

Expecting nothing in return? A tall order for those of us with bills to pay. Perhaps we might call it a leap of faith. In the mid-1990s, while writing my book *Don't Wait Until You Graduate*, I interviewed a Rice University medical student who was a student leader on campus. "Gandhi used an expression, *Sarvodaya*," I recall him telling me. "This term expresses how we serve others throughout our lives. We start by serving ourselves, by providing basic needs. Then we serve our family and friends. Beyond that, there is an element of risk, when we serve 'strangers.' Taking that step is one way communities are formed."

> "...there is an element of risk, when we serve 'strangers.' Taking that step is one way communities are formed."

And it is also how new relationships are built. On that note, let's get into the three top social media platforms used in business today.

Linking Up with LinkedIn

LinkedIn is a strictly business social network. It has become the industry standard for professional recruiters (whom I believe as a group really fueled its growth). Indeed, it was a professional recruiter who told me about LinkedIn in 2007 when I was scratching my head and figuring out what to do with my life and my career (I was rebuilding after a severe heart attack just before my 39th birthday, and all the repercussions in that followed).

I was introduced to LinkedIn by an executive recruiter as a resource for finding a job. However it has grown beyond that as a place where anyone in business can have a personal, professional web presence that creates a common standard for displaying service history and accomplishments. In fact, some believe it is replacing the traditional paper résumé. You will already see job postings where employers will only review applicants who have a minimum number of LinkedIn recommendations.

Recently, I was having coffee with a colleague, who asked my opinion of LinkedIn, and its role in prospecting. Indeed, the vast growth of LinkedIn and other business-networking web apps points to this: *It's all about prospecting.* If people didn't need to prospect, business networking web applications such as LinkedIn wouldn't be as popular and useful as they have become.

So, if business networking sites are all about prospecting, it begs the question: how does one best use them for this purpose? There are lots of ways to use—and abuse—them.

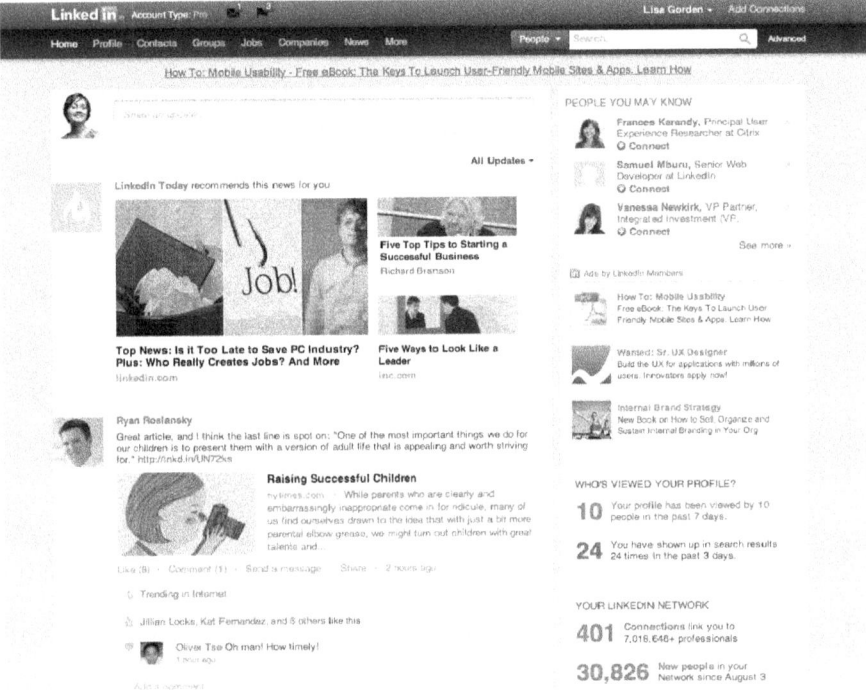

The LinkedIn home page.

LinkedIn is particularly powerful and designed specifically to help people maximize their business relationships—for everyone. In other words, it is as much about being a helper as it is about being helped. But what really strikes me about it is that it creates a platform where many of us who consider ourselves shy in a crowded room can really shine—if we put forth just a little effort.

> Some employers will only review applicants who have a minimum number of LinkedIn recommendations

Secondly, and this is perhaps the biggest bragging point of social media, is how *it shows us how many people we really do know.* How many of us have met with a friend and/or colleague seeking some referrals, and have asked the often ill-fated, open-ended question: "Who do you know...?"

Now, with LinkedIn, when conversing or seeking introductions from people with whom we have a positive relationship, we have a list from which to work—a list of our friend's network.

Now, before I go further, I want to emphasize one very important point: networks of people are sacred. Business connections are not commodities. Indeed they are assets. They are people with wants, needs, and feelings no different than your own and deserve to be treated that way. LinkedIn recognizes this very point when they stress that you should only be "linked" to people whom you know and trust. While this rule can be loosely interpreted, it overall has helped maintain integrity in the system.

Because of this integrity, when meeting with a person in your network with the hopes of seeking referrals, it gives both of you an advantage that makes the process much easier. Before going to a meeting, print out your friend's contact list (if it's brief enough) or look through it and jot down names of people to whom you would like to be introduced.

And while you are doing so, be prepared to reciprocate. Engage your colleague and learn more about who else he or she should be talking with concerning *their* business.

Yes, LinkedIn does allow for introductions to take place via email. And I have used that feature as well. However, if you are really interested in reaching out to another person, I have never been a fan of using regular email as a means of first contact—although I have made exceptions. Leverage the new technology with traditions of old. Touch your contacts on a regular basis, in person, or over the phone, or online.

Here are the basic components of LinkedIn, and how you can use them more effectively:

The Profile Page. Obviously, this is where most people start. It's where you start to begin building your online profile as well as where most people will browse to when they want to consider whether or not to connect with you. However, don't be fooled by its presence. It is not a static "resume" page as some people regard it to be. There are plenty of additional modules—some from LinkedIn and others from third parties—that you can incorporate into your online profile. These include the use of video, Powerpoint presentations and live links to your website and blogs (if you write one). There is even a feature that allows you to highlight books you have read, are reading and would recommend to others.

I think that one of the biggest mistakes people make in not leveraging this resource to its full potential is leaving out their photograph. Pictures can be stickier than names, and to not have

---

Networks of people are sacred.

Bonus Section III

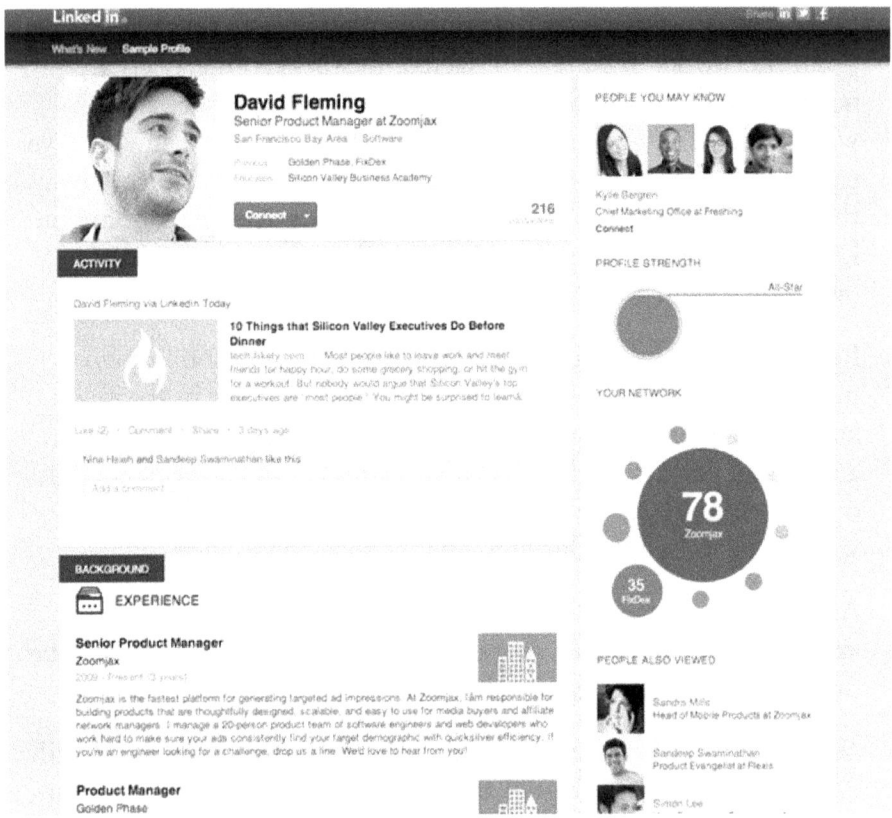

LinkedIn profile page.

a photo on your profile page is inexcusable. Just do it. If you don't have a decent picture, go outside during mid day (preferably when it's partly cloudy), stand in front of some foliage (three to six feet behind you), and have someone take a good head shot (obviously with a digital camera). Don't shoot it indoors against a wall. Flashes NEVER take good photos and cause red-eye—natural light will give you the best and fastest results. Do it in nature. You can't go wrong.

Recommendations. Here is another feature of LinkedIn that had to be fueled by recruiters. I have written elsewhere in this book about the value of testimonials. Recommendations on LinkedIn are no different. LinkedIn creates the structure for you not only to write recommendations for colleagues and others with whom you have worked, you can also request recommendations from others. When writing a recommendation, you are prompted to qualify it by disclosing the nature of your relationship with the other person, in terms of where you each worked at the time, whether one hired the other or worked as colleagues, etc.

And remember, if you are seeking employment, this is one of the first things potential employers will seek when screening out candidates. In many cases, no recommendations often means no phone call for a meeting.

Recommendations on LinkedIn are simply testimonials.

Groups. LinkedIn features countless groups of people who identify with each other by profession, industry, alma mater, interests, values, causes, current or previous employers, location, all of the above, or none of the above. I don't know how many groups there are; you can only belong to fifty of them.

Groups are a way of reaching out to others with whom you share some commonality. It is also the other members' way of reaching out to you. The groups feature has advanced quite a bit since it was created on LinkedIn, and it continues to evolve. First of all, if you want to join a group, you must submit a request, unless the group's manager/creator has set it up otherwise. Some groups are open in acceptance; others less so. Once in, you can see the profiles of other members, and it creates a foundation for extending a connection invite to someone you may not otherwise know—personally or virtually.

> Groups are a way of reaching out to others with whom you share some commonality.

There are many features to LinkedIn groups, which facilitate interaction between its members. Here are a few. Of course, you can get the best idea by going to LinkedIn and checking it out for yourself!

1. *Discussion boards.* This feature mimics perhaps one of the earliest forms of social media...the online bulletin boards where someone posts a question and other group members throw their two cents in. You can also post the discussion in the form of a link...perhaps to an article you wrote on your blog or found somewhere else. Some group managers will look upon that with scorn—just be warned. I know this from experience.

2. *Jobs.* LinkedIn has grown as one of the most sophisticated career advancement sites on the internet. Of course it offers employers the opportunity to post available jobs—and groups make it easier for them to zero in on their best prospects--and vice versa.

3. *Subgroups.* These are groups within your group where members can collaborate based on specialty, location, employer, project or anything else. Subgroups have many features including discussions, news, jobs and digest emails, etc. Only managers of the group can create subgroups and only members of this group can be members of a subgroup.

4. *Members.* This section is a directory of all the members of that particular group; each one is only open to fellow members of the main group. It allows you to see the profile of other members and reach out to them to connect.

5. Promotions. This is where members who are promoting something are *supposed* to post...and indeed in the larger groups when you visit the discussion boards, you will see plenty of spam—not truly topics for discussion but a blatantly promotional message. My observation—and I could be wrong—is that this section is not real friendly because it only allows links to be posted in the promotion content (not with a featured link with a complimentary image and descriptive content). It's almost like they put it there just for the sake of doing so but they really don't want you to use it.

Jobs. Fueled by recruiters, of course job postings will play a part. LinkedIn is a business-based networking and career resource. If you have searched through job openings through Monster, CareerBuilder or any of the others out there, you will see how LinkedIn's structure is comparable. It draws data from two sources: LinkedIn's exclusive job postings, and from a third-party database they contract with. Further, when you browse the postings, it gives you the guidance to track down who in your network may be connected to people at the companies that are hiring.

> Job postings on LinkedIn also tell you how you are connected to people at those companies.

Connections. The standard mantra of connecting with people on LinkedIn is that ideally, you should only connect with people you know personally and trust. Of course, this is one rule that people apply with discretion...or at best loosely interpret. The idea of a network is that you have a pool of individuals out there who in some circumstances are your extended eyes and ears on the lookout for opportunity. You, in turn, are looking out for them as well. It's a networking model that applies more directly to referral groups than necessarily to everyone who might be in your address book. Yet from what I have observed (as an experienced user) the quality-over-quantity approach is the preferred model. Indeed, if you extend an invitation to connect via LinkedIn with a person, and that person does not know you or recognize your name (all the more reason to have a photo...!), not only can they choose to ignore your invitation but, with a single click of a button, notify the LinkedIn powers-that-be that "they don't know you." This is like reporting you for spamming, and enough complaints can restrain your account activity or get you booted out all together!

I can always spot the member who has been restrained from extending LinkedIn invitations because they will send messages actually requesting that *I* extend a connection invite to *them*.

It is also why many LinkedIn users who have banded together to create the "Open Networker" code, which is a pledge NOT to ever click that button that we don't like to talk about. If you promote yourself as an Open Networker and you receive an invite from someone you don't personally know and with whom you do not wish to connect, you simply ignore the request and archive the email (i.e. sock it away to your "old mail" inbox).

To the best of my knowledge, I have only had one person claim to not know me...indeed it was someone I had once met at an American Marketing Association luncheon but he apparently did not remember me! Ouch...

One additional tip: When extending an invitation to connect, especially with someone you have met or had some interaction with, don't be lazy about it. Throw in a personal note to go along with the boilerplate message "I'd like to add you to my professional network on LinkedIn." When you reach out to someone, throw a little TLC into it, okay? Remember, people are not commodities. With my writing and publishing online, I get connection invites almost every day, and I get very annoyed when the person does not even take the time to inquire why they would like to connect. Unfortunately, the LinkedIn system makes this a little too easy. It will throw suggestions of profiles at you, as someone "...you may know." Next to the photo and name, is a "Connect" button—and with a single click, it sends a generic invite with no opportunity to add a custom note. So be careful.

Introductions. We have pointed out already how introductions make up the backbone of referral success. For example, if you are looking to meet Dave Johnson, a hiring manager at Midwest Plastics—someone you do not know and are thus not connected—then LinkedIn can show you the connection trail to Dave, if there is one.

Here is where you uncover the value of *tiered connections*. A **First Tier Connection** (marked by a semi-round icon with "1st" in it) is someone with whom you are directly connected.

A **Second Tier Connection** (the icon with "2nd" in it) indicates a person with whom you are not directly connected, but someone in your first tier is. So, when looking up Dave Johnson, his name may appear with the Second Tier Icon—that means he is connected to at least one person with whom you are also. His profile will reveal to you the names of those individuals. You can then choose any one of those connections of yours and request that person to "introduce" you to Dave. LinkedIn provides the email structure to do this.

When extending an invitation to connect, especially with someone you have met or had some interaction with, don't be lazy about it. Extend the invite with a personal note.

Suppose you look up Dave Johnson and his name is marked by an icon with "3rd" in it. You guessed it—Dave is a **Third Tier Connection**. That means that someone in his network is connected to someone else in yours. Introductions can still take place, but through one additional level.

Personally, I have not used this "introduction" feature on LinkedIn all that often. But others do use it, and some I am sure have had much success. However, this multi-tier structure does help reveal to you how truly connected you truly are. Each new connection can have an exponential impact on the growth of your network.

Overall, LinkedIn is, in my opinion as of this writing, still the primary social networking tool for business. But that does not mean it is the only resource. There are more out there than I would ever be able to learn, let alone tell you about. However, there are two others I will address, and I suggest you get to know all three, at minimum.

> The idea of a network is that you have a pool of individuals out there who in some circumstances are your extended eyes and ears on the lookout for opportunity.

"How Might I Build Connections on LinkedIn?"

Indeed, that is an excellent question. People with great connections don't have them by accident.

Let's step out of the virtual world for a moment. When you come across another person who has lots of connections in different places, that asset of "human capital" was built at a price. Someone had to work to build that asset.

This perspective was shared with me by Frank Agin, founder of AmSpirit Business Connections and co-author (with Lewis Howes) of the FANTASTIC book *LinkedWorking: Generating Success on the World's Largest Professional Networking Website*. If you are new to LinkedIn, this concise, easy read is exactly what you are looking for. Get it now.

"One of the things people tend to forget about networking is that it is work," Frank asserts. "That's why we call it networking... hence also the title of our book."

Networking is not—nor should it be—a low priority activity. The beauty of *LinkedWorking* is that it shows how timeless fundamentals in "face-to-face" networking apply equally to connecting online.

From Screen-2-Screen to Face-2-Face

For example, one of these timeless tenets is the notion of being a giver (does this sound familiar?). Share your expertise. Share your knowledge. Give advice when appropriate. It's a networking fundamental, and where better can you do this than on LinkedIn by answering questions posted by other members in group discussion boards?

This feature is not unique to LinkedIn...it is found on countless sites, including another one I have contributed to, *CollegeRecruiter.com*. Yet it is the personal stories that Frank and Lewis uncover in their book I find compelling...other people just like you and me who have built worldwide brands by simply paying it forward once per day.

That's the "nugget" I took from my first reading of this great book—not entirely new to me, but "relearned" with greater emphasis and a personal admission that it is one simple activity I should improve upon.

> When extending an invitation to connect, especially with someone you have met or had some interaction with, don't be lazy about it.

Want to be a giver? Is the thought of writing an article too overwhelming? Then don't. Answer a question, and improve someone else's life. One answer per day will bring people your way! Quite simply, it is just another form of social mobility.

Facebook

The odds are better that anyone reading this book has a Facebook account more than a LinkedIn account. If you are not on Facebook, you have no doubt heard of it.

A few years back I was having lunch with my friend Steve Baldzicki—President and Founder of Big Fish Networking—a ten-year old organization that is devoted to helping people in business come together and form new relationships. As Steve was telling me about some of the exciting developments on the horizon with Big Fish Networking, he also shared with me his insights on the value Facebook plays in helping him stay in touch with others.

"I like Facebook because it's fun," Steve points out. "It's great for staying connected with people—and it doesn't make any difference how that relationship started. It brings down the walls, and it's more laid back. If I haven't connected with someone in a while, where else can I throw a snowball at them? They throw it back, and next thing you know, we have a dialog going. I mean, how cool is that?" (Editor's note: a "snowball" on Facebook was a popular way to reach out to an online friend...to get their attention. It's a trend that is not really used any more.)

Facebook was begun in February 2004 by a couple of college students in their Harvard dorm room, as a social networking platform for their peers. By the following December it had almost one million users.

Here are some other basic statistics, taken directly from Facebook as of December, 2012:

- ☑ One billion monthly active users as of October 2012.

- ☑ Approximately 81% of their monthly active users are outside the U.S. and Canada.

- ☑ 584 million daily active users on average in September 2012.

- ☑ 604 million monthly active users who used Facebook mobile products as of September 30, 2012.

> "I like Facebook because it's fun...It brings down the walls, and it's more laid back."
> —Steve Baldzicki
> Founder, Big Fish Networking

Additional Statistics, according to the site AllFacebook.com:

- ☑ Facebook wins nine percent of all visits online.

- ☑ Facebook wins one of every five page views.

- ☑ The average visit to Facebook is 20 minutes.

- ☑ Fifty-seven percent of its members are female.

- ☑ Of all the popular online sites, Facebook's age distribution among members is the most even.

So, what does this mean to you? I'm not going to describe the structure of Facebook here the way that I did briefly for LinkedIn, primarily because it really would lead too far off on a tangent—plus you can learn far more by just getting on and exploring it for yourself if you have not been there. The other reason is that it is flexible and *always* changing. Many people are on Facebook for purely social enjoyment—indeed a population that began among the college crowd in the eastern United States boasts people age 35 and above as its fastest growing demographic.

One aspect of Facebook I like is that in my opinion, it's the most human of the applications available. This is one of the reasons I think it has become so popular so fast. It is as far wide and deep as each of us goes individually. You can share as much or as little information about yourself as you wish—and you can exercise a great amount of control in who has access to that information (despite occasional myths to the contrary).

For example, when you "add friends," you can assign those friends to your own different categories (known only to you). Some may be close friends and family members—and those people may have access to profile content that other friends—say people you connect with online yet do not know personally—may not (those of us who post photos of family members and children may appreciate this feature—yet it must be utilized correctly to make it work for you).

Facebook also allows you to keep a "passive channel of communication" going—to *passively prospect* if you will. By posting content that is visible to those in your FB network, you reach out and touch others. You stay visible—and on their radar screen. It's marketing that also strengthens weak ties. There really is no magic formula to using this media in order to prospect...it's simply a case of staying in front of people, doing so in a positive way. And you must do it *consistently*.

Further, what did we say earlier in the book about why people buy? They buy from you not because they like your company... they buy from you because they like you. Facebook is all about you. Business is personal. Facebook is personal. If you're shy in a crowded room, Facebook is one place where you can overcome this shyness.

Remember also that given so many people are "on" Facebook, they are each on for equally different reasons. For example, I have several friends who are teachers—and some of those individuals see Facebook as a means to connecting with their students. I have one very close teacher friend who will NOT do so, because for her it is a matter of privacy. And that's fine, too. It is up to the user.

You may find some people who are on Facebook primarily for business. You will see that they are posting stuff that is tied to their work or profession; they likely have a FB page for their business or employer (and have invited you to "like" their page); they are involved in FB groups that are so related (and have thus invited you to join). They are using these groups to plan and host events, and then drawing other people to attend.

At the same time, you may see that those folks on for business are less active in Facebook activities that are of purely entertainment

---

Facebook was begun in February 2004 by a couple of college students in their Harvard dorm room, as a social networking platform for their peers. By the following December it had almost one million users.

value. (Note: If you have not joined and experienced Facebook, you may need to do so before you will really get the gist of what I am writing about here.) These include the games such as Mafia Wars, or the endless quizzes that covertly gather consumer preference data from members ("What Color of the Rainbow are You? Take this Quiz and Find Out!"). If I ever wonder what character from *Gilligan's Island* with whom I would most identify, I at least know where I can go to find out. Until then, I will just keep it bookmarked.

Twitter: Can You Say it in 140 Characters or Less?

On to Twitter. Often described as a "mini-blog," at one point it was hailed as the latest and greatest tool for recruiters—a designation that was previously awarded (if not officially) to LinkedIn. Candidly, I suspect that LinkedIn may have won the title back.

Twitter is a social networking tool that uses the SMS text protocol (short messaging service) designed for mobile phones (which explains the character limit). Twitter was originally conceived to allow a user to broadcast these messages to a group of subscribers, or in this case, *followers*. While it is a web application and one of the most popular websites in the world, its use of the SMS protocol has allowed an array of third-party services and applications to be made available for *posting* and *receiving* content. In fact, it is believed that more Twitter users post using mobile devices than logging onto the actual website.

Which leads us to the inevitable question: *How can this simple tool be used to prospect for new business?*

This was my question until it was answered by the late **Brian Lockrey,** who was President/CEO at Assist Data Recovery until his sudden passing in 2013.

Brian had quite a bit to share with about his use of Twitter. In fact, he even ran an effective resource for Twitter users, called TwittGroups.com. So, how did Brian use Twitter to prospect for business?

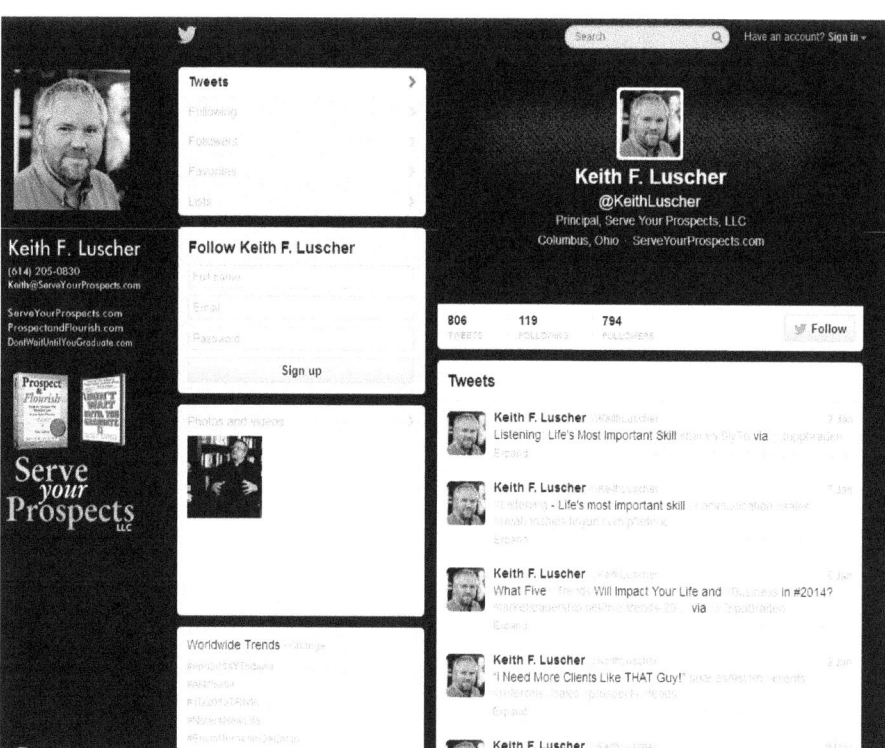

A Twitter home page.

Twitter is a social networking tool that uses the SMS text protocol (short messaging service) designed for mobile phones.

"I'll say this up front," Brian replied, "Like any other resource out there, it's going to be more useful for some people than it will be for others. It just depends on the kind of business you are in." Brian was in the data recovery business—so when someone's hard drive crashes (and it hasn't been properly backed up), and the data on that drive MUST be recovered, he was the man you would call. I know this from personal experience. Brian was the Jedi Master of data recovery—and he will be sorely missed.

"I'm a first responder." I recall Brian saying. "I have a growing base of people following me on Twitter. One example of how it helps me generate business is when Charlie, a Twitter user, runs into a computer problem, like a hard drive crash. Charlie doesn't know what to do, and hasn't backed up his data. So, Charlie sends out a "tweet" (the act of posting to Twittered.), saying something like `My hard drive crashed and I need my files! Help!'"

"Well, odds are Charlie and I are not following each other (directly connected.) on Twitter, even though we are both members of the community. But Jane, one of my followers, is also following Charlie. Jane knows me in the Twitter community and what I do. Maybe she has hired me before, maybe not. But either way, when she sees Charlie's tweet, she tweets back telling him to call me."

Brian said that this happens all the time. "There are several conditions that are required if you want to create these kinds of outcomes," he points out. "First, you become part of a community, and do so by investing just a few minutes per day on Twitter, and helping people out. (Editor's Note: does any of this sound familiar?) For example, like on a bulletin board, people will post all kinds of simple troubleshooting questions or maybe they are seeking a software solution to complete a specific task. If I can help that person in someway, either by directly answering a question or *referring* them to something (like a website or software application) or someone (a fellow Twitter user) who can help them solve their problem, I feed relationships through value. And I contribute to the community."

Taking Keith Farazzi's advice to "never eat alone," Brian would also use Twitter to have impromptu meetings for lunch or coffee. "If I find myself headed somewhere and have some time, I'll send out a tweet of where I am going with an open invitation to meet. Believe it or not, it works!"

Like any other online social networking vehicle—and so far they differ from each other greatly while still having fundamental traits in common—the value you get from using Twitter is going to parallel the value you offer to the community. It is not a forum for posting advertisements or content that is purely self-promotional. "That will get you marked very quickly," Brian used to caution.

For me, it's a tip I was glad to hear, and am pleased to share even though Brian is no longer with us. I have stated from the beginning: the best way to build and nurture long-term prosperous relationships is through value. Serve your prospects. Whether you are in the real world or the online world, what goes around comes around.

> The value you get from using Twitter is going to parallel the value you offer to the community.

How to Build Your Network of Followers

One of the interesting points about Twitter is the concept of having "followers" instead of "friends" or "connections." It's all semantics. Quite simply, when you create a Twitter account, you set up a simple profile. It doesn't take long—it's pithy just as all your posts will be.

Here are a few simple suggestions to manage your Twitter account and build followers.

Keyword your profile. Often, Twitter users (called "Peeps" among others, but it's my favorite) will seek out people to follow based upon industry, profession, location, who else they are connected with, etc. If your business is commercial real estate, then your profile should have key words that indicate so. You will also be sending out tweets that relate to what you do and those like interests of your prospective followers and clients. Such messages should also have keywords included so that potential followers will find you in their searches.

Don't fall into the "Twitter Trap!" Many Twitter users will get on their account and then start following as many people as possible indiscriminately in hopes that those people will in turn follow them back. This is a common mistake—and you can spot the people who do this by their follow-to-follower ratios. If John Smith has 5,145 followers, but also follows 4,989, then John *may* have a largely artificial following. Do 5,100 people really care what John has to tweet? Does John really spend his hours and days tracking the tweets of 5,000 fellow peeps? I doubt it. As a result, his following is artificial. He is just one of 5,000 people in a big room (I call it the "Twitter Trap"), most of whom are *talking to everyone, and listening to no one.*

> Avoid the Twitter Trap: Don't get stuck in a room of 5,000 other people, most of whom are talking to everyone, and listening to no one.

Take your time, and build a natural following. In other words, exercise discretion with who you follow. Follow someone on Twitter because you care about what they have to say, or are interested in pursuing a relationship with them of some kind.

In turn, if you indeed wish to use Twitter to prospect for your business, then those who follow you must have a genuine interest in what you have to say. For example, if you are in commercial real estate in Pittsburgh, PA, you can likely have prospects all over the country—people who may be involved in looking at Pittsburgh and its commercial locations for opening up an office for their company, or relocating altogether. Keep that in mind. Post messages and links to content that are of importance to them.

In this case, you can post content, thoughts and links that tie to your prospects' individual industries, or related to the location and community you represent! Obviously, you may also post content that is related directly to your own expertise and profession.

Also, be mindful of the posts from people you follow. Looking back to Brian's example, if someone tweets a question describing a problem or need, and you may have the solution, therein is your opportunity to help someone else out. It's just like people posting questions on a bulletin board. The more questions you answer, the more people you serve and the stronger your reputation will become (and your following will grow).

So how do people find you? Content is king. Post several times per day (two, three, maybe four times...?). Spread out those posts. Focus on a handful of topics. In the morning, post about the latest good news impacting your community; afternoon, focus on your industry or an aspect of your profession; evening tweets can be more laid back—with content that might be entertaining or contemplative (such as quotes of wisdom, etc.). Plan out your strategy—but keep it simple. More importantly, be consistent; most importantly, deliver value at every opportunity.

Those tweets will have keywords. You can even "tag" your tweets with key phrases to attract new followers, by placing hashtags (#) in front of those keywords.

> You can even "tag" your tweets with keyphrases to attract new followers, by placing hashtags (#) in front of those keywords.

For example, peeps use this feature to "broadcast" news announcements in real time. During the most recent Iranian elections, when the "winner" was announced within 15 minutes of the closing the last voting pole (which amounted to a logistical impossibility of counting the votes in that short a time), citizens began to protest in the streets, citing the election as a fraud. People in Tehran were tweeting what they saw happening—and were tagging those tweets with words like "#Iran", "#Elections" and "#Tehran."

In turn, these were among the most searched for keywords, as fellow peeps around the globe (including those in the news media) were clamoring for information that wasn't Iranian government-fed. (Twitter will regularly list the most popular searches in the sidebar on your home page.) During the uprising following this election, when you searched the keywords, the tweets of those Iranian peeps would come up faster than you could load them! At that point, you not only have access to their posted messages, but the option to follow those peeps as well.

Here is a simpler example. Suppose you like to write movie reviews. Let's say a new movie opens today, *The Big Heist*. You want to attract followers to your opinions. You go see the movie, and then write on your blog about it. You send out a tweet that includes "#bigheist" or the name of its star, and thus fellow peeps who are interested in that movie (or lead actor), and search for that keyword, will find your tweet. Will they follow you? It's up to them...and you. Did you deliver value? Did they like what you had to share?

Further, they can choose to "unfollow" you as easily as they choose to follow. So in that sense, you are feeding a relationship.

Some Twitter Terms

As you have already learned, Twitter has evolved into its own lingo and subculture. Here are just a couple basics. Check online for more.

@ScreenName. Peeps usually identify their screen names to others by including the "@" symbol in front of it. For example, my Twitter screen name is "KeithLuscher" (caps don't make a difference). So I will identify myself to other peeps as @KeithLuscher. If you attend a gathering of other peeps, this is likely what you will see written on their name tags.

Retweet (RT). When you receive a tweet from someone you follow and you wish to pass the word to the rest of your followers, you will "retweet" it. Often, this involves pasting the original message after you preface it with "RT @KeithLuscher." You are letting everyone know that you are passing the information along, and it originated with me.

#FollowFriday (FF). A custom of the Twitter community is to help each other build followers. Have some friends and people you follow, whom you think others might appreciate? Every Friday, you send out a tweet that begins with #FollowFriday or #FF and then list out the @ScreenNames. Get on and see how others do it!

Further, you will likely need to brush up on your knowledge of SMS/Instant Messaging acronyms. The dictionary evolved out of the timeless terms that predate SMS/IM such as FYI (for your information), AKA (also known as), ASAP (as soon as possible), and BTW (by the way).

A web search for the latest and greatest will reveal countless lists and references that also help to know if you are a parent with a teenager...

A custom of the Twitter community is to help each other build followers.

Bonus Section III

The 12 Laws of Social Media Prospecting

What we have shared here on these few pages really only scratches the surface of the growing and changing world of social media. We only went over a few of the tools out there, but at this point, I think it is safe to say that LinkedIn, Facebook and Twitter are among the most popular. But there are several other applications out there, including Plaxo (I recently began using this online address book and have really come to love it), Google+, Pinterest as well as bookmarking tools for information on the internet—most of which have included a social networking component to their structures (users can create online profiles and connect with other users.).

Yet, as in any community of people, be it virtual, geographical, professional, or otherwise, there do remain several key "universal" laws that must be followed if one is to prospect and flourish in these environments. I have outlined twelve of them, which at this time I believe covers the bases.

So, take these guidelines into account. See how they apply to whatever applications you use—LinkedIn, Facebook, Twitter, or Face2Face!

Law #1: Be a Giver.

You know, when we are out and about meeting people, those of us who are mindful of giving can always spot the givers and the takers. Every one of us has so much to give to others, and thereby we enable other people to really get to know who we are. This is called building relationships through value.

Effective business professionals know this. They are all about selling themselves and building relationships—and they do this through value. They give of themselves—both their time and their expertise. Most importantly, they do it from the heart. Quite simply: to sell yourself, you must give of yourself. I am not saying you must "give away the store;" nor am I saying that you give so much that it diminish the perception of your value. As I indicated earlier, you give of yourself when:

- ☑ You are socially mobile, volunteering and contributing to your community (such as leading online discussions and starting a special interest group.)

- ☑ You seek opportunities to help others, such as facilitating introductions between colleagues and friends (by forwarding profiles or connecting people via email)

- ☑ You exercise empathic listening, with genuine interest in the needs of others (by responding to questions and posts with a spirit of helping and answering questions, or referring others to resources and/or people you believe may be of benefit to them)

- ☑ You play a key role in helping another person create a positive outcome in their life, while expecting nothing in return.

It is how communities are formed whether they are virtual or "in the real." And it is also how new relationships are built.

Remember what Frank Agin and Brian Lockery said about helping people out and answering questions? It's all about giving and serving your prospects.

Law #2: Your Network is Sacred.

Do you know why some people are hesitant to use social media? Or perhaps why some people will absolutely never give out their email address (but are quick to hand over their phone number)? Or perhaps did you ever wonder why not everyone you meet will be immediately willing to put you in touch with everybody they know?

> "The central premise of social capital is that social networks have value."
> —Andrew Chiodo, Author, Social Capital

Your network, and the strength of relationships with people in your network, is one of your most valuable assets. A network of followers, friends, business contacts, colleagues, and clients is by no means a commodity. Therefore, it is not something you should take for granted.

Just as many of you read my ongoing feature (which can be found at http://www.KeithLuscher.com), you may do so via email subscription. My base of subscribers is one of my networks—and thus I want to be responsible and respectful of how I serve the people in that network. I send out value-based content typically once per week. If I were to begin sending out redundant messages or spam-like emails several times per week or even every day, what would happen to that subscriber base? It would shrink. People would remove themselves from the list, or tell their email clients to automatically send me to the junk folder.

Andrew Chiodo, a friend and colleague of mine refers to this asset as *Social Capital*. In fact, it's the title of a book he wrote and came out in 2007. According to Chiodo: "The central premise of social capital is that social networks have value. Social capital refers to the collective value of all 'social networks' [who people know] and the inclinations that arise from these networks to do things for each other ['norms of reciprocity']."

Further, your network is made up of people just like you and they deserve respect. You should treat them the way you know they want to be treated.

Just as you regard your own network as being sacred and a valuable asset, so do each of your own contacts and friends. In fact, your network's networks are indeed part of your own, just as the three-tier structure on LinkedIn illustrates. These are not people with whom you may be directly connected, but you are still connected.

When seeking referrals and introductions be them in person or online, you will need to show equal respect, consideration, and sensitivity to members in your friend's network. In fact, the more connected each of your own network members are, the deeper your network becomes. It's not just about width (your direct connections); it's about depth (the connections of your network members, and so on).

> The more connected each of your own network members are, the deeper your network becomes.

Law #3: Reciprocate.

As a member of the online community, you will no doubt be in the position to receive favors from others. Perhaps you might need to fill a position in your office, or your brother needs the advice of a good attorney. Social networks (where some people will be closer to you than others) can provide the foundation to be on the receiving end of the goodwill of others.

One example of online reciprocating is when one person writes a sincere recommendation for another, such as on LinkedIn. It is not unusual to write one in return, just as long as those recommendations are properly qualified, honest and sincere. Another example on Twitter is when someone retweets a post of yours, or mentions you in a Follow Friday, to do the same for that person return.

When I say reciprocate, which is another way of giving back, I say this in a spirit of being appreciative of the goodness of others. But it is *not* about always having to be even. I remember talking with one person who proudly claimed, "I do not accept the charity of others."

Well, I appreciated the spirit in which he spoke—but all we were talking about was a spare stylus for our identical smart phones (Yes, this was a few years ago.)! He had the same phone as mine, and had lost his stylus pen. I had a ton of spares because I bought a handful for next-to-nothing on Ebay! I offered him the one I had on hand; he insisted on paying me a couple bucks for it...

With some hesitation, I let him pay me back because it made HIM feel better. But when someone does something kind for you, whether it is referring you to a resource or answering an important question, be mindful of that. Remember it, and when the opportunity to reciprocate presents itself in some way shape or form, take it.

Law #4: Pay it Forward Once per Day.

We just talked about reciprocating to others, in the case of online posting recommendations and retweets. How about doing something like that for a network member, just for the heck of it? If someone in your network posts an exciting announcement or benefit available from their business or company...why not help spread the word?

> How about doing something positive for a network member, just for the heck of it?

On LinkedIn, look through your network. Who do you know for whom you can write a qualified, honest and sincere recommendation, yet haven't yet? Do it. Write one per day if you can.

Send a warm, kind message to someone with whom you may not have connected in a while. Not so you can "prospect" them...just do it because you want to make that person *feel* good. You never know—you might just make that person's day. Perhaps that lift will come on a day that they really need it.

Beyond writing sincere kind words about others, you can pay it forward online through:

- ☑ Retweeting posts on Twitter

- ☑ Tweeting followers you know on #FollowFriday

- ☑ Share online information from others to your Facebook wall or other information sharing web applications

- ☑ Introducing people in your own network to each other—perhaps they share a common interest either professionally or personally

☑ Scanning discussion boards on LinkedIn and Facebook (and others) and posting REAL answers and solutions that improves peoples' lives (but are not necessarily tied to your business).

It all comes down to doing something positive for someone else, and being completely selfless about it. When you do that, you are spreading good karma. You have heard the expression "What goes around, comes around." You have most likely also heard about the law of attraction—like attracts like. Paying it forward stems from this universal law. You will get back, what you put forward. Make sure it's good.

Law #5: Give Credit Where Credit Is Due.

Let me tell you something: *Nothing is new since the Earth cooled.*

> Nothing is new since the earth cooled.

Wow! That's a cool saying. It's also true. Wish I had thought it up. But in reality, I didn't. I first heard it from friend and mentor, I. David Cohen—the insurance veteran you may recall reading about in the introduction and elsewhere throughout this book. So when I speak to audiences, and this point will come up, I will typically say something like, "As a longtime friend and mentor has often said, nothing is new since the Earth cooled."

We all have things we share proudly, and sometimes privately wish we could take credit. When someone shares with you an article, resource, or helpful piece of advice that you in turn choose to pass on to others, be sure to mention the source. This is important for several key reasons:

1. *It gives that piece of information more credibility.* Perhaps you are not the best person to pass on information that gives financial advice...but your source is. Seeing this, your friends will likely give it more credence, and will also appreciate you for being a channel of helpful information.

2. *You serve your network; you also reciprocate.* A friend passes you information; you pass it on to others citing them as the source. That is reciprocation at its best. You build relationships on both fronts.

3. *You show humility.* Many of us are in the process of building our own personal brands, and online reputations are key to that success. However, none of us knows everything! Don't pretend that you do.

4. *It's just plain right.* Giving credit where credit is due is simply the most ethical and honest way to work, whether it is online, in the workplace, at home, or wherever.

Law #6: Speak Kindly and with Sincerity, or Don't Speak.

We have all heard the expression, if you can't say something nice, don't say anything at all. It's a timeless rule, yet one that is often ignored. The fact is, when you say something negative about another person, you only make yourself look bad—plus you spread bad karma (remember that what goes around…). You hurt yourself professionally, and you hurt yourself spiritually (this is the case whether you believe in that or not).

Here is a simple example: when I publish a new article on my blog, I will post it to the news boards of many groups on LinkedIn. That way, it gets plenty of exposure, brings in new readers and helps more people.

You can make comments to these various articles—and most of the time the comments will be positive, either affirming what I shared, or giving an additional example of my point. But every now and then, there will be a critic.

The problem is that the world has enough critics. So, what is a "critic?" For our example, a critic is someone who makes negative remarks without anything better or positive to offer up. Being critical is bad. Offering constructive criticism is good, and is altogether completely different.

The late Stephen Covey spoke of this when he would stress the principle of "loyalty to the absent." If you are to say something critical, say it constructively, with respect, and in a manner as though that person were present. When it is online, that person is always present…as are many others.

Let's say you read one of my articles that emphasizes the value of calling people back persistently until you get, as I sometimes say in jest, "…a restraining order."

Alas, you disagree. Your experience from being on both the phoning and the receiving end indicates that if a prospect does not return a call after the 47th voicemail message, the one doing the phoning should give it up and move on. You likely have a good point to share from your experience. How do you handle it? Here I am writing and sounding like a know-it-all when you definitely know better.

You can approach it two ways ....

> *Keith's article "Follow Up Until...The Art of Gentle Persistence," is very misleading to struggling sales people. My 35 years of experience tells me that if people don't want to talk to you, they won't call you. There is no reason for you to waste your time if they have not taken or returned your call by the third or fourth attempt..*

Well, *that's* helpful. In essence, the post above says to just give up! Yet, perhaps there are situations where one should simply move on and stop making calls to people who won't return them. Why not speak to your own experience or industry?

> *Keith's article, "Follow Up Until...The Art of Gentle Persistence," makes some valid points as to the importance of not giving up. Quite often, you just really never know if a prospect is truly interested until you receive a clear answer. However, my experience also tells me that in some professions or industries, one's time as a sales producer might better be invested in other prospects who are more responsive. There is no shortage of people out there who need—and want—our assistance. When prioritizing your calls, wouldn't you rather attempt to help people who are at least willing to help themselves?*

Wow. I think you just swayed my mind in that last post. Good job! Plus, it was constructive and provided value for everyone, instead of just being a critic attempting to one-up me. From an ego standpoint, I might still have been quietly miffed at the post above (depending on my level of insecurity that day), but you also began a constructive dialog to which others may feel compelled to respond. The sharing of ideas, and doing so with respect, is what we are all attempting to do online.

> A critic is someone who makes negative remarks without anything better or positive to offer up.

And if we were friends on Facebook, I might just send you a drink rather than throw a snowball at you (I know...no one does that anymore, but I wanted to close out this point with a whitty remark).

Law #7: Connecting Online Is Not an End; It is a Means.

Bob Kennedy has over five thousand friends on Facebook.

Bob is also 34, and stays home every night (including weekends) "interacting" with his friends online, and lives with his mother.

Note: If this is your name and I just described your life, it is pure coincidence.

From Screen-2-Screen to Face-2-Face

In reality, connecting with people online is merely a means of communication, just like talking to people on the phone, traditional email or even snail mail. It is no different than being part of a common organization, such as a place of worship, or a health club. It is no different than connecting with others who perhaps work at the same company or location. Or hang out a the same place after work, or for networking clubs.

> The sharing of ideas, and doing so with respect, is what we are all attempting to do online.

Being connected with other people online; racking up friends or online connections or followers should not be the goal in itself. It is a means to a goal. That goal, depending upon your situation (be them business or personal), is up to you.

Consider the online dating sites. If you join one of those matching sites, ideally your goal is to meet someone in person. You are prospecting, and you are doing it online.

So, when prospecting for business, the same dynamic exists. Perhaps your business does not always require face-to-face meetings (although this book does assume that for the majority of the readers of this book). Indeed, I have connections online who I can serve over the internet, if by nothing else by selling them one of my books. They can be anywhere in the world. If you bought this book and it's registered with me, you are eligible for electronic updates at no additional charge for life. There is a relationship here, and it began when we connected online.

Law #8: Not Everyone Online Is Online.

> "Currently, more than 60 percent of U.S. Twitter users fail to return the following month, or in other words, Twitter's audience retention rate, or the percentage of a given month's users who come back the following month, is currently about 40 percent."
>
> —David Martin, Vice President of Primary Research, Nielsen Online

I signed up my Twitter account in July of 2008, after hearing some buzz on the news. I didn't get engaged till almost six months later. It took me a while to figure it out. Candidly, I really only use it for sending out messages. I really don't follow anybody.

Let's say you attend a business function and meet Jane, a senior level, experienced corporate executive or business owner. You can trade business cards with her, and go back to LinkedIn and look up her profile. You find it!

Next to her name is her title, the company, and how many years she has been there. But there is nothing else; no photo, and a minimal description of the company. Oh yes, she has five connections. "How in the world did she become *soooo* successful?" you ask yourself.

Let me tell you something: with Jane, you got lucky. You only found one profile, *and not three duplicates!* The same can be true for Facebook or any of the others. Until recently, it was Plaxo. For years I had a profile and connections, but was never engaged there (I am now because it is truly a live online address book, and I needed that!).

> Social media is only going to help you connect with those who are engaged.

Lots of people are online. But many of those folks are not as engaged. They don't take to technology as well; nor do their business or social requirements demand that they learn it. They got on because someone told them to, or their 14-year-old kid walked them through it or did it for them.

So, remember that social media is only going to help you connect with those who are engaged. Others are not—so be prepared to follow up with them the old fashioned way: the telephone.

Law #9: Post As Though Your Mother Will See It...She Probably Will.

Here is where good old fashioned common sense comes into play. First, referring back to what we stated before about being negative...don't do it. Even cynicism or excess sarcasm can reflect poorly upon you. When in doubt, hold back or get a second or third opinion.

Second, do not post profanity of any kind. I would even avoid euphemisms. Anything that calls for such discourse is mostly likely going to be negative or cynical anyway—don't do it.

Facebook allows a great amount of control over who sees what in your profile. When you have friends, you can place them into categories that only you know about. You can control what groups see what content. That's good. But use that for your own discretion and privacy. Don't be irresponsible.

The fact is, tasteless photos, or even excessive party pics may not help you if you are using social media to earn a living or find a job. We have heard this on the news about how employers will research candidates through any and all means—especially at times when the economy gives them greater discretion in who they hire. Social media, MySpace pages, Facebook profiles, and LinkedIn pages are the first and easiest places to start. Further, they will hire professional hackers to uncover stuff you thought was private. Is that right or fair? No. But they do it nonetheless.

> If you join an online matching site, ideally your goal is to meet someone in person. You are prospecting, and you are doing it online.

If you find yourself about to post a remark or image that you would not want your mother or a potential employer and/or client to see, then do yourself a favor: click CANCEL.

Law #10: It's Not Who You Know. It's Who Knows You (Building A Brand).

In Chapter Two, we talked about the "two faces" of networking. Building contacts versus building relationships. It's like the difference on Twitter between who you follow versus who follows you. *It's the difference between who you know, versus who knows you.*

This is what building a "personal brand" is all about. It is about personal name recognition. It is about building a *positive* reputation that precedes you. It is about meeting people for the first time, and them already knowing just a little bit about you.

I introduced this concept to college students more than fifteen years ago in my book *Don't Wait Until You Graduate!* One of the things I stressed to students was "Volunteer!" Be a giver. Serve others and let other people *experience what you do*. This rule applies in real life, and it also applies in social media prospecting. Social media is a tremendous vehicle for getting your name out, doing it in a positive fashion, and building a reputation that precedes you. In essence, that is what building a personal brand is all about.

Law #11: Be Congruent and Consistent.

One of the expressions stated in this book and others of mine is this: When growing your own food, don't wait until you are hungry to plant your seeds.

When you plant your seeds, you need to water regularly. You need to feed the soil, to nurture the growth. What have we said here about twittering, about posting positive messages, about paying it forward once per day?

It's about being consistent. It's about your activity. That's what you learn in sales: it's all about your activity. That's all you can control.

As we indicated in the previous section, it's also the key element of success in marketing. Those who implement single-shot marketing efforts will most often be disappointed. However, those who consistently put themselves and their messages out there will see results. I know this from personal experience as well. When at times I have not been consistently visible, active and engaged, activity slows down. When I do the right thing on a regular basis, it picks up. It's not rocket science.

Law #12: Take Your Time.

For many of us, time is the one thing we feel we have the least. Begging back to the law of the harvest, and that relationships take time to build, effective leveraging of social media to build your career or your business will take time.

Don't be seduced by "gurus" or online services that promise to turn your name viral overnight. If someone promises you 10,000 Twitter followers in two days, those followers are not likely going to be interested in what you have to say (they likely will not even be real people).

Be patient. Be persistent. Be ethical. Most importantly: focus on helping people. What goes around comes around, in due time.

> This is what building a "personal brand" is all about...building a positive reputation that precedes you.

What's Strange about These Laws?

Let's look at these laws in a single list:

> Law #1: Be a Giver.
> Law #2: Your Network is Sacred.
> Law #3: Reciprocate.
> Law #4: Pay it Forward Once per Day.
> Law #5: Give Credit Where Credit Is Due.
> Law #6: Speak Kindly and with Sincerity, or Don't Speak.
> Law #7: Connecting Online Is Not an End; It is a Means.
> Law #8: Not Everyone Online Is Online.
> Law #9: Post As Though Your Mother Will See It...
>   She Probably Will.
> Law #10: It's Not Who You Know. It's Who Knows You
>   (Building A Brand).
> Law #11: Be Congruent and Consistent.
> Law #12: Take Your Time.

Read through this list. Give it some thought.

Every single one of them can be applied to building relationships *outside* the realm of social media. Indeed, these are fundamental ethics...*ethics of success in building prosperous human relationships.*

Afterward

Afterward:

Thinking About Giving Up?

You have read here and no doubt have heard elsewhere about the importance of persistence and of not giving up—of how good things happen when you truly believe in what you offer, and have faith in yourself.

This is all well and good, until you hit the wall. Although we addressed this topic in Chapter Four, it still merits some extra attention here at the end. After all, whether it is declining sales or being forced into the job market, these challenging times have taken their toll on many of us.

I was reminded of a book I read almost two years ago: Viktor Frankl's *Man's Search For Meaning*. To read Frankl's book is phenomenal; to read it realizing that he secretly wrote it in 1945 while a prisoner at Auschwitz (and not from the comfort of hindsight 15 years later) can be life transforming.

There was one paragraph that stood out in my memory that I would like to share with those of you who are feeling pushed to the edge—**and that perhaps it is time to give up.** The paragraph's context: the author is reflecting a particular (and then-recent) day while being marched by the Nazis one cold evening at dusk. For a mental respite, he begins to ponder the image of his wife, whom he has lost and misses terribly:

> ...for the first time in my life I saw the truth as it is set into song by so many poets, proclaimed as the final wisdom by so many thinkers. The truth — that love is the ultimate and the highest goal to which man can aspire. Then I grasped the meaning of the greatest secret that human poetry and human thought and belief have to impart: The salvation of man is through love and in love. I understood how a man who has nothing left in this world still may know bliss, be it only for a brief moment, in the contemplation of his beloved. In a position of utter desolation, when man cannot express himself in positive action, when his only achievement may consist in enduring his sufferings in the right way — an honorable way — in such a position man can, through loving contemplation of the image he carries of his beloved, achieve fulfillment. For the first time in my life I was able to understand the meaning of the words, "The angels are lost in perpetual contemplation of an infinite glory."

The salvation of man is through love and in love.

How powerful is this? That one can choose to focus on LOVE amidst circumstances so dreadful that they are beyond our imagination? Frankl points to the freedom that we have within us—a freedom that is connected with a deep "inner" life, fueled by a spiritual awareness that connects each of us with something that is outside and greater than ourselves.

Frankl's "beloved" was his wife; your beloved may include your spouse, your children, and even your closest friends and family. They are the people who lift and feed you...who give you purpose. The number one obstacle to effective prospecting, be it for clients or a job, is not understanding the value you provide for others. Quite simply—*it is numbness to your purpose*—to your meaning.

It is not enough just to identify your purpose...you must feel it. This delves into two facets: the WHAT—what you offer and the value it brings to others; and the WHY—why you do what you do.

What can first be gleaned by exploring your track record. Talk to previous/current clients and/or employers. Hear their stories—and feel the emotion behind their stories. Make notes of what they say, and write it up as a testimonial for their review and approval.

Understanding the **why** is simple. Who do you love? Who loves you? Your spouse? Your children? Your parents? Your pet? Your God? Whoever it may include, keep a reminder of these "whys" close to you at all times—and I mean CLOSE. On your phone, your computer, your key chain, everywhere. Savor the time you spend with them—every day, every moment, every hour. These feelings are not your defense; they are your offense. They keep you in a faithful and positive state of mind that holds that "wall" at bay.

And on days when you do and will "hit the wall," your connection to your purpose—your meaning—will give you the strength to break through. That's a promise.

Index

Index

A

access 50
accountability 93, 94
Adobe Systems 223
affinity 50
Agin, Frank 256, 267
AmSpirit 89, 92, 256
testimonials 220
appearance, personal 119
articles 76, 171–172
associations, professional 59, 80
attorneys 170
attributes, personal 52, 53
audio-video 217

B

Baldzicki, Steve 83, 257
Beckwith, Harry 248
behavior 136–137, 141. *See also* structure
belief 33, 137
benefit 28
Big Fish Networking 83, 257
blogs 76
BNI 89
board of advisors, personal 83, 154, 188
  enlisting 94
  meetings with 94–97
boards 79
books 216, 222
brochures 198, 206, 215, 222
budget, marketing 208
business cards 28, 86–99
Business Leads of America 89
business-to-business sales 103, 227–228

C

calls, follow up 26
canvassing, cold 25
CardMunch 87
caring 43
centers of influence 69, 101, 108–109, 109, 187, 189. *See also* talking points; *See also* board of advisors, personal
  and mentors 71
  getting started 72

Index

certified public accountants 170
Certus Professional Network 84–85
chain of command 176–177
character 34, 68
Chiodo, Andrew 267
Clemens, Samuel 175
client. *See also* service, client
   loyalty 163
   satisfaction 163
   total lifetime value of... 161
coach 94
coffee 88–89
COI. *See* centers of influence
cold calling. *See* canvassing, cold
CollegeRecruiter.com 257
communication skills 35–36
competition 55
contacts 68–69. *See* networking
content 28
content marketing 202–204, 214, 216, 238–239
cost-cutting 159
courage 37
creating 144, 145–146, 152. *See also* structure: and creating new realities
   structure of... 146–155
"creative tension" 152, 154
Customer Satisfaction is WORTHLESS; Customer Loyalty... 163–164

D

demographics 56, 57
difficulty
   in prospecting 38–40
discipline 57, 59–60, 129–142, 137, 189–190
   and choices 130
   and perseverance 131, 190
   delayed gratification and 129
   priorities and 130
   strengthening 129
"doers" 32, 43
Don't Wait Until You Graduate! 13, 249, 275

E

Ecclesiastes 195
Eight Rules of Outstanding Service 173, 191
Einstein, Albert 144
emotion 41
empathy 43
Encyclopedia of Associations 28
energy 35, 119
eye contact 118

F

Facebook 28, 125, 247, 257, 269, 272
   "passive prospecting" 259
   statistics 258–259
failures, previous 53–54
fear 137, 186. *See also* rejection: and fear
first impressions 102
fishing
   and prospecting 57–58
focus 54, 56–60, 194
fortitude 183, 184–185
Frankl, Viktor 279–280
freedom 185
Fritz, Robert 135, 137

G

geographics 56, 57
Gitomer, Jeffrey 163–164
goals 132
   "fit" goals 144, 147, 148, 190
   "stretch and leverage" 144–145, 148, 190
Goettler Associates 202
Gold Star Referral Clubs 89, 90–91, 92
green zone 193

H

honesty 43, 186
Howes, Lewis 256
How to Win Customers and Keep them for Life 175
humility 43

I

influence circle 232
interview, informational 67
introductions 30, 51, 187, 249. *See also* centers of influence
   and LinkedIn 255–256
   how to ask for 39–40
inverted pyramid 176
investment representatives 170
iTunes 221

K

Kennedy, John F. 36, 116

Index

L

laziness 18, 31, 186
Leadership and Golf: Swing to Balance 135
LeBoeuf, Michael, Ph.D. 175
LeTip 89
letters 26, 95
likability 42–43, 161
LinkedIn 28, 87, 125, 246, 247, 249–257, 268, 274
   Centers of Influence 74
   connections 254–255
   groups 253–254
   introductions 251, 255–256
   jobs 254
   "Open Networker" 254
   portrait photo 251
   profile page 251
   prospecting on 249–250
   recommendations 249, 252–253, 268, 269
   referrals 250–251
LinkedWorking 256–257
listening 86, 249, 267
   and your prospects 210
   how to listen 122
literature 28
Lockrey, Brian 267
Love the Work You're With 93
loyalty 160, 191
luck 30, 31

M

Mackay, Harvey 66
Man's Search For Meaning 279–280
Mariotti, Steve 32, 142
market 16, 47, 75, 108
   different models 48
   natural markets 50, 57, 59, 187
      identifying 51
   niche 54, 57, 187
      benefits of 55
      types of... 56
marketing 15–16, 48
   budget for 208
Marketing Action Plan 207
media, marketing 197
   and quality 224–225
   consistent use of 208
   print 213
meetings
   follow up 88–89, 251
   referral group 91
mentors 59, 71, 93, 187
message, marketing 16, 197

and media 206–207
consistent use of 208
moment of truth 191. *See* truth, moment of

N

names, remembering 123–126
National Foundation for Teaching Entrepreneurship 32, 143
natural markets. *See* market: natural markets
need, customer 17, 41, 51
networking 31, 63–83. *See also* centers of influence
   and building contacts 66, 68–69
   and "who you know" 69
   definition of 64, 187, 256–257
   events 83, 85, 188
   organizations 83
   the "awful truth" 67
   traditional 64–65
   "two faces" of... 65, 275
      differences between 68
newsletters 216
niche markets 207. *See* market: niche
Nightingale, Earl 30, 152
Nixon, Richard M. 116

O

observation, personal 30
occupations 56
opportunity
   recognizing 30, 68
oscillation. *See* structure

P

Panera 88–89
passion 41, 59, 131
PDF 222
Peck, M. Scott, M.D. 129, 133
perception
   vs. reality 116
perseverance 131
Plaxo 87, 125, 266, 274
podcasting 222
Podcasts 221
points, talking. *See* talking points
positioning 212
positive thinking 134
postcards 215
Powerpoint 218, 222
price, paying the... 185

Index

print. *See* media, marketing: print
problem-solving 135, 136–137, 142, 152
product distribution representatives 171
products 21
professionalism 117
prospecting
   and fishing... 57–58
   and marketing 15–16
   and selling 16
   and service 159
   and social media... 245–277
   definition of 15, 186, 245
   difficulty in... 38–40, 136
   five hurdles of successful... 18, 186
prospects
   identifying within different markets 47, 56–60, 65
   lack of 18, 185
   relative to income goal 149
   serve your 84
psychographics 56
punctuality 43, 186

R

rapport 52
real estate agents 170
reality, current 148
Really Simple Syndication (RSS) 222
red zone 193
ReferenceUSA 230–232
referral groups 82, 89, 188, 254
   and meetings 91
   key characteristics of 89–90
referrals 28, 53, 90
   and introductions 30, 51. *See also* centers of influence
   and LinkedIn 250–251
   and trust 29
   definition 29, 187
   how to ask for 39–40
rejection 18
   and fear 23
   and insecurity 22
relationships
   building 66, 67, 212, 266–267. *See also* centers of influence
resistance
   lowering prospect 58
respect 95, 118
responsibility 36, 162
responsiveness 43, 186
résumé 106–107, 249
reverse referrals 164
Risley, Sabrina 84–85
RSS. *See* Really Simple Syndication (RSS)

S

script 112–114
  and memorizing 112
  internalizing 112, 116, 189
  rehearsing 112, 113–114, 189
scripting 189, 198
seminars 172–173
SendOutCards 87
"Serve Your Prospects" 200
  in three steps 209
service, client 159, 190–191
  and attorneys 170
  and certified public accountants 170
  and complaints 174
  and convenience 174
  and investment representatives 170
  and product distribution representatives 171
  and real estate agents 170
  and selling 178, 178–179
  and your colleagues... 177–179
  decline of 159–160, 160
  definition 169
  Eight Rules of Outstanding... 173, 191
  how to provide outstanding... 169
  joy of... 173
  seeking opportunities for... 174
Sharkproof 66
short messaging service. *See* SMS
SlideShare 222
"SMART" formula 96
SMS 260
Social Capital 267
social media 125, 245–277
  prospecting with 266
social mobility 31, 74, 187, 247, 257
speaking
  fear of 79
  public 27, 77, 183
stories 104
stress 133
structure 135–142, 194
  and behavior 137, 141–142, 190
  and creating new realities 139–142, 146–155
  and oscillation 135–136
  definition of 137
  introduction to 135
subtext 115, 124, 162, 189
  components of... 115
  perception of 116
"success trap" 154
suspects 26

Index

T

talking points 109, 189
   creating your... 111
testimonials 21, 103, 200, 200–202, 237.
     See also LinkedIn: recommendations
The Millionaire Mind 35
The Path of Least Resistance 135, 137–138
The Road Less Traveled 133
time management 192–195
total lifetime value 212
trust 67, 114, 115, 199
truth, moment of 164–169
   examples 164–169
Twain, Mark 175
Twitter 247, 260
   followers 262
   "Follow Friday" 265, 268, 269
   hashtags 264
   keywords 263, 264
   "Retweeting" 265, 269
   terms 265
   the "Twitter Trap" 262

U

uniqueness 212

V

value 17, 28, 57. *See also* client: total lifetime value of...; *See also* Total Lifetime Value
   knowing your... 18, 19, 186, 198
   versus product 19
value proposition 19, 102, 111, 113, 198, 204–205, 229
   defined 102
value propositon 215
video 198, 206. *See also* audio-video
   effective use of 200, 220
vision 147
voice
   training 118
volunteering 75

W

wall, hitting the 131, 279–281
wants, customer 17, 51, 108
web applications 223
website 198, 206
   and web applications 223
Wedge, the 227
Wentz, Tom 135
Whiteley, Richard 93
writing 76

Y

yellow zone 194
YouTube 217, 219

About the Author

Keith F. Luscher as founder and principal of Serve Your Prospects, LLC, is a management consultant bringing more than twenty years of experience to content marketing and IP (intellectual property) development. His experience in content marketing predates the internet, back when it was referred to as "custom publishing"– and has remained a longtime advocate of what is at the heart of the matter: to serve your prospects (hence, the name of the operation).

Throughout his career Keith has advised colleagues on issues related to marketing and prospecting, and developed groundbreaking educational curriculum. In addition, Luscher is also a nationally known author, speaker, and expert in media, interpersonal communication and marketing.

Keith has served as a national spokesperson for a FORTUNE 50 company, and as a contributor to CollegeRecruiter.com—one of the nation's leading career sites for college students and recent graduates. He is currently a contributor to *Market Leadership Journal* (www.MarketLeadership.net). Further, Keith has developed successful marketing and public relations strategies for many organizations across the country (which include the assistance in raising more than $250 million for health-care, cultural, educational, and service organizations).

In addition to *Prospect & Flourish*, Keith is also the author of *Don't Wait Until You Graduate!* a widely acclaimed advanced career-planning book for college students that, in the past fifteen years, has become a part of the college landscape. It has also been translated into Chinese and is now in its second edition (with a third edition forthcoming).

As lead project consultant and ghost-writer, Keith also completed *Prospect or Perish: A Success Guide for Financial Services Professionals,* the textbook for a curriculum course for the Life Underwriter Training Council Fellow (LUTCF) program at The American College.

Keith is an active member of the American Marketing Association and is a graduate of The Ohio State University. He welcomes your connection invite on LinkedIn, Facebook and other social media.